FREUD'S "ON NARCISSISM: AN INTRODUCTION"

CONTEMPORARY FREUD
Turning Points and Critical Issues

Series Editor: Leticia Glocer Fiorini

On Freud's "Analysis Terminable and Interminable"
edited by Joseph Sandler

Freud's "On Narcissism: An Introduction"
edited by Joseph Sandler, Ethel Spector Person, Peter Fonagy

On Freud's "Observations on Transference-Love"
edited by Ethel Spector Person, Aiban Hagelin, Peter Fonagy

On Freud's "Creative Writers and Day-Dreaming"
edited by Ethel Spector Person, Peter Fonagy, Sérvulo Augusto Figueira

On Freud's "A Child Is Being Beaten"
edited by Ethel Spector Person

On Freud's "Group Psychology and the Analysis of the Ego"
edited by Ethel Spector Person

On Freud's "Mourning and Melancholia"
edited by Leticia Glocer Fiorini, Thierry Bokanowski, Sergio Lewkowicz

On Freud's "The Future of an Illusion"
edited by Mary Kay O'Neil & Salman Akhtar

On Freud's "Splitting of the Ego in the Process of Defence"
edited by Thierry Bokanowski & Sergio Lewkowicz

On Freud's "Femininity"
edited by Leticia Glocer Fiorini & Graciela Abelin-Sas Rose

On Freud's "Constructions in Analysis"
edited by Sergio Lewkowicz & Thierry Bokanowski, with Georges Pragier

On Freud's "Beyond the Pleasure Principle"
edited by Salman Akhtar & Mary Kay O'Neil

On Freud's "Negation"
edited by Mary Kay O'Neil and Salman Akhtar

FREUD'S "ON NARCISSISM: AN INTRODUCTION"

Edited By

Joseph Sandler
Ethel Spector Person
and Peter Fonagy

CONTEMPORARY FREUD
Turning Points and Critical Issues

Routledge
Taylor & Francis Group
LONDON AND NEW YORK

Grateful acknowledgement is made to Sigmund Freud Copyrights; The Institute of Psychoanalysis, London; The Hogarth Press; and Basic Books for permission to reprint "On Narcissism: An Introduction" as published in Sigmund Freud, *The Standard Edition of the Complete Works of Sigmund Freud*, Vol. 14, trans. and ed. by James Strachey, Hogarth Press, London; and in Sigmund Freud, *The Collected Papers of Sigmund Freud*, Vol. 4, ed. James Strachey, Basic Books, New York.

First published 1991 by Yale University Press for the International Psychoanalytical Association, London.

This edition published in 2012 by
Karnac Books Ltd.

Published 2019 by Routledge
2 Park Square, Milton Park, Abingdon, Oxon OX14 4RN
605 Third Avenue, New York, NY 10017

First issued in hardback 2019

Routledge is an imprint of the Taylor & Francis Group, an informa business

British Library Cataloguing in Publication Data
A C.I.P. for this book is available from the British Library

ISBN 13: 978-0-367-10142-8 (hbk)
ISBN 13: 978-1-78049-108-0 (pbk)

Contents

Preface

This is the second volume of the series "Contemporary Freud: Turning Points and Critical Issues," the first being *On Freud's "Analysis Terminable and Interminable."* The series was proposed by Robert Wallerstein, who appointed an IPA Committee on Publications under the chairmanship of Joseph Sandler; the proposal grew out of the desire to provide the IPA's membership with a new modality of intellectual interchange. Such an exchange seems more urgent now than ever before because of the increasingly rapid growth of psychoanalysis in different parts of the world, each with a unique and important perspective.

Each publication in this series will begin with one of Freud's classic papers and will be followed by essays by a number of distinguished psychoanalytic teachers from theoretically diverse and geographically dispersed backgrounds. Rather than merely reviewing the pertinent literature, each contributor has been asked to elucidate the essay's important points, to clarify what may be ambiguous in the essay, and to establish links between the original paper and important aspects of our present state of knowledge. The contributions are meant to be didactic and to express the contributor's views exactly as if he or she were conducting a seminar. Although each volume may be useful as a teaching text, it will also be of immeasurable value to anyone reading or re-reading Freud or exploring a given topic—in this case narcissism. It is the hope of the IPA Committee on Publications that each volume will draw the reader into an internal dialogue with the contributors, thus serving as a kind of personal study group.

Given the importance of narcissism to current theoretical concerns, the choice of focusing this volume on Freud's classic essay "On Narcissism: An Introduction" seems a happy one. Credit goes to Joseph Sandler, who served as chairperson of the Committee on Publications at the time the choice was made and who, with input from his advisory board, selected the contributors for this volume. They, in turn, have been generous in their participation in this project, and the excellent results thereof are self-evident.

Special thanks go to Lynne McIlroy of the IPA office for her prodigious help in securing permissions and coordinating such an international venture and to Doris Parker of the Columbia Psychoanalytic Center for checking the English references. I also want to thank Gladys Topkis, Eliza Childs, and Cecile Rhinehart Watters for their indispensable editorial input and their patience and care in bringing this volume into existence.

ETHEL SPECTOR PERSON

Introduction

Even to the casual observer of psychoanalysis it is abundantly apparent that in recent years issues of narcissism have taken center stage. The concept of narcissism is pivotal in revisions of theory, and the treatment of pathological narcissism central to technical innovations and to the evolving theory of technique. The growing interest in narcissism has found its way into popular culture as well, with the term being used in a pejorative sense to denote self-preoccupation and to describe certain aspects of contemporary life (although this is quite different from what clinicians mean when they use the term). But however contemporary the interest in narcissism may be, the first inkling of its importance in pathology and in everyday life, in love, and in normal development is to be found in Freud's seminal essay of 1914.

Although there is ample evidence for Freud's intuitive grasp of narcissistic issues and even some attempts on his part to theorize about narcissism prior to his writing "On Narcissism: An Introduction," it is in that essay that he first considers its broad implications for psychoanalysis. And, indeed, the essay may justly be considered as one of a series of turning points in Freud's thinking, opening up our understanding of motivation as stemming from something other than instinctual gratification, and presaging not only structural theory but object-relations theory, as well as the importance of the self concept as opposed to the ego, and many other subsequent theoretical developments. Freud, as he makes clear in the text, was well aware that he was initiating a long-running discussion, not preempting a topic—for example, when he lists a number of specific "themes which I propose to leave on one side, as an important field of work which still awaits exploration" (92). We are safe in assuming that Freud called his essay on narcissism "An Introduction" deliberately; he was being prescient, not coy.

"On Narcissism" is at first glance deceptively simple, because like all of Freud's prose it is easy to read; but it is, in fact, a densely packed, highly theoretical essay that introduces ideas still being debated today. Part I starts straightforwardly enough with Freud noting that he has borrowed the term "narcissism" from Näcke, who used it to describe a person who treated his own body as one generally treats a sexual object. Such an attitude, Freud observes, is frequently seen in homosexuals, and he thinks it likely that a narcissistic phase might be part of normal human development. Moreover, he feels that there is a narcissistic attitude in certain patients that limits their susceptibility to psychoanalytic intervention. In these cases he suggests that narcissism should be considered not perverse but "the libidinal complement to the egoism of the instinct of self-preservation" (73–74).

In part, Freud explains, his interest in schizophrenia has led him to explore narcissism. Schizophrenics display two fundamental characteristics: megalomania and a corresponding withdrawal of interest from the outside world. The schizophrenic's withdrawal is different both in kind and in degree from that of the neurotic. In analysis, the neurotic is shown to maintain an erotic relationship to a fantasized object if not a real one; the schizophrenic, by contrast, withdraws interest from the external world without investing in fantasy objects. (To the degree that the schizophrenic replaces his objects, this should be construed as part of a secondary restitutive process.) Translating his clinical observations into libidinal terms, Freud says that "object-libido" withdrawn and redirected to the self becomes "ego-libido." The libido withdrawn from the external world and so redirected constitutes "narcissism," accounting for the schizophrenic's megalomania. Since the narcissism of schizophrenia is a secondary phenomenon, the libido returns to the ego by a path previously traversed in the opposite direction, Freud hypothesizes that there must have been a primary infantile narcissism, adducing as evidence the omnipotent thinking observed in children and primitive peoples. In his famous amoeba metaphor, he postulates that the original libidinal cathexis of the ego and the subsequent redirection of much of that libidinal energy to objects is analogous to the amoeba's extension of pseudopodia from itself that changes its shape and direction.

Here he first suggests that there are two types of libido—object-libido and ego-libido—and that an increase in one causes a diminution in the other since libido is regarded as a fixed quantity. For example, in romantic love, in which the object is highly cathected, ego-libido diminishes; in schizophrenia, in which object cathexis almost disappears, the ego becomes more invested with libido. (Many of our commentators note that in this paper Freud is using the term "ego" as most of us today would use the "self.") Despite Freud's contention that libido is unitary, he continues to insist on a distinction between libido and ego-instincts. (Why this is so—the polemical and theoretical imperatives of 1914—is a subject addressed by several commentators.) By this point in the text, the reader is well aware that "On Narcissism" is a paper with an ambitious scope and far-reaching implications, but also one replete with ambiguities and obscurities, in part because of Freud's attempt to keep his arguments within an economic point of view.

Freud opens Section II with the comment that just as the study of transference neurosis enabled him to trace libidinal instinctual impulses, so will schizophrenia give him insight into the psychology of the ego. He describes narcissism as a predominant feature not only of schizophrenia, perversion, and homosexuality but also of organic disease and hypochondria. (The close relationship Freud posits between hypochondria and schizophrenia is challenged by several of our contributors.) One problem Freud raises is the question of why a buildup of ego-libido should perforce be associated with illness. He attempts to come to grips with this question by suggesting that hypochondria is an "actual" neurosis. Related to the problematic nature of the buildup of ego-libido is the question Freud raises of "what makes it necessary at all for a mental life to pass beyond the limits of narcissism and to attach libido to objects." He reiterates his belief that too much libidinal cathexis of the ego is hazardous and concludes that in the end "we must begin to love in order not to fall ill, and we are bound to fall ill, if, in consequence of frustration, we are unable to love" (88).

The study of love—in particular its different manifestations in men and women—provides still another look at narcissism. Freud distinguishes two types of object choice that may be followed because the child originally had two objects—himself and the woman who cared for him. In narcissistic object choice the individual may love someone who represents what he is, what he was, what he would like to be, or someone who was once part of himself. In anaclitic (dependent) attachment, he may love the woman who feeds him or the man who protects him. Freud concludes that though men are more likely to pick an anaclitic love object, women more often choose a narcissistic one. In a brilliant throwaway, he remarks that when we look at parents' feeling toward their children, we see that "it is a revival and reproduction of their own narcissism, which they have long since abandoned" (90–91). And he concludes, "At the most touchy point in the narcissistic system, the immortality of the ego, which is so hard pressed by reality, security is achieved by taking refuge in the child" (91). Despite his attempt to remain within an economic, libidinal framework, his psychological insights propel themselves into his essay.

In Section III, a true tour de force, Freud considers the fate of the child's megalomania, from which he had deduced the hypothesis of infantile primary narcissism. While part of the primary narcissism (ego-libido) is eventually directed to the object, another part is repressed. At this point Freud introduces the idea that foreshadows the structural theory he came to propose ten years later. He hypothesizes an ideal ego that becomes "the target of the self-love which was enjoyed in childhood by the actual ego." In a justifiably famous formulation, he says, "Man is not willing to forego the narcissistic perfection of his childhood; and when, as he grows up, he is disturbed by the admonitions of others and by the awakening of his own critical judgment, so that he can no longer retain that perfection, he seeks to recover it in the new form of an ego ideal. What he projects before him as his ideal is the substitute for the lost narcissism of his childhood in which he was his own ideal" (94). Freud is, however, careful to distinguish sublimation from idealization. Sublimation diverts object-libido toward some aim other than sexual satisfaction; by contrast, idealization aggrandizes or exalts the libidinal object and can pertain as readily to the sphere of the self as to that of the object.

Freud introduces the idea of a special psychic agency that attempts to guarantee narcissistic fulfillment through gratification of the ego-ideal. He equates this agency with what we experience as "conscience." He goes on to say that "what prompted the subject to form an ego ideal, on whose behalf his conscience acts as watchman, arose from the critical influence of his parents" (96). This insight enables him to explain delusions of being watched. And here he foreshadows not only structural theory but also object-relations theory and the importance accorded to the process of internalization and the influence of both parents and society.

Finally Freud tackles the issue of self-regard, demonstrating its close connection with narcissistic libido. As already suggested, primary narcissism is diminished in one of two ways; libido is invested either in an object or in the ideal. Self-regard, then, has three sources: utilizing residual primary narcissism, it is also a function of the reciprocity of love and of fulfillment of the ideal. Paradoxically, Freud speaks of increased self-regard in paraphrenia (a phenomenon most of us would regard as compensatory); but he also acknowledges the lowering of self-regard when one is unable to love.

In essence, then, Freud sees the development of the ego as a departure from primary narcissism, leaving the individual with the wish to recover that blissful state. In this single brief paper he explores narcissism in normal development, in love relationships, and in pathology, as well as in its relationship to the ego-ideal, the regulation of self-esteem, and group psychology. As Kernberg remarks, only two contemporary issues concerning narcissism are missing: "pathological narcissism considered as a specific type or spectrum of character pathology and narcissistic resistances as an important factor in psychoanalytic technique."

Any lengthier summary or elaboration would pale beside the sophisticated exegeses, elaborations, clarifications, and critiques provided by our contributors, each of them an outstanding psychoanalytic scholar. Each has a particular strategy in approaching Freud's essay: for example, citing its polemical value in 1914; teasing out those questions, previously either unasked or unanswered, that Freud was addressing; or placing the theme of narcissism in the context of psychoanalysis today.

The opening chapter, by Yorke, is truly a teaching text, placing Freud's essay in the context of Freud's evolving thinking. A wonderful guide for the first-time reader of Freud, Yorke takes us through the essay without sacrificing any subtleties. He points out that Freud approached the problem of narcissism from the perspectives of both normality and pathology. As with the perversions, Freud concluded that what may be pathological in later life is normal in early development. He came to posit narcissism as the stage in instinctual development between autoerotism and object choice. Yorke shows how Freud conceptualized libido as divided into ego-libido and object-libido and how this balance shifts in the pathological condition of schizophrenia as well as in the normal condition of falling in love. Most important, Yorke shows how considerations that arose in the narcissism paper led to the necessity for a theoretical shift to a structural model of the mind.

Etchegoyen views Freud's essay as one of the "basic writings in the corpus of psychoanalytic theory." He quotes Jones to the effect that this essay gave a jolt to instinct theory and reminds us that the primary narcissism posited by Freud remains central to many contemporary psychoanalytic controversies. Summarizing and discussing each of the three sections of Freud's essay, he raises what he feels are its problematic aspects. Reviewing Section I, he emphasizes that narcissism was introduced into libido theory in an attempt to explain schizophrenia. But narcissism is not restricted to schizophrenia, and it does not always issue forth in illness, as is demonstrated in Freud's discussion of primitive man and the child; and though in such normal instances one sees the same expansiveness of ego and belief in magic as in schizophrenia, here they do not indicate or catalyze illness. In schizophrenia, in contrast, narcissism is a result of excessive libido having flowed back to ego, deflected from its objects by virtue of illness. With this formulation, according to Etchegoyen, Freud has introduced a new stage in libido: narcissism falls between autoerotism and alloeroticism. Etchegoyen raises the question that, to his mind, Freud fails to answer successfully: why must one continue to distinguish between sexual instincts and ego-instincts once it has been acknowledged that the ego receives a libidinal cathexis from the very beginning? Etchegoyen points out that this was essentially the nature of Jung's 1912 objection to libido theory (part of the background political dispute that informs Freud's essay) and that Freud resorts to a biological (rather than psychological) argument in upholding an instinctual duality. In Etchegoyen's opinion, "the need to distinguish the sexual instincts from the ego-instincts is inherent not in libido theory but rather in the theory of conflict—the dynamic viewpoint." Raising a question as to why Freud related hypochondria so closely to "paraphrenia," Etchegoyen suggests that unlike the economic explanation that Freud proffers there is good evidence to suggest a psychological content to hypochondria. Etchegoyen sees a further limitation in Freud's formulation—namely, that he bases libido on an autoerotism that has dispensed with the need for an object, the latter's importance in Freud's theory guaranteed only through the ego-instincts. He also suggests that a consideration of aggression is missing from Freud's essay. Despite these caveats, Etchegoyen concludes that Freud's essay marks a momentous event in psychoanalytic history.

Treurniet points out that the biology of Freud's day not only predisposed him to a hydraulic point of view but also isolated the object of investigation, as though its environment were unimportant (in essence, treating the individual as a closed system). Nonetheless, Treurniet suggests that in the 1914 essay, "Freud carved the contours of the important developments to come without much regard for the rules of conceptual clarity." He suggests that through his amoeba metaphor Freud displays an intuitive grasp of the emotional vulnerability of narcissistic patients—a remarkable contrast to the economic point of view. Like Etchegoyen, Treurniet believes that Freud introduces a somewhat arcane and obscure argument in order to preserve the idea of ego-instincts, at the same time essentially replacing the contrast between libido and ego-instincts with a contrast between object-love and self-love, again indicating the beginning of a shift toward a psychological rather than an economic theory. He points out that though Freud spoke of the "ego" he was really referring to the "self." He believes that despite the essay's economic bias, the seeds of many offshoots of psychoanalytic theory were planted in the text. Freud first postulated that the development of the ego consists in a departure from primary narcissism; this ultimately results in the ego's rigorous attempts to recover that state by narcissistic object choice, by identification, and by trying to fulfill the ego ideal, in that (developmental) order. Treurniet points out that these concepts—object choice, identification, and ego-ideal—paved the way for the later structural theory. He also notes that although the amoeba metaphor intuitively conceptualized an individual's affective vulnerability, this insight could not be elaborated because Freud was still functioning within an almost exclusively economic point of view. Freud was able to put affects center stage only in 1926, with "Inhibitions, Symptoms and Anxiety." Treurniet sees Freud's intuitions of 1914 coming to fruition only in post-Freudian psychoanalytic thinking. He describes how the widening scope of psychoanalysis (especially the treatment of borderline and narcissistic personality organizations) opened up our ability to theorize about clinical, technical, and theoretical aspects of the self in relation to external reality, particularly within object-relations theory.

Grinberg, through the imaginative device of a letter to Sigmund Freud, also adds considerably to our understanding of the implications of Freud's essay. He admires Freud's paper but sees its limitations: "It contains fundamental innovations, such as the concept of the ego-ideal, the value of sublimation, self-regard, object choice, the self-observing agency, and conscience; but these are accompanied by certain contradictions and statements that are perhaps debatable, such as your uncompromising insistence on the importance of libidinal quantities in explaining the concept of narcissism, to the almost complete exclusion of object relations and their role in this concept." He, too, talks of the confusion in Freud's attempt to maintain a distinction between ego-libido and object-libido and sees it resolved only when Freud integrated the sexual and self-preservative instincts into the life instinct, which he then contrasted with the death instinct. Grinberg gives an interesting summary of the model of the "container/contained" and goes on to discuss many other topics, including hypochondria. He concludes by suggesting that our conception of narcissism has been rounded out by many ideas introduced after Freud's death—for example, the conceptualization of narcissism as the cathexis of the self rather than of the ego, the influence of object-relations theory, the redefinition of narcissism in noninstinctual terms, and narcissism as a defense against affects.

Baranger, too, stresses the pivotal importance of narcissism in psychoanalysis, regarding it as analogous to the concept of identification, both of which have led to a profound restructuring of theory. As he sees it, narcissism, once fully introduced into theory, "overturned the theory of instincts; the ultimate route of psychological conflict now became situated in the struggle between libido and destructiveness, Eros and Thanatos." He gives a close account of the history of the concept of narcissism in Freud's work, talking about how five terms—autoerotism as a stage of the libido, autoerotism as a mode of libidinal satisfaction, secondary narcissism, primary narcissism, and the ego-instincts—were continually reconceptualized. He points out that Freud's essay, though focusing on a study of the perversions, states of being in love, the ego-ideal, and groups, ultimately stimulated the study of object relations. Baranger's is a very insightful examination of the evolution of Freud's thinking on narcissism and how it has changed our fundamental psychoanalytic precepts.

In Kernberg's reading, Freud's most remarkable formulation is his insight into the intimate relationship between investment in the self and investment in objects. According to Kernberg, "in contemporary language we might say that the investments of libido oscillating between self and objects, brought about by introjective and projective mechanisms, determine the mutual reinforcement of affective investment of the self and of significant others, the simultaneous buildup of an internal and an external world of object relations, which strengthen each other." He, too, says that in today's world of science we would question Freud's assumption that the psyche originated in a closed system. He suggests instead, on the basis of the work of analysts and infant observers, that self and object relationships appear to develop very early and simultaneously; consequently, he would question the notion of the state either of autoerotism or of primary narcissism. In his framework, affects are intimately related to drives; there is a development of drives rather than a differentiated drive beginning in earliest life. After reviewing Freud's essay, Kernberg turns to his own classification of normal and pathological narcissism. He suggests that "pathological narcissism reflects a libidinal investment not in a normally integrated self-structure but in a pathological self-structure."

Segal and Bell are also interested in explicating not only the development of Freud's theory of narcissism but its post-Freudian theoretical elaborations, particularly by the Kleinians. Theirs is an important commentary because of its exegesis of Freud and its clear outline of some basic tenets of Melanie Klein's work, which will be extremely useful for those who are not intimately familiar with this line of development in psychoanalytic thinking. Klein was explicit in her disagreement with Freud's assertion that there is a stage of autoerotism and narcissism preceding object relations. She sees "narcissistic withdrawal" as a withdrawal to internalized objects. From her perspective there is no mental state, however regressed, in which the mental organization is either objectless or conflict-free. Rather than stages she posited the paranoid-schizoid and the depressive positions. In her frame of reference narcissistic object relations characterize the paranoid-schizoid position, in which the world is split between good and bad objects. This splitting takes place internally, but it is also projected. "The dominant anxieties are of a paranoid nature, and the defenses are aimed at protecting the self and the idealized objects from the murderous objects that contain split-off and projected aggression originating in the infant's self." Segal and Bell discuss Klein's "Notes on Some Schizoid Mechanisms," the key paper in her description of narcissism and the one in which she first detailed the mechanism of projective identification. As Segal and Bell point out, "patients who make excessive use of projective identification are trapped in a world made up of projective aspects of themselves." This excessive use weakens the ego, making it less able to cope with anxiety and leading to further splitting and projection. Segal and Bell describe patients who experience love as a threat to the self. Like many of our commentators, they speak to the necessity of an object-relations point of view. They conclude by emphasizing that the mythical Narcissus was not objectless but trapped by what he believed to be a lost love object, which was in fact an idealized aspect of self. Believing himself to be in love, he could not turn away and therefore died of starvation, lacking "a real object from whom he might have been able to get what he really needed."

Ornstein, writing from the perspective of self psychology, traces concepts of narcissism from Freud's essay through their elaboration in Kohut's work. He points out that questions raised through clinical observation have twice led psychoanalysts to consider the issue of narcissism, each time shaking the very foundation of psychoanalytic theory. The first such observations compelled Freud in 1914 to revise libido theory. According to Ornstein, both Freud's new theory of narcissism and, much later, Kohut's threatened the existing conflict theory of psychoanalysis. He describes the pedagogic background to which Freud was responding in writing the narcissism essay, specifically his need to counter the defections of Adler in 1911 and Jung in 1913. From there he proceeds to an explication of the key elements in Freud's theories of narcissism and a discussion of the fate of the concept in post-Freudian literature. What is unique to his chapter is the line of development he traces between Freud and Kohut. As he points out, Kohut began not by theorizing narcissism but by turning his attention to clinical observation and the two types of transference he observed in work with patients with narcissistic personality disturbances. These two transferences have become well known to us as the "mirror transference" and the "idealizing transference." Working from details of the transference, Kohut was able to reconstruct what he believed to be the infantile and childhood trauma that left the psyche insufficiently structuralized, so that there was manifest narcissistic pathology. A mirror transference was the response to the infantile "grandiose self"; the idealizing transference, a response to the "idealized parent imago." Ornstein points out that Kohut's first theoretical innovation was to posit separate lines of development for narcissism and for object love. He discusses the clinical and technical implications of this theoretical innovation and speaks of how it necessitated a revision of developmental theory. His clarification does for self psychology what Segal and Bell do for Kleinian theory.

Henseler notes that Freud encountered difficulties describing narcissistic phenomena in terms of economic considerations. He therefore turned in the 1914 paper, particularly in the second and third sections, to emotional states and fantasies deriving from the experiential world of relationships in order to explain narcissism—for example, in his discussion of megalomania, the omnipotence of thought, and the magical power of gestures, fantasies, and the like, each of which implies a relationship to an object. Henseler then seeks to expand the concept of primary narcissism as an archaic form of relationship. For example, turning to Freud's exegesis of parental love,

Henseler suggests that the parent identifies not only with the baby but with the entire interaction. He suggests that "in reality, the parents' efforts are directed toward the creation of a relationship in which laws do not apply, boundaries dissolve, and subject and object interpenetrate—a relationship in which the bliss of oneness and eternal harmony beckons." Following this he introduces a marvelous discussion of the psychology of the *unio mystica*, which he describes as a primary narcissistic experience. He goes on to mention "oceanic feeling," certain religious experiences, and responses to art as related phenomena. Henseler suggests that empathy may be based on primary identification. He discusses the differences between primary and secondary identification as explicated not only in the 1914 essay but also in "Group Psychology and Analysis of the Ego" (1921). Drawing on Freud's distinction between object-love and identification, Henseler makes the important point that this distinction mandates acknowledgment of a distinction between the pleasure of instinctual satisfaction as opposed to the pleasure of fusion with the object of identification. He concludes that primary narcissism is a myth "composed out of memory traces of a psychophysiological state, satisfying experiences with objects, and wishful fantasies of happiness and harmony—which can be understood as reaction formations to frustrating reality. Hence, primary narcissism and the narcissistic constellations that later develop from it are a wonderful human achievement, a subsequent invention, offering us universal withdrawal from harsh reality."

In contrast to Henseler, Grünberger speaks of primary narcissism not as a mythical formation or reconstruction but as a real entity with prenatal origins. According to Grünberger, it is in intrauterine life that the wish for self-sufficiency is a reality, and the self may be regarded as omnipotent in a state where time and space do not exist. It is the memory of intrauterine life that he thinks leaves traces that later reappear in our creation of the God image. Perhaps the most important point of his essay is that the projection of a lost omnipotence onto the analyst is distinct from transference proper. As he puts it,

> For me, the analytic situation is characterized much more by the narcissistic regression than by the transference. What I mean is that the transference—and here I am faithfully following Freud—is a universal phenomenon: people have a transference to their cardiologist, to their milkman, to the caretaker of their block of flats. It is true that the analytic situation constitutes a laboratory where the manifestations of

> the transference are observed in a privileged and, as it were, aseptic manner (by virtue of the neutrality of the analyst, who "does not reply" but interprets). But the analytic coordinates, more than anything else, set in motion the narcissistic aspects of the psyche.

He traces many phenomena to what he believes is the experience of intrauterine life, including belief in the body-mind duality and religious and mystical experiences. Essentially he suggests that these experiences are not acts of the wishful imagination (as Henseler, for example, has proposed) but are derived from the memory traces of something once experienced, however fleetingly. His, then, is a strikingly original point of view. He ends his essay by asking whether Freud has not projected onto women the lost fetal self-sufficiency recovered by fusion with the mother, which would then be seen as a successor to the feelings of oneness experienced in uterine life.

Our brief summaries of these extremely complex and often brilliant essays do not do them justice. The contributors display an ability not only to read Freud's text closely but also to use it to chart new developments of psychoanalysis and to point toward still unsolved problems. They certainly demonstrate that narcissism is a key element in all our contemporary psychoanalytic theories.

JOSEPH SANDLER
ETHEL SPECTOR PERSON
PETER FONAGY

PART ONE

On Narcissism: An Introduction (1914)

SIGMUND FREUD

ON NARCISSISM: AN INTRODUCTION

I

The term narcissism is derived from clinical description and was chosen by Paul Näcke[1] in 1899 to denote the attitude of a person who treats his own body in the same way in which the body of a sexual object is ordinarily treated—who looks at it, that is to say, strokes it and fondles it till he obtains complete satisfaction through these activities. Developed to this degree, narcissism has the significance of a perversion that has absorbed the whole of the subject's sexual life, and it will consequently exhibit the characteristics which we expect to meet with in the study of all perversions.

Psycho-analytic observers were subsequently struck by the fact that individual features of the narcissistic attitude are found in many people who suffer from other disorders—for instance, as Sadger has pointed out, in homosexuals—and finally it seemed probable that an allocation of the libido such as deserved to be described as narcissism might be present far more extensively, and that it might claim a place in the regular course of human sexual development.[2] Difficulties in psycho-analytic work upon neurotics led to the same supposition, for it seemed as though this kind of narcissistic attitude in them constituted one of the limits to their susceptibility to influence. Narcissism in this sense would not be a perversion, but the libidinal

[1] [In a footnote added by Freud in 1920 to his *Three Essays* (1905*d*, *Standard Ed.*, 7, 218 *n.*) he said that he was wrong in stating in the present paper that the term 'narcissism' was introduced by Näcke and that he should have attributed it to Havelock Ellis. Ellis himself, however, subsequently (1928) wrote a short paper in which he corrected Freud's correction and argued that the priority should in fact be divided between himself and Näcke, explaining that the term 'narcissus-like' had been used by him in 1898 as a description of a psychological attitude, and that Näcke in 1899 had introduced the term '*Narcismus*' to describe a sexual perversion. The German word used by Freud is '*Narzissmus*'. In his paper on Schreber (1911*c*), near the beginning of Section III, he defends this form of the word on the ground of euphony against the possibly more correct '*Narzissismus*'.]

[2] Otto Rank (1911*c*).

complement to the egoism of the instinct of self-preservation, a measure of which may justifiably be attributed to every living creature.

A pressing motive for occupying ourselves with the conception of a primary and normal narcissism arose when the attempt was made to subsume what we know of dementia praecox (Kraepelin) or schizophrenia (Bleuler) under the hypothesis of the libido theory. Patients of this kind, whom I have proposed to term paraphrenics,[1] display two fundamental characteristics: megalomania and diversion of their interest from the external world—from people and things. In consequence of the latter change, they become inaccessible to the influence of psychoanalysis and cannot be cured by our efforts. But the paraphrenic's turning away from the external world needs to be more precisely characterized. A patient suffering from hysteria or obsessional neurosis has also, as far as his illness extends, given up his relation to reality. But analysis shows that he has by no means broken off his erotic relations to people and things. He still retains them in phantasy; i.e. he has, on the one hand, substituted for real objects imaginary ones from his memory, or has mixed the latter with the former; and on the other hand, he has renounced the initiation of motor activities for the attainment of his aims in connection with those objects. Only to this condition of the libido may we legitimately apply the term 'introversion' of the libido which is used by Jung indiscriminately.[2] It is otherwise with the paraphrenic. He seems really to have withdrawn his libido from people and things in the external world, without replacing them by others in phantasy. When he *does* so replace them, the process seems to be a secondary one and to be part of an attempt at recovery, designed to lead the libido back to objects.[3]

The question arises: What happens to the libido which has been withdrawn from external objects in schizophrenia? The megalomania characteristic of these states points the way. This megalomania has no doubt come into being at the expense of

[1] [For a discussion of Freud's use of this term, see a long Editor's footnote near the end of Section III of the Schreber analysis (1911*c*).]

[2] [Cf. a footnote in 'The Dynamics of Transference' (1912*b*).]

[3] In connection with this see my discussion of the 'end of the world' in [Section III of] the analysis of Senatspräsident Schreber [1911*c*]; also Abraham, 1908. [See also below, p. 86.]

object-libido. The libido that has been withdrawn from the external world has been directed to the ego and thus gives rise to an attitude which may be called narcissism. But the megalomania itself is no new creation; on the contrary, it is, as we know, a magnification and plainer manifestation of a condition which had already existed previously. This leads us to look upon the narcissism which arises through the drawing in of object-cathexes as a secondary one, superimposed upon a primary narcissism that is obscured by a number of different influences.

Let me insist that I am not proposing here to explain or penetrate further into the problem of schizophrenia, but that I am merely putting together what has already been said elsewhere,[1] in order to justify the introduction of the concept of narcissism.

This extension of the libido theory—in my opinion, a legitimate one—receives reinforcement from a third quarter, namely, from our observations and views on the mental life of children and primitive peoples. In the latter we find characteristics which, if they occurred singly, might be put down to megalomania: an over-estimation of the power of their wishes and mental acts, the 'omnipotence of thoughts', a belief in the thaumaturgic force of words, and a technique for dealing with the external world—'magic'—which appears to be a logical application of these grandiose premisses.[2] In the children of to-day, whose development is much more obscure to us, we expect to find an exactly analogous attitude towards the external world.[3] Thus we form the idea of there being an original libidinal cathexis of the ego, from which some is later given off to objects, but which fundamentally persists and is related to the object-cathexes much as the body of an amoeba is related to the pseudopodia which it puts out.[4] In our

[1] [See, in particular, the works referred to in the last footnote. On p. 86 below, Freud in fact penetrates further into the problem.]

[2] Cf. the passages in my *Totem and Taboo* (1912-13) which deal with this subject. [These are chiefly in the third essay, *Standard Ed.*, **13**, 83 ff.]

[3] Cf. Ferenczi (1913*a*).

[4] [Freud used this and similar analogies more than once again, e.g. in Lecture XXVI of his *Introductory Lectures* (1916-17) and in his short paper on 'A Difficulty in the Path of Psycho-Analysis' (1917*a*), *Standard Ed.*, **17**, 139. He later revised some of the views expressed here. See the end of the Editor's Note, p. 71 above.]

researches, taking, as they did, neurotic symptoms for their starting-point, this part of the allocation of libido necessarily remained hidden from us at the outset. All that we noticed were the emanations of this libido—the object-cathexes, which can be sent out and drawn back again. We see also, broadly speaking, an antithesis between ego-libido and object-libido.[1] The more of the one is employed, the more the other becomes depleted. The highest phase of development of which object-libido is capable is seen in the state of being in love, when the subject seems to give up his own personality in favour of an object-cathexis; while we have the opposite condition in the paranoic's phantasy (or self-perception) of the 'end of the world'.[2] Finally, as regards the differentiation of psychical energies, we are led to the conclusion that to begin with, during the state of narcissism, they exist together and that our analysis is too coarse to distinguish between them; not until there is object-cathexis is it possible to discriminate a sexual energy—the libido—from an energy of the ego-instincts.[3]

Before going any further I must touch on two questions which lead us to the heart of the difficulties of our subject. In the first place, what is the relation of the narcissism of which we are now speaking to auto-erotism, which we have described as an early state of the libido?[4] Secondly, if we grant the ego a primary cathexis of libido, why is there any necessity for further distinguishing a sexual libido from a non-sexual energy of the ego-instincts? Would not the postulation of a single kind of psychical energy save us all the difficulties of differentiating an energy of the ego-instincts from ego-libido, and ego-libido from object-libido?[5]

As regards the first question, I may point out that we are

[1] [This distinction is drawn here by Freud for the first time.]

[2] [See footnote 3, p. 74 above.] There are two mechanisms of this 'end of the world' idea: in the one case, the whole libidinal cathexis flows off to the loved object; in the other, it all flows back into the ego.

[3] [Some account of the development of Freud's views on the instincts will be found in the Editor's Note to 'Instincts and their Vicissitudes', below p. 113 ff.]

[4] [See the second of Freud's *Three Essays* (1905*d*), *Standard Ed.*, 7, 181-3.]

[5] [Cf. a remark on this passage in the Editor's Note to 'Instincts and their Vicissitudes', p. 115 below.]

bound to suppose that a unity comparable to the ego cannot exist in the individual from the start; the ego has to be developed. The auto-erotic instincts, however, are there from the very first; so there must be something added to auto-erotism—a new psychical action—in order to bring about narcissism.

To be asked to give a definite answer to the second question must occasion perceptible uneasiness in every psycho-analyst. One dislikes the thought of abandoning observation for barren theoretical controversy, but nevertheless one must not shirk an attempt at clarification. It is true that notions such as that of an ego-libido, an energy of the ego-instincts, and so on, are neither particularly easy to grasp, nor sufficiently rich in content; a speculative theory of the relations in question would begin by seeking to obtain a sharply defined concept as its basis. But I am of opinion that that is just the difference between a speculative theory and a science erected on empirical interpretation. The latter will not envy speculation its privilege of having a smooth, logically unassailable foundation, but will gladly content itself with nebulous, scarcely imaginable basic concepts, which it hopes to apprehend more clearly in the course of its development, or which it is even prepared to replace by others. For these ideas are not the foundation of science, upon which everything rests: that foundation is observation alone. They are not the bottom but the top of the whole structure, and they can be replaced and discarded without damaging it. The same thing is happening in our day in the science of physics, the basic notions of which as regards matter, centres of force, attraction, etc., are scarcely less debatable than the corresponding notions in psycho-analysis.[1]

The value of the concepts 'ego-libido' and 'object-libido' lies in the fact that they are derived from the study of the intimate characteristics of neurotic and psychotic processes. A differentiation of libido into a kind which is proper to the ego and one which is attached to objects is an unavoidable corollary to an original hypothesis which distinguished between sexual instincts and ego-instincts. At any rate, analysis of the pure transference neuroses (hysteria and obsessional neurosis) compelled me to make this distinction and I only know that all attempts to

[1] [This line of thought was expanded by Freud in the opening passage of his paper on 'Instincts and their Vicissitudes' (1915*c*), below, p. 117.]

account for these phenomena by other means have been completely unsuccessful.

In the total absence of any theory of the instincts which would help us to find our bearings, we may be permitted, or rather, it is incumbent upon us, to start off by working out some hypothesis to its logical conclusion, until it either breaks down or is confirmed. There are various points in favour of the hypothesis of there having been from the first a separation between sexual instincts and others, ego-instincts, besides the serviceability of such a hypothesis in the analysis of the transference neuroses. I admit that this latter consideration alone would not be unambiguous, for it might be a question of an indifferent psychical energy which only becomes libido through the act of cathecting an object. But, in the first place, the distinction made in this concept corresponds to the common, popular distinction between hunger and love. In the second place, there are biological considerations in its favour. The individual does actually carry on a twofold existence: one to serve his own purposes and the other as a link in a chain, which he serves against his will, or at least involuntarily. The individual himself regards sexuality as one of his own ends; whereas from another point of view he is an appendage to his germ-plasm, at whose disposal he puts his energies in return for a bonus of pleasure. He is the mortal vehicle of a (possibly) immortal substance—like the inheritor of an entailed property, who is only the temporary holder of an estate which survives him. The separation of the sexual instincts from the ego-instincts would simply reflect this twofold function of the individual.[1] Thirdly, we must recollect that all our provisional ideas in psychology will presumably some day be based on an organic substructure. This makes it probable that it is special substances and chemical processes which perform the operations of sexuality and provide for the extension of individual life into that of the species.[2] We are taking this probability into account in replacing the special chemical substances by special psychical forces.

I try in general to keep psychology clear from everything that

[1] [The psychological bearing of Weismann's germ-plasm theory was discussed by Freud at much greater length in Chapter VI of *Beyond the Pleasure Principle* (1920*g*), *Standard Ed.*, **18**, 45 ff.]

[2] [See below, footnote 2, p. 125.]

is different in nature from it, even biological lines of thought. For that very reason I should like at this point expressly to admit that the hypothesis of separate ego-instincts and sexual instincts (that is to say, the libido theory) rests scarcely at all upon a psychological basis, but derives its principal support from biology. But I shall be consistent enough [with my general rule] to drop this hypothesis if psycho-analytic work should itself produce some other, more serviceable hypothesis about the instincts. So far, this has not happened. It may turn out that, most basically and on the longest view, sexual energy—libido—is only the product of a differentiation in the energy at work generally in the mind. But such an assertion has no relevance. It relates to matters which are so remote from the problems of our observation, and of which we have so little cognizance, that it is as idle to dispute it as to affirm it; this primal identity may well have as little to do with our analytic interests as the primal kinship of all the races of mankind has to do with the proof of kinship required in order to establish a legal right of inheritance. All these speculations take us nowhere. Since we cannot wait for another science to present us with the final conclusions on the theory of the instincts, it is far more to the purpose that we should try to see what light may be thrown upon this basic problem of biology by a synthesis of the *psychological* phenomena. Let us face the possibility of error; but do not let us be deterred from pursuing the logical implications of the hypothesis we first adopted[1] of an antithesis between ego-instincts and sexual instincts (a hypothesis to which we were forcibly led by analysis of the transference neuroses), and from seeing whether it turns out to be without contradictions and fruitful, and whether it can be applied to other disorders as well, such as schizophrenia.

It would, of course, be a different matter if it were proved that the libido theory has already come to grief in the attempt to explain the latter disease. This has been asserted by C. G. Jung (1912) and it is on that account that I have been obliged to enter upon this last discussion, which I would gladly have been spared. I should have preferred to follow to its end the course embarked upon in the analysis of the Schreber case without any discussion of its premisses. But Jung's assertion is,

[1] ['*Ersterwahlte*' ('first selected') in the editions before 1924. The later editions read '*erstenwähnte*' ('first mentioned'), which seems to make less good sense and may be a misprint.]

to say the least of it, premature. The grounds he gives for it are scanty. In the first place, he appeals to an admission of my own that I myself have been obliged, owing to the difficulties of the Schreber analysis, to extend the concept of libido (that is, to give up its sexual content) and to identify libido with psychical interest in general. Ferenczi (1913*b*), in an exhaustive criticism of Jung's work, has already said all that is necessary in correction of this erroneous interpretation. I can only corroborate his criticism and repeat that I have never made any such retractation of the libido theory. Another argument of Jung's, namely, that we cannot suppose that the withdrawal of the libido is in itself enough to bring about the loss of the normal function of reality,[1] is no argument but a dictum. It 'begs the question',[2] and saves discussion; for whether and how this is possible was precisely the point that should have been under investigation. In his next major work, Jung (1913 [339–40]) just misses the solution I had long since indicated: 'At the same time', he writes, 'there is this to be further taken into consideration (a point to which, incidentally, Freud refers in his work on the Schreber case [1911*c*])—that the introversion of the *libido sexualis* leads to a cathexis of the " ego", and that it may possibly be this that produces the result of a loss of reality. It is indeed a tempting possibility to explain the psychology of the loss of reality in this fashion.' But Jung does not enter much further into a discussion of this possibility. A few lines[3] later he dismisses it with the remark that this determinant 'would result in the psychology of an ascetic anchorite, not in a dementia praecox'. How little this inapt analogy can help us to decide the question may be learnt from the consideration that an anchorite of this kind, who 'tries to eradicate every trace of sexual interest' (but only in the popular sense of the word 'sexual'), does not even necessarily display any pathogenic allocation of the libido. He may have diverted his sexual interest from human beings entirely, and yet may have sublimated it into a heightened interest in the divine, in nature, or in the animal kingdom, without his libido having undergone an introversion on to his phantasies or a return to

[1] [The phrase is from Janet (1909): '*La fonction du réel*'. See the opening sentences of Freud, 1911*b*.]

[2] [In English in the original.]

[3] [All the German editions read '*Seiten*' ('pages'), a misprint for '*Zeilen*'.]

his ego. This analogy would seem to rule out in advance the possibility of differentiating between interest emanating from erotic sources and from others. Let us remember, further, that the researches of the Swiss school, however valuable, have elucidated only two features in the picture of dementia praecox —the presence in it of complexes known to us both in healthy and neurotic subjects, and the similarity of the phantasies that occur in it to popular myths—but that they have not been able to throw any further light on the mechanism of the disease. We may repudiate Jung's assertion, then, that the libido theory has come to grief in the attempt to explain dementia praecox, and that it is therefore disposed of for the other neuroses as well.

II

Certain special difficulties seem to me to lie in the way of a direct study of narcissism. Our chief means of access to it will probably remain the analysis of the paraphrenias. Just as the transference neuroses have enabled us to trace the libidinal instinctual impulses, so dementia praecox and paranoia will give us an insight into the psychology of the ego. Once more, in order to arrive at an understanding of what seems so simple in normal phenomena, we shall have to turn to the field of pathology with its distortions and exaggerations. At the same time, other means of approach remain open to us, by which we may obtain a better knowledge of narcissism. These I shall now discuss in the following order: the study of organic disease, of hypochondria and of the erotic life of the sexes.

In estimating the influence of organic disease upon the distribution of libido, I follow a suggestion made to me orally by Sándor Ferenczi. It is universally known, and we take it as a matter of course, that a person who is tormented by organic pain and discomfort gives up his interest in the things of the external world, in so far as they do not concern his suffering. Closer observation teaches us that he also withdraws *libidinal* interest from his love-objects: so long as he suffers, he ceases to love. The commonplace nature of this fact is no reason why we should be deterred from translating it into terms of the libido theory. We should then say: the sick man withdraws his libidinal cathexes back upon his own ego, and sends them out again when he recovers. 'Concentrated is his soul', says Wilhelm Busch of the poet suffering from toothache, 'in his molar's narrow hole.' [1] Here libido and ego-interest share the same fate and are once more indistinguishable from each other. The familiar egoism of the sick person covers both. We find it so natural because we are certain that in the same situation we should behave in just the same way. The way in which a lover's feelings, however strong, are banished by bodily ailments, and

[1] [Einzig in der engen Höhle
Des Backenzahnes weilt die Seele.
Balduin Bahlamm, Chapter VIII.]

suddenly replaced by complete indifference, is a theme which has been exploited by comic writers to an appropriate extent.

The condition of sleep, too, resembles illness in implying a narcissistic withdrawal of the positions of the libido on to the subject's own self, or, more precisely, on to the single wish to sleep. The egoism of dreams fits very well into this context. [Cf. below, p. 223.] In both states we have, if nothing else, examples of changes in the distribution of libido that are consequent upon a change in the ego.

Hypochondria, like organic disease, manifests itself in distressing and painful bodily sensations, and it has the same effect as organic disease on the distribution of libido. The hypochondriac withdraws both interest and libido—the latter specially markedly—from the objects of the external world and concentrates both of them upon the organ that is engaging his attention. A difference between hypochondria and organic disease now becomes evident: in the latter, the distressing sensations are based upon demonstrable [organic] changes; in the former, this is not so. But it would be entirely in keeping with our general conception of the processes of neurosis if we decided to say that hypochondria must be right: organic changes must be supposed to be present in it, too.

But what could these changes be? We will let ourselves be guided at this point by our experience, which shows that bodily sensations of an unpleasurable nature, comparable to those of hypochondria, occur in the other neuroses as well. I have said before that I am inclined to class hypochondria with neurasthenia and anxiety-neurosis as a third 'actual' neurosis.[1] It would probably not be going too far to suppose that in the case of the other neuroses a small amount of hypochondria was regularly formed at the same time as well. We have the best

[1] [This seems to have been first hinted at in a footnote near the end of Section II of the Schreber case (1911*c*). It was again briefly, though more explicitly, mentioned by Freud in his closing remarks on masturbation at a discussion in the Vienna Psycho-Analytical Society (1912*f*). He returned to the subject later towards the end of Lecture XXIV of the *Introductory Lectures* (1916–17). At a much earlier period, Freud had already approached the question of the relation between hypochondria and the other 'actual' neuroses. See Section I (2) of his first paper on anxiety neurosis (1895*b*).]

example of this, I think, in anxiety neurosis with its superstructure of hysteria. Now the familiar prototype of an organ that is painfully tender, that is in some way changed and that is yet not diseased in the ordinary sense, is the genital organ in its states of excitation. In that condition it becomes congested with blood, swollen and humected, and is the seat of a multiplicity of sensations. Let us now, taking any part of the body, describe its activity of sending sexually exciting stimuli to the mind as its 'erotogenicity', and let us further reflect that the considerations on which our theory of sexuality was based have long accustomed us to the notion that certain other parts of the body—the 'erotogenic' zones—may act as substitutes for the genitals and behave analogously to them.[1] We have then only one more step to take. We can decide to regard erotogenicity as a general characteristic of all organs and may then speak of an increase or decrease of it in a particular part of the body. For every such change in the erotogenicity of the organs there might then be a parallel change of libidinal cathexis in the ego. Such factors would constitute what we believe to underlie hypochondria and what may have the same effect upon the distribution of libido as is produced by a material illness of the organs.

We see that, if we follow up this line of thought, we come up against the problem not only of hypochondria, but of the other 'actual' neuroses—neurasthenia and anxiety neurosis. Let us therefore stop at this point. It is not within the scope of a purely psychological inquiry to penetrate so far behind the frontiers of physiological research. I will merely mention that from this point of view we may suspect that the relation of hypochondria to paraphrenia is similar to that of the other 'actual' neuroses to hysteria and obsessional neurosis: we may suspect, that is, that it is dependent on ego-libido just as the others are on object-libido, and that hypochondriacal anxiety is the counterpart, as coming from ego-libido, to neurotic anxiety. Further, since we are already familiar with the idea that the mechanism of falling ill and of the formation of symptoms in the transference neuroses—the path from introversion to regression—is to be linked to a damming-up of object-libido,[2] we may come to closer quarters with the idea of a damming-up

[1] [Cf. *Three Essays* (1905*d*), *Standard Ed.*, **7**, 183 f.]

[2] Cf. [the opening pages of] 'Types of Onset of Neurosis' (1912*c*).

of ego-libido as well and may bring this idea into relation with the phenomena of hypochondria and paraphrenia.

At this point, our curiosity will of course raise the question why this damming-up of libido in the ego should have to be experienced as unpleasurable. I shall content myself with the answer that unpleasure is always the expression of a higher degree of tension, and that therefore what is happening is that a quantity in the field of material events is being transformed here as elsewhere into the psychical quality of unpleasure. Nevertheless it may be that what is decisive for the generation of unpleasure is not the absolute magnitude of the material event, but rather some particular function of that absolute magnitude.[1] Here we may even venture to touch on the question of what makes it necessary at all for our mental life to pass beyond the limits of narcissism and to attach the libido to objects.[2] The answer which would follow from our line of thought would once more be that this necessity arises when the cathexis of the ego with libido exceeds a certain amount. A strong egoism is a protection against falling ill, but in the last resort we must begin to love in order not to fall ill, and we are bound to fall ill if, in consequence of frustration, we are unable to love. This follows somewhat on the lines of Heine's picture of the psychogenesis of the Creation:

> Krankheit ist wohl der letzte Grund
> Des ganzen Schöpferdrangs gewesen;
> Erschaffend konnte ich genesen,
> Erschaffend wurde ich gesund.[3]

We have recognized our mental apparatus as being first and foremost a device designed for mastering excitations which would otherwise be felt as distressing or would have pathogenic effects. Working them over in the mind helps remarkably towards an internal draining away of excitations which are incapable of direct discharge outwards, or for which such a

[1] [This whole question is discussed much more fully in 'Instincts and their Vicissitudes' (1915*c*), below, p. 119 ff. For the use of the term 'quantity' in the last sentence, see Part I, Section 1, of Freud's 'Project' (1950*a*), written in 1895.]

[2] [A much more elaborate discussion of this problem too will be found in 'Instincts and their Vicissitudes' (1915*c*), p. 134 ff. below.]

[3] [God is imagined as saying: 'Illness was no doubt the final cause of the whole urge to create. By creating, I could recover; by creating, I became healthy.' *Neue Gedichte*, 'Schöpfungslieder VII'.]

discharge is for the moment undesirable. In the first instance, however, it is a matter of indifference whether this internal process of working-over is carried out upon real or imaginary objects. The difference does not appear till later—if the turning of the libido on to unreal objects (introversion) has led to its being dammed up. In paraphrenics, megalomania allows of a similar internal working-over of libido which has returned to the ego; perhaps it is only when the megalomania fails that the damming-up of libido in the ego becomes pathogenic and starts the process of recovery which gives us the impression of being a disease.

I shall try here to penetrate a little further into the mechanism of paraphrenia and shall bring together those views which already seem to me to deserve consideration. The difference between paraphrenic affections and the transference neuroses appears to me to lie in the circumstance that, in the former, the libido that is liberated by frustration does not remain attached to objects in phantasy, but withdraws on to the ego. Megalomania would accordingly correspond to the psychical mastering of this latter amount of libido, and would thus be the counterpart of the introversion on to phantasies that is found in the transference neuroses; a failure of this psychical function gives rise to the hypochondria of paraphrenia and this is homologous to the anxiety of the transference neuroses. We know that this anxiety can be resolved by further psychical working-over, i.e. by conversion, reaction-formation or the construction of protections (phobias). The corresponding process in paraphrenics is an attempt at restoration, to which the striking manifestations of the disease are due. Since paraphrenia frequently, if not usually, brings about only a *partial* detachment of the libido from objects, we can distinguish three groups of phenomena in the clinical picture: (1) those representing what remains of a normal state or of neurosis (residual phenomena); (2) those representing the morbid process (detachment of libido from its objects and, further, megalomania, hypochondria, affective disturbance and every kind of regression); (3) those representing restoration, in which the libido is once more attached to objects, after the manner of a hysteria (in dementia praecox or paraphrenia proper), or of an obsessional neurosis (in paranoia). This fresh libidinal cathexis differs from the primary one in that it starts from another level and under other conditions.[1] The difference between the transference neuroses brought about in the case of this fresh kind of libidinal cathexis and the corresponding formations where the ego is normal should be able to afford us the deepest insight into the structure of our mental apparatus.

A third way in which we may approach the study of narcissism is by observing the erotic life of human beings, with its many kinds of differentiation in man and woman. Just as object-libido at first concealed ego-libido from our observation, so too in connection with the object-choice of infants (and of growing children) what we first noticed was that they derived their sexual objects from their experiences of satisfaction. The first auto-erotic sexual satisfactions are experienced in connection with vital functions which serve the purpose of self-preservation. The sexual instincts are at the outset attached to the satisfaction of the ego-instincts; only later do they become independent of these, and even then we have an indication of that original attachment in the fact that the persons who are concerned with a child's feeding, care, and protection become his earliest sexual objects: that is to say, in the first instance his mother or a substitute for her. Side by side, however, with this type and source of object-choice, which may be called the 'anaclitic' or 'attachment' type,[2] psycho-analytic research has revealed a second

[1] [See some further remarks on this at the end of the paper on 'The Unconscious' (pp. 203–4 below).]

[2] ['*Anlehnungstypus*.' Literally, 'leaning-on type'. The term has been rendered in English as the 'anaclitic type' by analogy with the grammatical term 'enclitic', used of particles which cannot be the first word in a sentence, but must be appended to, or must lean up against, a more important one, e.g. the Latin '*enim*' or the Greek '*δέ*'. This seems to be the first published appearance of the actual term '*Anlehnungstypus*'. The idea that a child arrives at its first sexual object on the basis of its nutritional instinct is to be found in the first edition of the *Three Essays* (1905*d*), *Standard Ed.*, **7**, 222; but the two or three explicit mentions in that work of the 'anaclitic type' were not added to it until the 1915 edition. The concept was very clearly foreshadowed near the beginning of the second of Freud's papers on the psychology of love (1912*d*), *Standard Ed.*, **11**, 180–1. The term '*angelehnte*' ('attached') is used in a similar sense near the beginning of Section III of the Schreber case history (1911*c*), but the underlying hypothesis is not stated there.—It should be noted that the 'attachment' (or '*Anlehnung*') indicated by the term is that of the sexual instincts to the ego-instincts, not of the child to its mother.]

type, which we were not prepared for finding. We have discovered, especially clearly in people whose libidinal development has suffered some disturbance, such as perverts and homosexuals, that in their later choice of love-objects they have taken as a model not their mother but their own selves. They are plainly seeking *themselves* as a love-object, and are exhibiting a type of object-choice which must be termed 'narcissistic'. In this observation we have the strongest of the reasons which have led us to adopt the hypothesis of narcissism.

We have, however, not concluded that human beings are divided into two sharply differentiated groups, according as their object-choice conforms to the anaclitic or to the narcissistic type; we assume rather that both kinds of object-choice are open to each individual, though he may show a preference for one or the other. We say that a human being has originally two sexual objects—himself and the woman who nurses him—and in doing so we are postulating a primary narcissism in everyone, which may in some cases manifest iself in a dominating fashion in his object-choice.

A comparison of the male and female sexes then shows that there are fundamental differences between them in respect of their type of object-choice, although these differences are of course not universal. Complete object-love of the attachment type is, properly speaking, characteristic of the male. It displays the marked sexual overvaluation which is doubtless derived from the child's original narcissism and thus corresponds to a transference of that narcissism to the sexual object. This sexual overvaluation is the origin of the peculiar state of being in love, a state suggestive of a neurotic compulsion, which is thus traceable to an impoverishment of the ego as regards libido in favour of the love-object.[1] A different course is followed in the type of female most frequently met with, which is probably the purest and truest one. With the onset of puberty the maturing of the female sexual organs, which up till then have been in a condition of latency, seems to bring about an intensification of the original narcissism, and this is unfavourable to the development of a true object-choice with its accompanying sexual overvaluation. Women, especially if they grow up with good looks, develop a certain self-contentment which

[1] [Freud returned to this in a discussion of being in love in Chapter VIII of his *Group Psychology* (1921*c*), *Standard Ed.*, **18**, 112 f.]

compensates them for the social restrictions that are imposed upon them in their choice of object. Strictly speaking, it is only themselves that such women love with an intensity comparable to that of the man's love for them. Nor does their need lie in the direction of loving, but of being loved; and the man who fulfils this condition is the one who finds favour with them. The importance of this type of woman for the erotic life of mankind is to be rated very high. Such women have the greatest fascination for men, not only for aesthetic reasons, since as a rule they are the most beautiful, but also because of a combination of interesting psychological factors. For it seems very evident that another person's narcissism has a great attraction for those who have renounced part of their own narcissism and are in search of object-love. The charm of a child lies to a great extent in his narcissism, his self-contentment and inaccessibility, just as does the charm of certain animals which seem not to concern themselves about us, such as cats and the large beasts of prey. Indeed, even great criminals and humorists, as they are represented in literature, compel our interest by the narcissistic consistency with which they manage to keep away from their ego anything that would diminish it. It is as if we envied them for maintaining a blissful state of mind—an unassailable libidinal position which we ourselves have since abandoned. The great charm of narcissistic women has, however, its reverse side; a large part of the lover's dissatisfaction, of his doubts of the woman's love, of his complaints of her enigmatic nature, has its root in this incongruity between the types of object-choice.

Perhaps it is not out of place here to give an assurance that this description of the feminine form of erotic life is not due to any tendentious desire on my part to depreciate women. Apart from the fact that tendentiousness is quite alien to me, I know that these different lines of development correspond to the differentiation of functions in a highly complicated biological whole; further, I am ready to admit that there are quite a number of women who love according to the masculine type and who also develop the sexual overvaluation proper to that type.

Even for narcissistic women, whose attitude towards men remains cool, there is a road which leads to complete object-love. In the child which they bear, a part of their own body confronts them like an extraneous object, to which, starting out from their narcissism, they can then give complete object-love. There are other women, again, who do not have to wait for a child in order to take the step in development from (secondary) narcissism to object-love. Before puberty they feel masculine and develop some way along masculine lines; after this trend has been cut short on their reaching female maturity, they still retain the capacity of longing for a masculine ideal—an ideal which is in fact a survival of the boyish nature that they themselves once possessed.[1]

What I have so far said by way of indication may be concluded by a short summary of the paths leading to the choice of an object.

A person may love:—

(1) According to the narcissistic type:
- (*a*) what he himself is (i.e. himself),
- (*b*) what he himself was,
- (*c*) what he himself would like to be,
- (*d*) someone who was once part of himself.

(2) According to the anaclitic (attachment) type:
- (*a*) the woman who feeds him,
- (*b*) the man who protects him,

and the succession of substitutes who take their place. The inclusion of case (*c*) of the first type cannot be justified till a later stage of this discussion. [P. 101.]

The significance of narcissistic object-choice for homosexuality in men must be considered in another connection.[2]

The primary narcissism of children which we have assumed and which forms one of the postulates of our theories of the libido, is less easy to grasp by direct observation than to confirm by inference from elsewhere. If we look at the attitude of affectionate parents towards their children, we have to recog-

[1] [Freud developed his views on female sexuality in a number of later papers: on a case of female homosexuality (1920*a*), on the effects of the physiological distinctions between the sexes (1925*j*), on the sexuality of women (1931*b*) and in Lecture XXIII of his *New Introductory Lectures* (1933*a*).]

[2] [Freud had already raised this point in Section III of his study on Leonardo (1910*c*), *Standard Ed.*, **11**, **98 ff.**]

nize that it is a revival and reproduction of their own narcissism, which they have long since abandoned. The trustworthy pointer constituted by overvaluation, which we have already recognized as a narcissistic stigma in the case of object-choice, dominates, as we all know, their emotional attitude. Thus they are under a compulsion to ascribe every perfection to the child —which sober observation would find no occasion to do—and to conceal and forget all his shortcomings. (Incidentally, the denial of sexuality in children is connected with this.) Moreover, they are inclined to suspend in the child's favour the operation of all the cultural acquisitions which their own narcissism has been forced to respect, and to renew on his behalf the claims to privileges which were long ago given up by themselves. The child shall have a better time than his parents; he shall not be subject to the necessities which they have recognized as paramount in life. Illness, death, renunciation of enjoyment, restrictions on his own will, shall not touch him; the laws of nature and of society shall be abrogated in his favour; he shall once more really be the centre and core of creation—'His Majesty the Baby',[1] as we once fancied ourselves. The child shall fulfil those wishful dreams of the parents which they never carried out—the boy shall become a great man and a hero in his father's place, and the girl shall marry a prince as a tardy compensation for her mother. At the most touchy point in the narcissistic system, the immortality of the ego, which is so hard pressed by reality, security is achieved by taking refuge in the child. Parental love, which is so moving and at bottom so childish, is nothing but the parents' narcissism born again, which, transformed into object-love, unmistakably reveals its former nature.

[1] [In English in the original. Perhaps a reference to a well-known Royal Academy picture of the Edwardian age, which bore that title and showed two London policemen holding up the crowded traffic to allow a nursery-maid to wheel a perambulator across the street.—'His Majesty the Ego' appears in Freud's earlier paper on 'Creative Writers and Day-Dreaming' (1908*e*).]

III

The disturbances to which a child's original narcissism is exposed, the reactions with which he seeks to protect himself from them and the paths into which he is forced in doing so—these are themes which I propose to leave on one side, as an important field of work which still awaits exploration. The most significant portion of it, however, can be singled out in the shape of the 'castration complex' (in boys, anxiety about the penis—in girls, envy for the penis) and treated in connection with the effect of early deterrence from sexual activity. Psycho-analytic research ordinarily enables us to trace the vicissitudes undergone by the libidinal instincts when these, isolated from the ego-instincts, are placed in opposition to them; but in the particular field of the castration complex, it allows us to infer the existence of an epoch and a psychical situation in which the two groups of instincts, still operating in unison and inseparably mingled, make their appearance as narcissistic interests. It is from this context that Adler [1910] has derived his concept of the 'masculine protest', which he has elevated almost to the position of the sole motive force in the formation of character and neurosis alike and which he bases not on a narcissistic, and therefore still a libidinal, trend, but on a social valuation. Psycho-analytic research has from the very beginning recognized the existence and importance of the 'masculine protest', but it has regarded it, in opposition to Adler, as narcissistic in nature and derived from the castration complex. The 'masculine protest' is concerned in the formation of character, into the genesis of which it enters along with many other factors, but it is completely unsuited for explaining the problems of the neuroses, with regard to which Adler takes account of nothing but the manner in which they serve the ego-instincts. I find it quite impossible to place the genesis of neurosis upon the narrow basis of the castration complex, however powerfully it may come to the fore in men among their resistances to the cure of a neurosis. Incidentally, I know of cases of neurosis in which the 'masculine protest', or, as we regard it, the castration complex, plays no pathogenic part, and even fails to appear at all.[1]

Observation of normal adults shows that their former megalomania has been damped down and that the psychical characteristics from which we inferred their infantile narcissism have been effaced. What has become of their ego-libido? Are we to suppose that the whole amount of it has passed into object-cathexes? Such a possibility is plainly contrary to the whole trend of our argument; but we may find a hint at another answer to the question in the psychology of repression.

We have learnt that libidinal instinctual impulses undergo the vicissitude of pathogenic repression if they come into conflict with the subject's cultural and ethical ideas. By this we never mean that the individual in question has a merely intellectual knowledge of the existence of such ideas; we always mean that he recognizes them as a standard for himself and submits to the claims they make on him. Repression, we have said, proceeds from the ego; we might say with greater precision that it proceeds from the self-respect of the ego. The same impressions, experiences, impulses and desires that one man indulges or at least works over consciously will be rejected with the utmost indignation by another, or even stifled before they enter consciousness.[2] The difference between the two, which contains the conditioning factor of repression, can easily be expressed in terms which enable it to be explained by the libido theory. We can say that the one man has set up an *ideal* in himself by which he measures his actual ego, while the other has formed no

[1] [In a letter dated September 30, 1926, replying to a question from Dr. Edoardo Weiss (who has kindly brought it to our attention), Freud wrote: 'Your question, in connection with my assertion in my paper on Narcissism, as to whether there are neuroses in which the castration complex plays no part, puts me in an embarrassing position. I no longer recollect what it was I had in mind at the time. To-day, it is true, I could not name any neurosis in which this complex is not to be met with, and in any case I should not have written the sentence to-day. But we know so little of the whole subject that I should prefer not to give a final decision either way.'—A further criticism of Adler's views on the 'masculine protest' will be found in the 'History of the Psycho-Analytic Movement', p. 54 f. above.]

[2] [Cf. some remarks in the paper on repression (1915*d*), below, p. 150.]

such ideal. For the ego the formation of an ideal would be the conditioning factor of repression.[1]

This ideal ego is now the target of the self-love which was enjoyed in childhood by the actual ego. The subject's narcissism makes its appearance displaced on to this new ideal ego, which, like the infantile ego, finds itself possessed of every perfection that is of value. As always where the libido is concerned, man has here again shown himself incapable of giving up a satisfaction he had once enjoyed. He is not willing to forgo the narcissistic perfection of his childhood; and when, as he grows up, he is disturbed by the admonitions of others and by the awakening of his own critical judgement, so that he can no longer retain that perfection, he seeks to recover it in the new form of an ego ideal. What he projects before him as his ideal is the substitute for the lost narcissism of his childhood in which he was his own ideal.[2]

We are naturally led to examine the relation between this forming of an ideal and sublimation. Sublimation is a process that concerns object-libido and consists in the instinct's directing itself towards an aim other than, and remote from, that of sexual satisfaction; in this process the accent falls upon deflection from sexuality. Idealization is a process that concerns the *object*; by it that object, without any alteration in its nature, is aggrandized and exalted in the subject's mind. Idealization is possible in the sphere of ego-libido as well as in that of object-libido. For example, the sexual overvaluation of an object is an idealization of it. In so far as sublimation describes something that has to do with the instinct and idealization something to do with the object, the two concepts are to be distinguished from each other.[3]

The formation of an ego ideal is often confused with the sublimation of instinct, to the detriment of our understanding of the facts. A man who has exchanged his narcissism for homage to a high ego ideal has not necessarily on that account succeeded in sublimating his libidinal instincts. It is true that the ego

[1] [A comment on this sentence will be found in a footnote to Chapter XI of *Group Psychology* (1921*c*), *Standard Ed.*, **18**, 131 *n.*]

[2] [In the editions previous to 1924 this read '. . . is only the substitute . . .']

[3] [Freud recurs to the topic of idealization in Chapter VIII of his *Group Psychology* (1921*c*), *Standard Ed.*, **18**, 112 f.]

ideal demands such sublimation, but it cannot enforce it; sublimation remains a special process which may be prompted by the ideal but the execution of which is entirely independent of any such prompting. It is precisely in neurotics that we find the highest differences of potential between the development of their ego ideal and the amount of sublimation of their primitive libidinal instincts; and in general it is far harder to convince an idealist of the inexpedient location of his libido than a plain man whose pretensions have remained more moderate. Further, the formation of an ego ideal and sublimation are quite differently related to the causation of neurosis. As we have learnt, the formation of an ideal heightens the demands of the ego and is the most powerful factor favouring repression; sublimation is a way out, a way by which those demands can be met *without* involving repression.[1]

It would not surprise us if we were to find a special psychical agency which performs the task of seeing that narcissistic satisfaction from the ego ideal is ensured and which, with this end in view, constantly watches the actual ego and measures it by that ideal.[2] If such an agency does exist, we cannot possibly come upon it as a *discovery*—we can only *recognize* it; for we may reflect that what we call our 'conscience' has the required characteristics. Recognition of this agency enables us to understand the so-called 'delusions of being noticed' or more correctly, of being *watched*, which are such striking symptoms in the paranoid diseases and which may also occur as an isolated form of illness, or intercalated in a transference neurosis. Patients of this sort complain that all their thoughts are known and their actions watched and supervised; they are informed of the functioning of this agency by voices which characteristically speak to them in the third person ('Now she's thinking of that again', 'now he's going out'). This complaint is justified; it describes the truth. A power of this kind, watching, discovering and criticizing all our intentions, does really exist. Indeed, it exists in every one of us in normal life.

[1] [The possible connection between sublimation and the transformation of sexual object-libido into narcissistic libido is discussed by Freud towards the beginning of Chapter III of *The Ego and the Id* (1923*b*).]

[2] [It was from a combination of this agency and the ego ideal that Freud was later to evolve the super-ego. Cf. Chapter XI of *Group Psychology* (1921*c*) and Chapter II of *The Ego and the Id* (1923*b*).]

Delusions of being watched present this power in a regressive form, thus revealing its genesis and the reason why the patient is in revolt against it. For what prompted the subject to form an ego ideal, on whose behalf his conscience acts as watchman, arose from the critical influence of his parents (conveyed to him by the medium of the voice), to whom were added, as time went on, those who trained and taught him and the innumerable and indefinable host of all the other people in his environment—his fellow-men—and public opinion.

In this way large amounts of libido of an essentially homosexual kind are drawn into the formation of the narcissistic ego ideal and find outlet and satisfaction in maintaining it. The institution of conscience was at bottom an embodiment, first of parental criticism, and subsequently of that of society—a process which is repeated in what takes place when a tendency towards repression develops out of a prohibition or obstacle that came in the first instance from without. The voices, as well as the undefined multitude, are brought into the foreground again by the disease, and so the evolution of conscience is reproduced regressively. But the revolt against this 'censoring agency' arises out of the subject's desire (in accordance with the fundamental character of his illness) to liberate himself from all these influences, beginning with the parental one, and out of his withdrawal of homosexual libido from them. His conscience then confronts him in a regressive form as a hostile influence from without.

The complaints made by paranoics also show that at bottom the self-criticism of conscience coincides with the self-observation on which it is based. Thus the activity of the mind which has taken over the function of conscience has also placed itself at the service of internal research, which furnishes philosophy with the material for its intellectual operations. This may have some bearing on the characteristic tendency of paranoics to construct speculative systems.[1]

It will certainly be of importance to us if evidence of the

[1] I should like to add to this, merely by way of suggestion, that the developing and strengthening of this observing agency might contain within it the subsequent genesis of (subjective) memory and the time-factor, the latter of which has no application to unconscious processes. [For some further light on these two points see 'The Unconscious', pp. 187 and 188–9 below.]

activity of this critically observing agency—which becomes heightened into conscience and philosophic introspection—can be found in other fields as well. I will mention here what Herbert Silberer has called the 'functional phenomenon', one of the few indisputably valuable additions to the theory of dreams. Silberer, as we know, has shown that in states between sleeping and waking we can directly observe the translation of thoughts into visual images, but that in these circumstances we frequently have a representation, not of a thought-content, but of the actual state (willingness, fatigue, etc.) of the person who is struggling against sleep. Similarly, he has shown that the conclusions of some dreams or some divisions in their content merely signify the dreamer's own perception of his sleeping and waking. Silberer has thus demonstrated the part played by observation—in the sense of the paranoic's delusions of being watched—in the formation of dreams. This part is not a constant one. Probably the reason why I overlooked it is because it does not play any great part in my own dreams; in persons who are gifted philosophically and accustomed to introspection it may become very evident.[1]

We may here recall that we have found that the formation of dreams takes place under the dominance of a censorship which compels distortion of the dream-thoughts. We did not, however, picture this censorship as a special power, but chose the term to designate one side of the repressive trends that govern the ego, namely the side which is turned towards the dream-thoughts. If we enter further into the structure of the ego, we may recognize in the ego ideal and in the dynamic utterances of conscience the *dream-censor*[2] as well. If this censor is to some extent on the alert even during sleep, we can

[1] [See Silberer (1909 and 1911). In 1914—the year in which he wrote the present paper—Freud added a much longer discussion of this phenomenon to *The Interpretation of Dreams* (*Standard Ed.*, **5**, 503–6).]

[2] [Here and at the beginning of the next sentence, as well as below on p. 100, Freud makes use of the personal form, '*Zensor*', instead of his almost universal '*Zensur*' ('censorship'). Cf. a footnote to the passage in *The Interpretation of Dreams*, referred to in the last footnote (*Standard Ed.*, **5**, 505). The distinction between the two words is clearly brought out in a sentence near the end of Lecture XXVI of the *Introductory Lectures* (1916–17): 'We know the self-observing agency as the ego-censor, the conscience; it is this that exercises the dream-censorship during the night.']

understand how it is that its suggested activity of self-observation and self-criticism—with such thoughts as, 'now he is too sleepy to think', 'now he is waking up'—makes a contribution to the content of the dream.[1]

At this point we may attempt some discussion of the self-regarding attitude in normal people and in neurotics.

In the first place self-regard appears to us to be an expression of the size of the ego; what the various elements are which go to determine that size is irrelevant. Everything a person possesses or achieves, every remnant of the primitive feeling of omnipotence which his experience has confirmed, helps to increase his self-regard.

Applying our distinction between sexual and ego-instincts, we must recognize that self-regard has a specially intimate dependence on narcissistic libido. Here we are supported by two fundamental facts: that in paraphrenics self-regard is increased, while in the transference neuroses it is diminished; and that in love-relations not being loved lowers the self-regarding feelings, while being loved raises them. As we have indicated, the aim and the satisfaction in a narcissistic object-choice is to be loved.[2]

Further, it is easy to observe that libidinal object-cathexis does not raise self-regard. The effect of dependence upon the loved object is to lower that feeling: a person in love is humble. A person who loves has, so to speak, forfeited a part of his narcissism, and it can only be replaced by his being loved. In all these respects self-regard seems to remain related to the narcissistic element in love.

The realization of impotence, of one's own inability to love, in consequence of mental or physical disorder, has an exceedingly lowering effect upon self-regard. Here, in my judgement, we must look for one of the sources of the feelings of inferiority which are experienced by patients suffering from the transference neuroses and which they are so ready to report. The main source of these feelings is, however, the impoverishment of the ego, due to the extraordinarily large libidinal cathexes

[1] I cannot here determine whether the differentiation of the censoring agency from the rest of the ego is capable of forming the basis of the philosophic distinction between consciousness and self-consciousness.

[2] [This subject is enlarged on by Freud in Chapter VIII of his *Group Psychology* (1921*c*), *Standard Ed.*, **18**, 113 f.]

which have been withdrawn from it—due, that is to say, to the injury sustained by the ego through sexual trends which are no longer subject to control.

Adler [1907] is right in maintaining that when a person with an active mental life recognizes an inferiority in one of his organs, it acts as a spur and calls out a higher level of performance in him through overcompensation. But it would be altogether an exaggeration if, following Adler's example, we sought to attribute every successful achievement to this factor of an original inferiority of an organ. Not all artists are handicapped with bad eyesight, nor were all orators originally stammerers. And there are plenty of instances of excellent achievements springing from *superior* organic endowment. In the aetiology of neuroses organic inferiority and imperfect development play an insignificant part—much the same as that played by currently active perceptual material in the formation of dreams. Neuroses make use of such inferiorities as a pretext, just as they do of every other suitable factor. We may be tempted to believe a neurotic woman patient when she tells us that it was inevitable she should fall ill, since she is ugly, deformed or lacking in charm, so that no one could love her; but the very next neurotic will teach us better—for she persists in her neurosis and in her aversion to sexuality, although she seems more desirable, and is more desired, than the average woman. The majority of hysterical women are among the attractive and even beautiful representatives of their sex, while, on the other hand, the frequency of ugliness, organic defects and infirmities in the lower classes of society does not increase the incidence of neurotic illness among them.

The relations of self-regard to erotism—that is, to libidinal object-cathexes—may be expressed concisely in the following way. Two cases must be distinguished, according to whether the erotic cathexes are ego-syntonic, or, on the contrary, have suffered repression. In the former case (where the use made of the libido is ego-syntonic), love is assessed like any other activity of the ego. Loving in itself, in so far as it involves longing and deprivation, lowers self-regard; whereas being loved, having one's love returned, and possessing the loved object, raises it once more. When libido is repressed, the erotic cathexis is felt as a severe depletion of the ego, the satisfaction of love is impossible, and the re-enrichment of the ego can be effected only by a withdrawal of libido from its objects. The return of the object-libido to the ego and its transformation into narcissism represents,[1] as it were, a happy love once more; and, on the other hand, it is also true that a real happy love corresponds to the primal condition in which object-libido and ego-libido cannot be distinguished.

The importance and extensiveness of the topic must be my justification for adding a few more remarks which are somewhat loosely strung together.

The development of the ego consists in a departure from primary narcissism and gives rise to a vigorous attempt to recover that state. This departure is brought about by means of the displacement of libido on to an ego ideal imposed from without; and satisfaction is brought about from fulfilling this ideal.

At the same time the ego has sent out the libidinal object-cathexes. It becomes impoverished in favour of these cathexes, just as it does in favour of the ego ideal, and it enriches itself once more from its satisfactions in respect of the object, just as it does by fulfilling its ideal.

One part of self-regard is primary—the residue of infantile narcissism; another part arises out of the omnipotence which is corroborated by experience (the fulfilment of the ego ideal), whilst a third part proceeds from the satisfaction of object-libido.

The ego ideal has imposed severe conditions upon the satisfaction of libido through objects; for it causes some of them to be rejected by means of its censor,[2] as being incompatible. Where no such ideal has been formed, the sexual trend in question makes its appearance unchanged in the personality in the form of a perversion. To be their own ideal once more, in regard to sexual no less than other trends, as they were in childhood—this is what people strive to attain as their happiness.

Being in love consists in a flowing-over of ego-libido on to the object. It has the power to remove repressions and re-instate perversions. It exalts the sexual object into a sexual ideal. Since, with the object type (or attachment type), being in love occurs

[1] ['*Darstellt.*' In the first edition only: '*herstellt*', 'establishes'.]
[2] [See footnote, p. 97.]

in virtue of the fulfilment of infantile conditions for loving, we may say that whatever fulfils that condition is idealized.

The sexual ideal may enter into an interesting auxiliary relation to the ego ideal. It may be used for substitutive satisfaction where narcissistic satisfaction encounters real hindrances. In that case a person will love in conformity with the narcissistic type of object-choice, will love what he once was and no longer is, or else what possesses the excellences which he never had at all (cf. (*c*) [p. 90]). The formula parallel to the one there stated runs thus: what possesses the excellence which the ego lacks for making it an ideal, is loved. This expedient is of special importance for the neurotic, who, on account of his excessive object-cathexes, is impoverished in his ego and is incapable of fulfilling his ego ideal. He then seeks a way back to narcissism from his prodigal expenditure of libido upon objects, by choosing a sexual ideal after the narcissistic type which possesses the excellences to which he cannot attain. This is the cure by love, which he generally prefers to cure by analysis. Indeed, he cannot believe in any other mechanism of cure; he usually brings expectations of this sort with him to the treatment and directs them towards the person of the physician. The patient's incapacity for love, resulting from his extensive repressions, naturally stands in the way of a therapeutic plan of this kind. An unintended result is often met with when, by means of the treatment, he has been partially freed from his repressions: he withdraws from further treatment in order to choose a love-object, leaving his cure to be continued by a life with someone he loves. We might be satisfied with this result, if it did not bring with it all the dangers of a crippling dependence upon his helper in need.

The ego ideal opens up an important avenue for the understanding of group psychology. In addition to its individual side, this ideal has a social side; it is also the common ideal of a family, a class or a nation. It binds not only a person's narcissistic libido, but also a considerable amount of his homosexual libido,[1] which is in this way turned back into the ego. The want of satisfaction which arises from the non-fulfilment of this ideal

[1] [The importance of homosexuality in the structure of groups had been hinted at in *Totem and Taboo* (1912–13), *Standard Ed.*, **13**, 144, and was again referred to in *Group Psychology* (1921*c*), *Standard Ed.*, **18**, 124 *n.* and 141.]

liberates homosexual libido, and this is transformed into a sense of guilt (social anxiety). Originally this sense of guilt was a fear of punishment by the parents, or, more correctly, the fear of losing their love; later the parents are replaced by an indefinite number of fellow-men. The frequent causation of paranoia by an injury to the ego, by a frustration of satisfaction within the sphere of the ego ideal, is thus made more intelligible, as is the convergence of ideal-formation and sublimation in the ego ideal, as well as the involution of sublimations and the possible transformation of ideals in paraphrenic disorders.

PART TWO

Discussion of "On Narcissism: An Introduction"

Freud's "On Narcissism": A Teaching Text

CLIFFORD YORKE

Anyone coming to Freud's paper "On Narcissism" for the first time may find the going rough. For one thing, there is the sheer profusion of ideas, so densely packed as to make heavy demands on the reader. And the subject matter itself is not easy; there are many conceptual problems in the issues under discussion. It is difficult to be a student these days without realizing that a great deal of controversy surrounds the concepts of "narcissism," "the self," and "self-esteem." These subjects bristle with complexities. This fact in itself may be a very good reason for going back to the first psychoanalytic attempts to grapple with some of them. It will probably come as no surprise to learn from Strachey's introduction that Freud found the paper difficult to write and that he said in a letter to Abraham: "The 'Narcissism' had a difficult labor and bears all the marks of a corresponding deformation."

For all that, it is easy to feel very involved in Freud's explorations. As always with his developing ideas, it is helpful to relate any particular formulation to those that have gone before and to keep an eye on those that lie ahead. In reading the paper on narcissism, for example, you may find it useful to keep in mind that it already has the makings of a tripartite model of the mind, even if there is still a long way to go before the formulations of *The Ego and the Id*, which clarified so many problems and set up a major landmark. Here, for example, we are already dealing with an important development in the theory of the instinctual drives, with the "ego," and with an internal self-observing agency that anticipates a more fully developed concept of the superego; and we are concerned with the relations of these agencies both to one another and to the outside world.

In the *Standard Edition*, as is well known, Strachey almost invariably translates the term *das Ich* as "the ego," and he himself traces, on more than one occasion, the shift in the meaning Freud attached to it in the course of developing his ideas. The detailed history of these shifts is rather complicated, but Strachey's brief discussion of it in his Editor's Note is perfectly serviceable. In the early papers, the "ego," though often ill-defined, usually stands for the "self" (a term not without its own complexities), whereas from 1923 onward it has a more definite if restricted meaning, referring to a mental agency with its own attributes and functions. In this sense, it can perhaps be thought of as the executive apparatus of the mind, holding the balance among the often conflicting demands of the instinctual drives, the superego, and external reality. As Strachey observes, in the paper on narcissism the concept of the ego "occupies a transitional point." In practice this means that one has to be particularly careful about the meaning of the term whenever it is met in the course of the argument. I shall try to clarify this as I go along. But "the ego" is not the only term that may trouble the reader in this paper; many difficulties are encountered with the concepts of primary and secondary narcissism, and I will also give some attention to such questions.

Let us now take a look at some of the principal ideas in the paper, bearing these points in mind as we do so. In trying to tackle the problem of narcissism Freud discusses both the normative and the pathological. He talks about "His Majesty the Baby" and about falling in love. From the side of pathology, he draws inferences from schizophrenia and paranoia, from physical pain in organic states as well as in hypochondriasis, and he starts and ends his discussion with reference to sexual deviation.

Freud begins by reminding us that the term "narcissism" was initially a descriptive one, first used by Näcke at the turn of the century to refer to the attitudes of certain people to their own body, which they treat in much the same way as other people treat the bodies of those with whom they have a sexual relationship—that is, they look at it, admire it, stroke it, fondle it, and find it entirely self-satisfying. Carried to this degree, narcissism has all the characteristics of a sexual deviation. Freud takes the view that the phenomenon does not exist in this extreme or pure form. He may be right: certainly, if it *does* exist, it might not come to notice. It would be unlikely to offend the public or attract the attention of the police, and since people do not "suffer" from disorders such as this, they would be unlikely to seek help on account of it. But it is certainly met with in less extreme forms. As Freud points out, it is an important component in homosexuality. And it may very well be met, in some degree, in the course of an analysis. A patient I know once described the phenomenon in talking about her adolescence. She recalled looking at herself in the mirror and admiring her body, but to become really aroused she would wear diapers soaked in very warm water as she gazed at her reflection. Perhaps this particular example comes to mind because the regressive element in the experience is so striking, perhaps because of its bearing on childhood narcissism. These adolescent episodes did not persist as a deviation into the adult life of this patient. They did, however, involve a flight from object relations and to that extent are of further pertinence to our immediate concerns.

But the example also illustrates Freud's long-standing view, so well argued in *Three Essays on the Theory of Sexuality*, that what appears as deviation in later life is to be found in normative child development. Certainly, the pleasure derived by the infant from the warmth of the urine and feces in her diapers is unlikely to be thought of as perverse. This is in line with Freud's conclusion that narcissism is not a deviation as such but the sexual "complement to the egoism of the instinct of self-preservation." It is the libidinal contribution to self-attachment and self-interest.

The point will bear repeating: in this context, "narcissism" means self-love and "egoism" means the self-regard manifested in the drive for self-preservation. In order to grasp the point it is necessary to bear in mind the state of instinct theory in 1914. In the first edition of the *Three Essays* in 1905 Freud had used the term "auto-erotism" and regarded the activity as an expression of the sexual instinct before *self- and object-differentiation had occurred*. He had borrowed the term from Havelock Ellis and had already used it in a letter to Fliess. "Auto-erotism" referred to the very first stage in instinctual development. It was succeeded by instinctual "object choice," but the child's first "choice" was his own body or bodily self, and it was this stage to which Freud gave the name of "narcissism" in 1911, in the third part of his discussion of the Schreber case. The sexual instincts were already distinguished from the "ego-instincts"—the self-preservative instincts of the "self," including hunger. The concept of "ego-instincts" was maintained in this paper; but the concept of narcissism posed difficulties for instinct theory that called for some measure of reappraisal.

Freud turned to certain psychotic phenomena to assist this reappraisal. The Schreber case opened up a number of important new issues for him, some of which had a significant bearing on the theory of the instincts. In particular, he was concerned with the question of whether, or to what extent, the schizophrenic and paranoiac could be understood with the help of libido theory. He considered that patients of this kind had two striking and basic characteristics. The first of these was "megalomania," in which the overvaluation of the self went side by side with the second feature—a withdrawal of interest from people and things. (This second characteristic led Freud to believe that such patients were inaccessible to psychoanalytic treatment.) He maintained that the megalomania was the direct result of this withdrawal from objects.

Freud had already taken the view that neurosis involved a withdrawal from the external world, from the world of objects, precipitated by loss of the object, by loss of object love, or by an inability to adapt to the instinctual claims of objects—in short, by what is at bottom instinctual frustration. In the neuroses, an erotic relationship to objects is not given up, though: it is retained, but only in fantasy. Disappointment or frustration in the real world leads to the cathexis of fantasy objects, based largely, if unconsciously, on the object relationships of childhood. In this sense, the cathexes are still object-cathexes and not the narcissistic or self-cathexes of psychosis.

The reader will be familiar with the next steps in neurotic symptom formation as Freud conceptualized them, of how the withdrawal of instincts from real to fantasy objects (a process he used to call "introversion") leads to a regressive shift, how the defensive ego (in this sense a structure) opposes and disguises the return of the repressed, leading to symptom formation through compromise. All this is germane to the general question, which I shall touch on presently, of the relationship of the neuroses to the psychoses—not only a matter of importance in this essay but a continuing problem and still a source of controversy.

In schizophrenia, then, it is the withdrawal of libido from objects to the self that gives rise to the pathological narcissism characteristic of this disorder. But this narcissism is a secondary one, since it was originally directed to external objects, and it augments the preexisting primary narcissism that has remained attached to the self (a point worth remembering, since primary narcissism is often confused with what, in this paper, Freud calls autoerotism). The result is a *hypercathexis* of the "self" (or, as we put it nowadays in more structural terms, of the mental representation of the self). Unlike the neurotic, the narcissist does not replace the object in the external world by a fantasized one. But when an attempt *is* made to restore object investment, it does appear in delusional form.

At this point, it may be helpful to set aside Freud's main argument for the moment and to look back to the Schreber case—a case of persecutory paranoia. The apparent first step in Schreber's illness was the delusional belief that his former physician, Flechsig, would emasculate him, turning him into a woman to be sexually abused. The next step was the belief that God had called upon him to carry out a divine mission and that he could accomplish this only if he *did* turn into a woman. He believed he had come to possess breasts and female genitals and that God would send divine rays in order to impregnate him so that he could give birth to a new race of men. In the process Schreber had to suffer a great deal at God's hands. (This was the stage designated at the time as "dementia paranoides"—a term long since abandoned. In any case, far from showing signs of what would nowadays be called dementia, Schreber was sufficiently unimpaired in his intellectual powers to be able to write the memoirs of his illness.) But how did Freud's formulation of the Schreber case fit in with the notion of megalomania? And how do grandiose wish-fulfilling beliefs lead to persecutory delusions?

You have to remember Freud's conception of the steps by which Schreber's illness came about and to think of them in two phases. The first of these was the morbid process itself; the second was the formation of the overt paranoid illness. Freud had come to the conclusion that the first stage was brought about when Schreber's homosexual wishes toward Flechsig were subjected to a form of repression. The libidinal cathexis was withdrawn from Flechsig (or, rather, from Schreber's mental representation of him) and was returned to the self, leading to the grandiose delusions, the megalomanic belief in building a new race of men. The paranoid delusions came about by a return of the libido, hitherto repressed, to the object of Schreber's love—to Flechsig. But the repressed homosexual wish could reappear only in altered form, and so Flechsig was hated instead of loved. Even this alteration could not be accepted as it stood; it had to be projected, so that Schreber experienced the hatred as coming from without—from Flechsig. The unconscious underlying wish was to play the role of a woman in relation to the man or, more correctly if we take into account a regressive process, of a girl in relation to the father. So, although in this formulation the first step in the formation of the illness was a libidinal cathexis of the self and not of a fantasy object, the object relation was restored through a process of restitution. The initial steps, and the final outcome, are very different from those in the neuroses. But what is clear, in this account at any rate, are the striking similarities between the two groups of disorders.

All this should be borne in mind when reading the paper on narcissism, even though Freud rightly emphasized that he was not concerned, in this paper, with the intricacies of schizophrenia and paranoia. It is almost always useful, when reading anything of Freud's, to have an idea of the concepts that were in his mind at the time he wrote as well as some of the directions in which he was heading. So it may be helpful to think of the Schreber case when reading this paper, since much of his thinking then was carried forward to influence it. It is also recommended that you look ahead to "Instincts and Their Vicissitudes" and even "Mourning and Melancholia." In this work, the schizophrenic psychoses and paranoia are introduced to cast fresh light on the problems of narcissism. What then, in particular, did this paper add to what had gone before?

In the first place, it drew a distinction for the first time between "ego-libido" and "object-libido" to show how, under certain circumstances, the one could replace the other in part or in whole. Freud also introduced the concept of the ego-ideal and of a self-observing function, but I want to defer discussion of this until a little later. Incidentally, when one is thinking about the new terminology, it is important not to confuse narcissistic libido with the ego-instincts: both appear to refer to the self. We have already looked at the fact that the self-preservative instinct of the ego is in many ways in opposition to the libidinal drives themselves, whenever those drives might be dangerous or threatening to the individual's safety or peace of mind. But in referring to the concept of "repression" in both the neuroses and the psychoses, Freud is also pointing to an opposing structure within the mental apparatus that can interfere with or oppose drive discharge. In this respect the ego has an adaptive, even executive function and cannot be simply or satisfactorily equated with the "self."

If Freud describes the mechanisms by which grandiosity arises in terms of a decathexis of objects and a hypercathexis of the self, he is at pains to emphasize that the grandiosity itself is not a "new creation" but must be regarded as a heightened state of a preexisting condition, one belonging to a normative stage in child development. This analogue or precursor of "megalomania" can be found in early childhood, in what Freud referred to as the "omnipotence of thoughts"—the child's belief in the magical power of words stemming from overestimation of the power of his wishes and of his mental acts. This is the attitude of "His Majesty the Baby," which would, if it occurred in later life, be regarded as decidedly grandiose. Freud examines this infantile attitude, from the instinctual side, in terms of an initial libidinal overinvestment of the self; and, indeed, any attachment to the external world of objects can be withdrawn at any time. (The famous analogy is with the pseudopodia of the amoeba.)

Freud thought that an opposite state of affairs is encountered in the phenomenon of falling in love. According to this view, it is the object, not the self as in childhood omnipotence or in paranoia, that is libidinally overinvested. The loved one is exalted and there is a corresponding devaluation of the self. Many people are impatient with any idea that falling in love involves a depletion of self-esteem. They regard Freud's concept as a kind of mathematical manipulation of relationships that may well serve an economic point of view but does no great service to our understanding of everyday experience. They point to the elation that is such a common concomitant of being in love: surely, they argue, this suggests a rise in self-esteem as well as esteem of the object.

It is true that this view of falling in love is an "economic" one, but you need to keep a number of points in mind if you are to decide its value for your own thinking about the subject. To start with, Freud had in mind the economics of *narcissism* in *self-esteem*: the two terms are not synonymous. Furthermore, he made clear in the metapsychological papers that followed this essay his firm opinion that any given psychological process could be understood only if *all* metapsychological points of view were taken into account. From this standpoint, the dynamic and structural aspects of falling in love would have to complement the economic one; and a number of writers have commented on the need to consider the developmental and adaptive points of view also. Although there are some structural considerations and some dynamic ones in the paper on narcissism, the discussion is unmistakably and by design an economic one, and to that extent is far from complete, even in the light of Freud's psychoanalytic understanding at the time it was written. Again, the paper is about falling in love, the state of being in love, and not about loving itself. Had it been about the latter it would have been far more difficult to restrict the discussion to an economic viewpoint. Furthermore, the discussion, if taken as a whole, makes clear that any exalted feeling that comes from the state of being in love derives from an awareness that the love is returned. Unrequited love, after all, can be a very painful state indeed.

Moreover, Freud speaks of *two* types of object choice, of which this is but one. We need to look more closely at his reasoning. He approaches the question developmentally and argues that the child's first sexual objects are those who care for him and look after him and from whom he experiences satisfaction. Using the terminology of the time, he points out that the earliest autoerotic satisfactions are linked with vital functions so that those satisfactions also serve the purpose of self-preservation. Thus at the start of life, there is a close relationship between the sexual instincts and the ego-instincts, though these become independent at a later stage in development. But even when that independence is arrived at, those concerned with the child's feeding, care, and protection—generally speaking, the mother or mother substitute—are the first sexual objects. This is the "anaclitic," or attachment type of object choice. This kind of object choice, however modified, may persist and become the basis of adult object choice. Of course, if it is insufficiently modified by a healthy adult sexuality and regard for the object, it leads to the kind of relationship in which the man is looking for a mother rather than a wife. There is another type of object choice, to be found very often in women, though Freud emphasized that it is by no means universal or confined to them. This can properly be called "narcissistic object choice." The two types are not sharply differentiated, though the individual may show a preference for one or the other.

Freud, however, derived his concepts of narcissistic object choice not only from observations of the normative but also from considerations of the homosexual and the sexually perverse. These conditions all display a high degree of narcissism: indeed, it is not difficult to argue that love for one's own sex is founded on love of oneself. And homosexual love also involves the persistence of, or return to, a childhood state of affairs. This is particularly clear in homosexual pedophilia but is readily traceable in many other conditions. It should be remembered that the term "homosexuality" includes a very wide range of conditions indeed, involving, inter alia, different types of identification. If, for example, you read Richard Ellmann's biography of Oscar Wilde, you may easily form the opinion that Wilde's effeminacy included an identification with an adoring mother and that his passion for beautiful boys (usually, it seems, adolescents and very boyish young men) involved narcissistic love of himself as a boy through identification with a beautiful mother. These are complex issues that I can only touch on here.

Any adequate discussion of narcissistic love would involve detailed attention to the perversions: for present purposes it may be enough to keep in mind that a considerable overinvestment in a particular part-instinct and erotogenic zone of the body at the expense of genital heterosexual intercourse is a regular feature. The relationship between this group of disorders and the hypochondriases is something that calls for a later comment.

To return to the normative, Freud thought that object love of the attachment type, with its pronounced sexual overvaluation of the loved one stemming from the child's original narcissism, was more characteristic of the male. In most women, on the other hand, the maturation of the sexual organs, which had come about at puberty, meant that the original narcissism was intensified. It was an important reason that object choice leading to sexual overvaluation was less likely to be the first step in a woman's falling in love. The initial need was to be loved, with narcissism reinforced from the outside: the woman's love of the object came in response to feeling loved. No doubt we would all be inclined to consider that, whereas the man generally derives his sexual excitement from the exciting quality of the woman herself, the woman gets her excitement from the fact that she can excite the man.

Freud was of the opinion that feminine narcissism was particularly attractive to men. That is an opinion we can share if we think of the appeal of film stars or fashion models. Freud thought that part of the attraction for men of beautiful and narcissistic women came from their apparent independence and self-confidence, and envy of the invulnerability of their apparently blissful state of mind. Their narcissism was of an order that men had had to renounce early on. Freud made the striking observation that narcissistic animals such as cats often excite admiration, as do "criminals and humourists." I suppose we can all think of the narcissistic displays of comedians to which we respond with a pleasure comparable with their self-enjoyment; and certainly criminals have a fascination—in books and television, at any rate.

Many men will recognize what Freud meant when he referred to a reverse side to the charm and attraction of the narcissistic woman: to a considerable extent, the man's doubts about the woman's love, his dissatisfaction with the "enigma" she presents, stem from the different underlying nature of the two types of object choice. *Her* type of love is different from his. But Freud reemphasized the fact that there are a number of women who love according to the masculine type and develop a corresponding sexual overvaluation of the object, just as some men love according to the feminine type. Perhaps many of us would want to add that, whatever the type of object choice, where love is returned, *being in love* as opposed to *loving* contains a mutual idealization, even if the factors that lie behind it have different origins. And last, we should bear in mind Freud's observation that, in narcissistic love, a person can delight in someone who represents what he himself is, what he himself was, what he himself would like to be, or in someone who was once part of himself. Love of the anaclitic, or attachment type can be directed to someone who represents the woman who fed him or the man who protected him.

We now come to one of the most important parts of Freud's paper—the major contribution to our understanding of mental structure and functioning brought about by the introduction of the concept of an "ego ideal." Freud's discussion of the concept is generally very clear, although there are a few points that may appear obscure, at least at first. I shall try to clarify some of these, without oversimplifying, in the brief summary that follows.

Freud's conceptual forward leap springs from his question: what is the fate of "infantile megalomania?" To find an answer, he reexamines the concept of repression, observing that instinctual impulses are repressed when they come into conflict with the individual's cultural and ethical standards. So although repression has always been held to be imposed from the side of the ego, it would be more accurate to say that it arises from the "self-respect of the ego." Instinctual impulses and wishes that one person may indulge, or at least consciously entertain, would be put out of court by another without even entering consciousness. The difference between the two (the operation of repression) can be explained by the fact that one man has set up an ideal in himself by which he measures his "actual ego"—that is, the current state of the self or, in later terminology, the self-representation. The other man has not formed any such ideal. The formation of the ideal would be the factor that conditions repression. The self-love of childhood with its narcissistic sense of self-perfection is now directed to the ego ideal: it is to this ideal that the state of childhood perfection is now attributed.

Freud then asks a further question: what is the relation between this ideal and sublimation? In sublimation *object-libido* is directed or deflected to a nonsexual aim. In idealization, on the other hand, an object itself is "aggrandised and exalted in the subject's mind." And since an object can be the self as well as another person, both ego-libido and object-libido can lead to the exaltation. The formation of an ego-ideal should not be confused with the sublimation of instinct. As Freud puts it, rather tellingly, an ego-ideal may demand sublimation, "but it cannot enforce it"; the execution is independent of its promptings. Sublimation meets instinctual demand without any contribution from repression.

The next step in Freud's argument is perhaps the most crucial. There must be a psychic agency that tries to make sure that narcissistic gratification from the ego-ideal is maintained. Its task is to observe the state of the ego (self) and to measure it and assess it from the standpoint and standards of the ideal. We can recognize and identify this agency by simple introspection; it is, at a conscious level, our "conscience." And if we follow Freud and turn, once again, to paranoia for further enlightenment, we can recognize the operation of the agency in the delusions of being watched. The patient's thoughts are known to others, and his actions are observed. Auditory hallucinations in the form of voices may tell him of this—for example, by recounting his movements in the third person. The patient complains of this and rebels against it. His complaint has a real justification, because the experience is a regressive one in which he is once again observed from the outside by controlling and supervising parental figures whose power is augmented by teachers and other influential people. The patient's rebellion can be understood and justified in this way. Since the investment of the ego-ideal is narcissistic, it is also homosexual. In paranoia a homosexually driven conscience confronts the patient, in a regressive form, as an external and hostile witness.

What I have presented here is a guide to Freud's paper, not a substitute for it. He deals with a great many subjects, some of which I have not touched on at all; nor have I tried to compare the views expressed in the paper with those of recent and contemporary writers such as Kohut and Kernberg. I believe very strongly that it is not possible to understand and evaluate the formulations of these thinkers unless you already know your Freud. And the paper on narcissism represents a transitional stage in his thinking that is of such importance that it must be put into historical perspective before it is possible to move on. So at this point it seems appropriate to offer some suggestions for the next step in your Freud reading.

READING

The Freudian revaluations that were still to come included, from the standpoint of metapsychology, the clarification of instinct theory, major structural refinements in the concept of the ego, and the development and elucidation of the theory of the superego. They also included a major reformulation of the theory of anxiety. In terms of the special interests exemplified in the paper on narcissism, the later contributions to the understanding of sexual development, and to the sexual perversions, in both men and women were of special importance.

"Instincts and Their Vicissitudes" is the natural successor to the present paper. It is necessary to understand this work in order to appreciate the need for a wholesale revision of theory in *The Ego and the Id* in 1923. (*Beyond the Pleasure Principle*, which foreshadowed that theory somewhat controversially, speculatively, and whose emphasis was on the biological rather than the psychological, can be set aside for the time being.) A reading of "Instincts" should be followed by a study of the other metapsychological papers of 1915. They are indispensable and in some ways the most neglected of Freud's theoretical works. This may be partly a reflection of the fact that, in many quarters, metapsychology is unfashionable; but it is, to my mind, synonymous with psychoanalytic psychology both then and now. Personally, I can't do without it in my own clinical and theoretical thinking, but some people neglect it with insouciance. At any rate, in order to follow through the thinking in "On Narcissism," you will need to turn to the papers on repression and the unconscious. "A Metapsychological Supplement to the Theory of Dreams" and "Mourning and Melancholia" are essential reading for the theory of psychosis and much else besides. You will also need to pursue Freud's other papers on psychosis, because his comments in the present work are unsatisfactory if left to stand by themselves. I will say a little more about this under a different heading.

You may want to defer the reading on psychosis until you have familiarized yourself with structural theory. There are two ways of doing this. One is to turn next to *The New Introductory Lectures* before reading *The Ego and the Id*. In this case you will find the chapter on anxiety and instinctual life takes you first to the revised instinct theory, and the chapter on mental anatomy introduces you in a very lucid way to the tripartite model. This method has the further advantage of acquainting you with the revision of the theory of anxiety—a later development than that of instinct and mental structure.

The other way is to go straight to *The Ego and the Id* and use *The New Introductory Lectures* for clarification. But before following either of these methods, let us ask ourselves why some of these changes were necessary.

The necessity for formulating a structural *model* of the mind, as distinct from a structural *point of view*, came about for two reasons, one theoretical, the other clinical. The older topographical model had placed the repressing agencies of the mind within the preconscious system, and this created a serious anomaly. How could defenses operate unless they themselves were unconscious? After all, if a defense were accessible to consciousness, how could you be aware of it without knowing what it was defending against? The clinical reason was equally compelling. Freud was impressed by the "negative therapeutic reaction." He repeatedly observed patients who had worked diligently with the analyst in the treatment and had gained important insights and yet not only failed to get better but actually got worse. He was able to explain this only on the basis of unconscious guilt—a notion that led him to extend his earlier discussions of conscience and the ego ideal to the concept of a superego which itself had important unconscious roots. So the superego became much more than an internal watchdog, and it certainly could not be equated merely with "conscience"—conscience cannot be regarded as "conscience" unless it is open to awareness.

If you have chosen to begin your study of the structural model with *The New Introductory Lectures*, you will find that the chapter on female sexuality will now help clarify some of the problems posed by Freud's earlier thinking on the subject; and differences in gender development are, to say the least, one of the important considerations touched on but not developed in the paper on narcissism.

And last, when reading Freud's later contributions to the theory of the perversions, special attention should be paid to "A Child Is Being Beaten" and "The Economic Problem of Masochism." They have a great deal to say that links childhood experience with perverse activities that seem to contradict and go against the "Pleasure Principle."

NARCISSISM AND SELF-ESTEEM

It is important not to confuse narcissism and self-esteem. Although narcissism is an instinctual component of self-esteem, it is not identical with it. It is worth remembering that Freud points to two other components of self-regard. We have already touched on the second of these: the residue of childhood omnipotence that is reinforced by experience. It represents a fulfillment of the early ideal state of the self for the later attainment of the self-ideal. The third contributor comes from satisfaction, including instinctual satisfaction, via the object. But we should not forget Freud's comment that the "ego-ideal" imposes restrictions on the degree and quality of instinctual satisfaction through objects especially where infantile forms of gratification have become unacceptable. The interrelationship of the three components of self-regard is no simple matter.

It is worth seeing if, armed with the structural model, you can translate these earlier formulations on self-regard into structural terms. It will be necessary to start by revising the terminology in order to accommodate the new concepts. You have to take account of the substantial revisions of drive theory now that aggression has been given a status comparable to that of sexuality; and you will have to ask how far the concept of a structural defense organization has replaced the older concept of ego-instincts. (Your conclusion may very well be that the concepts of internal and external adaptation are helpful here; certainly structural theory brings the adaptive viewpoint into greater prominence and clarity.)

But to continue: when thinking about the term "ego" you should use the term "self" when you *mean* the self (or, more precisely, its representation within the mind) and the term "ego" when you refer to the ego as an adaptive and executive structure. The term "superego" is more difficult. It is to be seen not only as an agency that sets aims and standards and acts as an internal policeman whose operation gives rise to a sense of guilt but also as an internal source of love and approval. Such an exercise should prove rewarding, and it may also help make clear why further work was needed on the concept of the superego, why it gave rise to an extensive later literature, and why a number of associated concepts still need further clarification.

SCHIZOPHRENIA AND PARANOIA

Freud's remarks on the role played by narcissism in the development of paranoid and schizophrenic psychoses, and my discussion of it in relation to this particular paper, may suggest that he saw a close relationship between these disorders and the neuroses. But if you set these observations in the context of his other contributions to the subject, you may recognize, as many writers in recent times have done, that he was by no means single-minded about the matter. He held to the possibility that the instinctual decathexis of objects did not simply serve a defensive function but might be brought about, at least in part, by defects arising in ego functioning (one contemporary, Nathaniel London, called it a "psychological deficiency state"). In our book *Development and Psychopathology: Studies in Psychoanalytic Psychiatry*, Tom Freeman, Stanley Wiseberg, and I have discussed this question at some length, as well as some important issues arising from it; but I need to make one or two brief points to clarify my earlier comments.

Freud always acknowledged his debt to the English neurologist Hughlings Jackson and his theory of evolution and dissolution of the nervous system. Freud applied these formulations to his own thinking about mental illness. The loss or impairment of the most recently acquired ego functions gave rise to two sets of symptoms: the negative symptoms stemming from the loss itself, and the positive ones that came to light when developmentally older mental functioning, hitherto prevented from reaching full expression by an intact ego, came to the fore. In these terms, the loss of object cathexes would represent the negative symptoms, and the phase of restitution would be better understood in terms of the positive ones.

These two views of the psychotic process have given rise to opposing schools of thought, both very much alive today. Broadly speaking, positive symptoms (such as delusions, hallucinations, and negativism) may be thought of either as the repetition and regressive expression of infantile fantasies and defenses—a view taken by Melanie Klein, Harold Blum, Ping-nie Pao, and other writers—or as the result of an ego dissolution that allows earlier mental content, such as oedipal wishes, to reappear and serve the purpose of reconstruction. This is a view that can be traced through Freud from Hughlings Jackson and is represented by such writers as Maurits Katan, Robert Bak, and John Frosch.

It is not necessary to jettison a link between neurosis and psychosis if you follow this second line of thinking. Katan, in particular, devoted his life to Freud's thinking about the psychoses but found the concepts of decathexis and restitution difficult to accept as processes leading to symptom formation in the schizophrenic and paranoid psychoses. He has shown that the difficulties can be substantially resolved if a distinction is drawn between a prepsychotic phase and the psychosis itself. The symptoms of the prepsychotic phase, when these have been observed or reconstructed, can be explained on the basis of regression and the return of the repressed—that is, of the neurotic model. In the psychotic phase neurotic compromise formations between defense and drive representations no longer exist, because the ego is disorganized by the psychotic process and cannot function in a comparable way. It comes, to a much greater degree, under the sway of the primary process, which now plays a leading part in bringing about the form and content of delusions and hallucinations, once a defect in and loss of ego functions has led to the break with reality. The underlying conflicts are no different in the prepsychotic and psychotic phases, but the partial ego dissolution in the latter alters the way in which they are dealt with and hence the clinical presentation. Indeed, it is the fact that comparable conflicts are to be found in the neuroses and psychoses that has made the continuum theory so attractive to so many analysts.

Before passing on to one or two concluding matters, I should like to go back for a moment to Freud's view of "megalomania" in terms of withdrawal of object cathexis and its reinvestment of the self. Older critics of this view, like Paul Federn and Paul Schilder, have argued that if, in psychosis, this hypercathexis of the self always follows the decathexis, then grandiose delusions ought to be found in every acute attack. But this is not the case. In the majority of schizophrenic psychoses with persecutory delusions, grandiose delusions *follow* rather than precede or accompany the persecutory features. Indeed, Federn went so far as to assert that a fall, rather than an increase, in the libidinal investment of the self not only preceded a persecutory schizophrenic illness but was a precondition for it.

Perhaps the key point to be taken from these comments is one made over twenty years ago by Edith Jacobson and reemphasized more recently by writers like London and Frosch. It is that, in formulating a theory of what ought properly to be called "the schizophrenias," nosography is of central importance. There is a wide range and variety of symptoms not only between but within a given type, and psychoanalysts and general psychiatrists alike have to take due account of this. Any theory that restricts itself to one particular clinical presentation is bound to pose difficulties for those who try to understand disturbances that show different clinical features, are brought about differently, and have a different result. Some schizophrenias clear up without recurrence and others have a moderately severe or very severe end state. Delusional object relations in the remitting schizophrenias are different from those in the nonremitting; and the dynamic, economic, and structural considerations of each need to be given adequate consideration and weight. Many of the writers I have mentioned here have made valuable contributions to a better understanding of these disorders. Although Freud's formulation, as presented in the paper on narcissism, has some limitations, his thinking has nevertheless proved a fertile basis for later contributors in the field.

Last, when reading "Mourning and Melancholia," it is useful to keep in mind your own experiences with manic depressive psychosis. The question of mania and hypomania in relation to narcissism is an interesting one. Certainly the expression of grandiose delusions can be found in abundance (if you are lucky enough to see the patient before medication has affected the clinical picture) even though it is often possible to detect traces of painful underlying states. But it may also be worth asking whether the instinctual component in certain delusions invests the self with a sexual quality that is more or less unmodified and is not subject to aim inhibition. Much can be said about, and learned from, the manic depressive illnesses.

ORGANIC ILLNESS AND HYPOCHONDRIASIS

I will not say much about the increased narcissism of organic illness, for Freud's comments speak for themselves, and one's own experiences confirm them. But I do want to say a few words about hypochondria to which, Freud suggests, the same economic considerations apply.

Perhaps most people would prefer to speak of the "hypochondriases" rather than "hypochondria," since the symptom of hypochondriasis can appear as a clinical feature in a very wide range of conditions. It is a repeated manifestation in the psychoses, including the schizophrenias; indeed, a schizophrenic psychosis can first attract attention when a patient complains of distortion, malfunction, or injury to his body that turns out to be delusional. There is an example of this condition in "A Metapsychological Supplement to the Theory of Dreams," and everyone with experience in psychiatry or psychology will have encountered many such instances. It is well known, too, that depressive hypochondriasis with delusional body disorders—such as a belief that the body is rotting or falling to pieces—is not uncommon in severe psychotic manic depressive depressions and in the involutional form of that disorder. There are also those instances in which a severe hypochondriasis, which may reach delusional intensity, is superimposed on an existing organic disturbance that in itself is of minor significance. Certainly, the forms hypochondriases can take are protean; I can think of a patient who suffered in reality from a serious blood disorder, which he totally ignored, repeatedly placing himself in peril, while at the same time believing he had an incurable cancer.

There is, however, a form of hypochondriasis that is often monosymptomatic and does *not* present as part of any other disorder. The narcissistic attachment to the offending part of the body is intense, and, indeed, it may be almost impossible to get the patient to show interest in anything else. Object cathexis is so minimal that it is often impossible to gain the patient's attention long enough to take a history. Such patients are often refractory to any psychological intervention, so that therapy, analytic or not, is out of the question. Incidentally, Schilder once put forward the interesting idea that certain forms of depersonalization, often similarly refractory to treatment, may include in the context of their pathology a *decathexis* of a part of the body and even, sometimes, the whole of it.

It cannot be pretended that cases of this kind are well understood. They have not generally been subjected or amenable to the kind of analytic scrutiny that would make them more comprehensible, at least psychologically. This is particularly true of the monosymptomatic conditions. But it is very important to differentiate these states from other psychological disturbances presenting with somatic disorders. From the standpoint of narcissism, I believe you can draw a very important distinction between a monosymptomatic hypochondriasis and a somatic conversion hysteria. In the case of the latter the symptom itself includes an important residue of an infantile object relationship, whereas in the hypochondriasis no object relationship is represented in the symptom and the instinctual investment in it is entirely narcissistic. This observation is in line with Freud's formulations in the paper on narcissism and with his comments on the instinctualization of the organs involved.

Freud's discussion of infantile narcissism and infantile omnipotence underlines the central importance of the developmental principle in psychoanalytic thinking. Some work might therefore be studied that draws on the clinical and theoretical findings of child analysis; and I don't think you can do better than read Anna Freud's book *Normality and Pathology in Childhood*. In any child studies, it is useful to bear in mind Anna Freud's distinction between hypochondriacal *symptoms* and hypochondriacal *attitudes* in children. We have all come across children who have not been given adequate bodily care by their mother or mother substitute and who respond by taking over, prematurely, the care of their own body. This may sometimes lead to a degree of bodily concern that is absent from children more fortunate in this respect. But hypochondriacal attitudes can stem from many sources.

LOOKING AHEAD

Looking ahead again, this time beyond Freud's contributions to our knowledge of narcissism, the self, and self-esteem, I would suggest that even those who feel they have a good working knowledge of Freud not rush straight to the literature on what has been called "self psychology" or to contemporary writers on "narcissistic disturbance." There is a vast output, to be sure, and it will have to be tackled sometime. But I would be inclined to look first at some other key, if earlier, writings—for example, at Hartmann's clarifications of the distinctions between the concepts of "ego" and "self." His discussion of "narcissism" in terms of the libidinal investment of the structured representation of the self within the system ego (a point I have touched on before) clarifies some important issues. His formulation was particularly attractive to Edith Jacobson and led her to provide an extensive discussion, in 1964, of what she called "the self and the object world." She had seized on Hartmann's distinction between the self as the *person* and the self *representation*. Hartmann had already suggested that this term be used for the unconscious, preconscious, and conscious endopsychic representations of the bodily and mental self in the structured ego.

Other essential reading includes Erikson on pride and shame, Schafer on the "self" in his book on internalization, Piers and Singer on shame and guilt, and the work of Sandler and his colleagues at the Anna Freud Centre on the concepts of the superego as well as the representational world. Such concepts as an "ideal self" and an "ideal parent" will no doubt be both clinically and theoretically useful. I have not supplied any references: the search for these writings will not be a difficult one and may itself provide a learning experience. From then on, you can, I hope, look further ahead without too much guidance and perhaps make your own evaluation of later contributions.

"On Narcissism: An Introduction": Text and Context

R. HORACIO ETCHEGOYEN

"On Narcissism: An Introduction," has always been regarded as one of the basic writings in the corpus of psychoanalytic theory, because Freud here deals with a number of important and complex problems. Many of these problems remain as valid as when the work was written, whereas others are no longer so relevant; however, I would venture to assert that the proposition of a primary narcissism as the starting point of psychic life is at the root of the fundamental controversies of psychoanalysis today. To understand Freud's paper, a thorough and attentive reading is essential; one might even say that it should be read word by word. At the same time, it must be placed in its historical context, and due account must be taken not only of its theoretical determinants but also of the demands of the contemporary situation it was designed to satisfy. For this purpose, we must address ourselves to the major figures of that time, when the psychoanalytic establishment was forming and this newly created structure was in the process of breaking up through the defection of two important protagonists, Adler and Jung. This task must be performed as objectively and dispassionately as possible, and we must, of course, never forget that we, too, are a part of this history and that our judgments are delivered from the position we necessarily occupy—a position that is not only theoretical but also affective and political.

CHRONOLOGY

Although I intend to follow Freud's essay step by step as if Freud himself were speaking, I do not nurture excessive illusions about my impartiality; it is precisely because of this distrust of myself, however, that I have some hope of achieving a certain balance. Again, to be honest, I must say that the difficulties are due not only to the commentator but also to the text itself, which is not always clear and sharply defined. Indeed, why should it be? "On Narcissism" is a transitional work, a worrying paper, says Jones, because "it gave a disagreeable jolt to the theory of instincts on which psychoanalysis had hitherto worked" (1955, 339). We may add that Freud not only changes the theory of instincts but also foreshadows a new conception of the psychic apparatus. In fact, while establishing the principles of his metapsychology, to be formulated in his 1915 papers, Freud was prefiguring the upheaval that ensued some years later, which culminated in the structural theory of *The Ego and the Id* (1923). Freud was at the time immersed in these acute theoretical conflicts (which by themselves more than suffice to explain his difficulties) as well as the major theme of psychosis, and he was also caught up in the turmoil of personal arguments that induced all those involved to take up passionately and disputatiously held positions. It is this, of course, that provoked its author to say that this paper had had a difficult birth (letter to Abraham, March 16, 1914; Freud and Abraham, 1965).

Although it is true that Freud formally introduced the concept of narcissism into his theory at this point, the term was already known, although it was not in common use. According to Jones, Freud used it for the first time in the work on Leonardo (Freud, 1910a). He used it again a year later to explain Schreber's megalomania (Freud, 1911), but he had already told the Vienna Psychoanalytical Society on November 10, 1909, that narcissism was a necessary intermediate stage in the passage from autoerotism to alloerotism (Jones, 1955, 2:304). Both the second edition of the *Three Essays on the Theory of Sexuality* (1905), which appeared in 1910, and *Leonardo da Vinci and a Memory of His Childhood*, which dates from the same year, are concerned with narcissism, or more specifically with narcissistic object choice, which leads the future homosexual, identified with his mother, to seek a person of his own sex who represents him.

In the third essay of *Totem and Taboo* (1912–13), Freud discusses narcissism in relation to omnipotence (Section 3): at the animistic stage, men ascribe omnipotence of thoughts to themselves; this they will subsequently have to delegate to the parents. At this point, Freud recalls his comments in the *Three Essays* (in particular, from the third edition of 1915) on psychosexual development. Childhood sexuality is not unitary and is not directed toward an object; it is at first anarchic, its various components each seeking its own pleasure and finding its satisfaction in the subject's own body. Freud calls this the stage of "autoerotism"; it precedes "alloerotism," in which the object appears. There is a stage between these two, in which the unified sexual instincts take as their object the individual's own ego, which has been constituted at about the same time. In this intermediate stage, called "narcissism," the subject behaves as if he were in love with himself; his egoistic instincts cannot yet be separated from his libidinal wishes. It is worth emphasizing that this condition is for Freud not only a stage of development but also a stable structure in the human being, who remains narcissistic even after finding an object. As elsewhere in his work, Freud says here that the cathexes of objects are merely emanations of the libido that remains in the ego.[1] It is to this narcissism that Freud ascribes the omnipotence of thoughts.

The ideas sketched out above converge and are powerfully developed in the 1914 paper. Let us now review the three sections of "On Narcissism" in sequence.

I

Freud borrowed the term "narcissism" from Paul Näcke, who used it in 1899 to denote a perversion in which a person treats his own body as a sexual object, and from Havelock Ellis, who introduced it a year earlier to describe a psychological attitude comparable to that of the mythical figure ("Narcissus-like"). Following Freud's classification of the perversions in the first of his *Three Essays*, we might say that Näcke's narcissism is a perversion in regard to the sexual *object*.

1. "A human being remains to some extent narcissistic even after he has found external objects for his libido. The cathexes of objects which he effects are as it were emanations of the libido that still remains in his ego and can be drawn back into it once more" (*Totem and Taboo*, 89).

Clinical experience revealed that narcissistic features were also displayed by other patients—for example, homosexuals, as Sadger pointed out. Finally, Otto Rank concluded in 1911 that narcissistic allocations of libido might claim a place in normal human sexual development. In this way, narcissism ceased to be merely a perversion and became also "the libidinal complement to the egoism of the instinct of self-preservation" (Freud, 1914, 73–74). At this point it is worth dwelling for a moment on Rank's forgotten essay, which emphasizes the importance of narcissism and understands it as a normal phenomenon, as an inescapable transition from autoerotism to object love taking place in adolescence. Rank's case is that of a woman in whom, as he pointed out, love for her own body not only determined normal female vanity but was also closely bound up with a homosexual inclination. Rank maintained that self-love in adolescent women also had to do with the state of being in love with the mother in childhood, which was subsequently transformed into an identification with her and the search for the subject herself in the female homosexual partner (as had already been described in men). In this way the fantasy of rejuvenation was crystallized—a fantasy that was to play an important part in Rank's subsequent ideas about the double as a narcissistic ideal of immortality.

The hypothesis of normal narcissism proved to be an essential link for Freud when he tried to understand schizophrenia in the light of libido theory.[2] The big difference between these patients and neurotics is that, in the former, the libido has truly been withdrawn from the object; the process thus goes further than the phenomenon of introversion described by Jung in his fine essay of 1910, "Psychic Conflicts in a Child."[3] This is a vital point in the paper, and we shall return to it; for the present, however, I wish to

2. As we know, Freud (1911) proposed the term "paraphrenia" to replace Kraepelin's "dementia praecox," which Bleuler called "schizophrenia." The word used by the eminent superintendent of Burghölzli is preferred in this essay not only because it has become accepted but also because I consider it most appropriate. It may also be pointed out that Freud altered the meaning of his paraphrenia in 1914 to embrace Bleuler's schizophrenia and Kraepelin's paranoia. It will also be remembered that Kraepelin distinguished paranoia from paraphrenia from 1912 onward. Finally, for the sake of accuracy, we should point out that Eugen Bleuler's book was finished in 1908, as the author says in his prologue, although it was not published until 1911.

3. Jung here describes the behavior of four-year-old Anna after the birth of a younger brother; he says that the little girl's reveries "express the fact that part of the love which formerly belonged, and should belong, to a real object is now *introverted* —that is, it is turned inwards into the subject and there produces an increased fantasy activity" (13).

stress that narcissism was introduced into libido theory to take account of schizophrenia.

Freud characterizes schizophrenia by two features: lack of interest in the outside world, and megalomania.[4] He finds that the hypothesis of a narcissistic libido fully resolves the matter: the libido withdrawn from the outside world explains the lack of interest, its application to the ego, and the megalomania. Without embarking upon a lengthy psychiatric discussion, I must point out that this characterization is, to say the least, questionable. Megalomania is not a pathogenic symptom of illness but rather is "pathoplastic," to use Birnbaum's old, consistent classification of symptoms. In my opinion, the symptoms that are pathogenic of schizophrenia are better covered by Bleuler's classic trio—dissociation, ambivalence, and autism.

But let us return to Freud. The economic change that transfers object-libido to the ego, which is thereby enlarged, is not an entirely new phenomenon; it is not something that generates illness. In the third essay of *Totem and Taboo*, Freud says that primitive man and the boy containing him in our ontogenic development display this same expansion of the ego, this overvaluation of wishes and of the power of the mind—that is, ultimately, the belief in magic as an infallible way of dominating the surrounding world. On the basis of this developmental assumption, Freud was to say that the narcissism of the schizophrenic is secondary, that the libido flows back to the ego by virtue of the illness, following an already existing path, which must then necessarily stem from a primary narcissism.

With this argument, Freud has introduced a major change into libido theory: between autoerotism and alloerotism, he has interpolated a stage in which the libido is applied to the ego, which is thereby constituted.

It is at this point that Freud, for the first time in his work, distinguishes between two types of libido—object-libido and ego-libido, which contrast with and complement each other. The one always grows at the expense of the other. From then on, Freud was to play with these two concepts and to maintain always (or almost always) that ego-libido was the original phenomenon that subsequently gave rise to the cathexes given to objects. The model Freud used repeatedly is that of the amoeba and its pseudopodia.

Object-libido attains its peak of expression in love, where the ego appears to dissolve while the object is enlarged; on the other hand, narcissistic libido

4. This word is used in Strachey's translation and, of course, refers to normal individuals, not psychotics.

is totally predominant in the schizophrenic fantasy of the "end of the world," which Freud had studied in 1911 in his explanation of some aspects of the mental illness of Judge Schreber.

With the postulation of a primary narcissism, two questions immediately arise concerning the future position in the theory of, first, autoerotism and, second, the ego-instincts. Autoerotism had been a fundamental premise since the first edition of the *Three Essays*, and Abraham had made use of it in 1908 in his convincing explanation of the psychosexual differences between hysteria and dementia praecox—that is, between neurosis and psychosis. Freud places these two pieces of the theory in order of development and specifically states that instincts are present in the individual from the start, whereas the ego, in contrast, has to be developed. Autoerotism is replaced by narcissism precisely when the libidinal cathexis of the ego comes about as a new psychic act (Freud, 1914, 77). This satisfactorily answers the first question, at least for the time being. The second is more complex, and the reply to it contains the fundamental controversy with Jung, to which we will return. For a better understanding of our present subject, let us go back for a moment to "The Psycho-Analytic View of Psychogenic Disturbance of Vision" (1910b), in which Freud for the first time clearly distinguishes two types of instincts, sexual and ego-instincts, which may conflict. The sexual instincts seek pleasure, while the ego-instincts have as their aim the self-preservation of the individual, so that "all the organic instincts that operate in our mind may be classified as 'hunger' or 'love'" (Freud, 1910b, 214–15). Note that the word *hunger* is used here in a very wide sense, to encompass all the self-preservative instincts, and that Freud unequivocally attributes the function of repression to these "ego-instincts." Every organ (in this case, the eye) is subject to a double claim (from the ego and from sexuality), making it vulnerable to psychogenic alteration. By the theoretical construction recalled above, Freud redefines the psychic conflict, the dynamic of mental processes, contrasting sexual and ego-instincts, love and hunger—two instinctual forces always at odds with each other.

But once it had been admitted that the ego receives a libidinal cathexis at the outset, might it not be appropriate to abandon the distinction between sexual instincts and ego-instincts? This is precisely what Jung (1912) had in effect proposed in widening the concept of libido and placing it on a par with ego interest. Freud, of course, rejects this proposal and argues that the differentiation of libido into two classes arises from the intimate characteristics of neurotic and psychotic processes and "is an unavoidable corollary to an original hypothesis which distinguished between sexual instincts and ego-instincts" (1914, 77). He adds that this differentiation arises from the study of the transference neuroses (hysteria and obsessional neurosis), whose symptomatic dynamics are explained by a psychic conflict between sexuality and the ego. Freud is obviously basing his argument on the study of neurosis and does not wish to give up well-earned ground to Jung, who not only asserts that libido theory is inapplicable to the psychoses but claims that it should be dropped altogether.

Freud gives further reasons for maintaining the distinction between the ego-instincts and the sexual instincts. First, he considers that it corresponds to the popular distinction between the fundamental instinctual categories of hunger and love; second, it takes account of man's twofold existence, both as an individual and as a carrier of germ-plasm. This argument is based on Weismann's theory, which was then in vogue, but it could hold up equally well in terms of present-day genetic theories. At the end of his argument, Freud finds himself impelled to admit, at any rate, that libido theory, in upholding this instinctual duality, is based more than anything on biological arguments: "the hypothesis of separate ego-instincts and sexual instincts (that is to say the libido theory) rests scarcely at all upon a psychological basis, but derives its principal support from biology" (1914, 79). Careful consideration shows that the need to distinguish the sexual instincts from the ego-instincts is inherent not in libido theory but rather in the theory of conflict—the dynamic viewpoint. Although Freud does not say so in this paragraph, libido theory can be maintained without the "ego-instincts." In fact, before 1910 (and, of course, from 1923 on), Freud speaks of an ego as opposed to instinct, and in 1920 he declared that narcissistic libido could be identified with the instincts of self-preservation (1920, chap. 6).

II

Having introduced the concept of narcissism in Section I, Freud devotes the next section to a consideration of the pathways leading to it. He begins by asserting that the chief means of access appears to be the study of schizophrenia; just as the neuroses opened the way to the observation of object-libido, it will be the psychoses that will afford an insight into the psychology of the ego—that is, of narcissistic libido. There are other means of approaching this complex phenomenon, however—for example, organic disease, hypochondria, and erotic life.

Following a suggestion by Ferenczi, Freud considered that organic disease affected the distribution of libido. Ferenczi subsequently wrote a number of papers on this subject. One of the first was "Disease—or Patho-Neurosis" (1917), pathoneurosis being psychological illness stemming from organic disease. In the pathoneuroses, libido is withdrawn from objects in the external world and concentrated on a specific organ; however, the disturbance of libidinal economy is secondary and not primary as in the psychoneuroses. Ferenczi claims that this disturbance not only affects the narcissistic positions of the libido; the concentration of libido on an organ may, he suggests, stimulate a particular component instinct, so that the object relation is maintained. Ferenczi here obviously sets less store than Freud by the idea that libido, if located in the body, must necessarily be narcissistic.

For Freud, as well as for Ferenczi, organic suffering causes the individual to withdraw from the world of objects and concentrate on himself; in terms of the theory formulated above, this means that the libido has flowed back to the ego, which is here in fact identified with the body. Ego-libido and the ego-instincts (interest) then share a common fate and again become indistinguishable: egoism covers both (1914, 82). Something similar occurs in dreaming, where the libido is also withdrawn onto the subject's own self. Freud returned to this theme in 1917 when he wrote that the "psychic state of a sleeping person is characterized by an almost complete withdrawal from the surrounding world and a cessation of all interest in it" (1917, 222). In the sleeping state, a profound change takes place, whereby the ego returns to the stage of hallucinatory fulfillment of wishes, and the libido, to primary narcissism.

The hypochondriac, Freud continues, also withdraws his libido from the external world and makes it narcissistic, by directing it toward the organ that is engaging his attention, the difference here being that there are no signs of organic disease. Nevertheless, if we regard the "sick" organ of the hypochondriac as an erotogenic zone, it may be compared with the genitals in a state of excitation. The libido withdrawn from the objects of the external world in hypochondria and transformed into narcissistic libido has cathected an erotogenic zone; in this way, hypochondria is explained, like organic disease, in terms of distribution of libido. As we know, Freud placed hypochondria among the actual neuroses. But whereas anxiety neurosis and neurasthenia operate with object-libido, hypochondria uses narcissistic libido; and just as anxiety neurosis is the actual neurosis of the hysterias and neurasthenia that of obsessional neurosis, so hypochondria is constituted in accordance with the actual-neurosis model of schizophrenia. From the point of view of ego-libido, hypochondriacal anxiety is, for Freud, the counterpart of neurotic anxiety (1914, 84). Freud had arrived at the same conclusions in the case of Schreber, where he states that a theory of paranoia that does not include hypochondriacal symptoms is not trustworthy (1911, 56, n. 3). I have no doubt that Freud's thinking here was profoundly influenced by the illness of Schreber, who first suffered an attack of severe hypochondria, which remitted, followed years later by his succumbing to paranoia or dementia paranoides.[5] Freud must also surely have had in mind the analysis of the Wolf Man, with his hypochondriacal symptoms and megalomania (Freud, 1918).

In any case, Freud does not give many reasons for classifying hypochondria among the actual neuroses—that is, in a group of illnesses that express an alteration of libido at the level of the organism and not of the mind, whose symptoms have no psychological content and must be regarded as being of toxic origin (as Freud said in 1895 and at the symposium on masturbation held by the Vienna Psychoanalytical Society [Freud, 1912a, 248]). Nor is it clear to me why Freud relates hypochondria so closely to "paraphrenia," to use the term he prefers. Hypochondria is as frequent in schizophrenia as in manic-depressive psychosis (without going any further, we may recall Cotard's syndrome); indeed, following the work of Rosenfeld (1958, 1964), there is good reason to believe that hypochondria does in fact have a psychological content.[6] For these reasons, Freud goes a step further and maintains that the starting point for schizophrenia is the damming-up of ego-libido.

To obtain the best possible understanding of Freud's reasoning on this complex subject, it is appropriate to recall "Types of Onset of Neurosis" (Freud, 1912b). The mechanism of illness and symptom formation in the transference neuroses is explained by a frustration (*Versagung*), which initiates introversion of libido. The subject withdraws his libido from reality objects and finds satisfaction in fantasy life; however, if the libido is not satisfied in this way, damming-up occurs. The libido then follows the path of regression, infantile aims are reactivated, and a conflict is triggered. This conflict is resolved by the formation of symptoms (1912b, 231–33).

5. "Dementia paranoides" means paranoid dementia praecox or paranoid schizophrenia.

6. We may recall the argument between Freud and Stekel when Stekel published his book on anxiety neurosis, which rejected the concept of actual neurosis (Stekel, 1908).

In this argument, the mental apparatus is regarded as a device designed for mastering excitations that would otherwise give rise to unpleasure or have pathogenic effects. Working over the excitation in the mind performs an important service as it allows a draining away of excitations that are incapable of direct discharge outward (or where such a discharge is undesirable). It is initially irrelevant whether this internal process of discharge is carried out on real or imaginary objects; this becomes important only when the libido turned onto the imaginary object is insufficiently discharged and damming-up occurs.

Using this model, Freud explains what happens in schizophrenia when the libido returns to the ego and therefore becomes narcissistic: megalomania arises to process this narcissistic libido, and "perhaps it is only when the megalomania fails that the damming-up of libido in the ego becomes pathogenic and starts the process of recovery which gives us the impression of being a disease" (1914, 86).

It follows from Freud's explanation that megalomania is a normal process that tends to drain away excitation within an ego overloaded by the libido, which has flooded it and which, in the event of failure, is converted to hypochondria; this is the onset of what phenomenologically constitutes the illness with its symptoms. If I am not mistaken, megalomania can be understood in this context as an attempt to increase the self-regard of the ego (perhaps reduced by frustration); Kohut (1971) would certainly take this view.

To sum up, in order to explain schizophrenia by the theory of the damming-up of libido and actual neurosis, Freud postulates a blockage of ego-libido, with the ad hoc hypothesis that this blockage gives rise to unpleasure because of increased tension. He needs this second hypothesis because the flowing back of libido onto the ego cannot be unpleasant for the Freudian dialectic, as it must be for object-libido. Here we see clearly emerging the Freud of the "Project" (1950 [1895])—the Freud who sought to explain mental phenomena by sums of excitation (Q), the Freud who put forward the economic view of the metapsychology of the years around 1915, the Freud who produced the unpublished "Project" and also wrote on neurasthenia and anxiety neurosis (Freud, 1895). With these conceptual instruments, Freud was not only to approach the mystery of psychosis but also to propose an explanation of an even greater mystery—why mental life finds itself compelled to go beyond the boundaries of narcissism and assign libido to the objects of the external world: "this necessity arises when the cathexis of the ego with libido exceeds a certain amount" (1914, 85). Freud ends this argument with the following comforting words: "A strong egoism is a protection against falling ill, but in the last resort we must begin to love in order not to fall ill." For those who believe, like Melanie Klein (1928) and Fairbairn (1941), that the ego and object relations exist from the beginnings of mental life, this problem is solved by definition, although other, no less thorny, problems certainly confront them.

Freud then concludes that the megalomania of schizophrenia allows an internal working over of the libido turned back onto the ego, and when this fails—that is, when megalomania fails—the libido is pathogenically dammed up in the ego, giving rise to hypochondria and thence to the singular process of recovery that gives the impression of being a disease.

Let us once again examine Freud's rigorous argument. Both the transference neuroses and schizophrenia (narcissistic neurosis) are initiated when a certain amount of libido is withdrawn from the objects of the real world, owing to frustration, and applied to imaginary objects (in the transference neuroses) or to the ego (in the narcissistic neuroses). In the former case, the process is called introversion; in the latter, megalomania. As long as no damming-up of libido occurs, everything is all right; but if it does, anxiety appears in the transference neuroses, the libido then following the path of regression, and hypochondria arises in schizophrenia and initiates the illness. Megalomania "would thus be the counterpart of the *introversion* onto phantasies that is found in the transference neuroses; a failure of this psychic function gives rise to the hypochondria of paraphrenia and this is homologous to the anxiety of the transference neuroses" (1914, 86). In other words, megalomania is to ego-libido what introversion is to object-libido; when these fail, hypochondria and anxiety respectively arise. Just as anxiety can be conquered in the transference neuroses by the construction of neurotic symptoms (conversions, phobias, reaction formations, and so on), in schizophrenia hypochondria can be worked over by a process of restoration that gives rise to manifest pathological phenomena. Hence the symptoms of schizophrenia are an attempt to attach the libido once again to objects. This new cathexis is certainly very different from the original one, as Freud explains in "The Unconscious" (1915).

After considering hypochondria with a view to approaching closer to the problem of narcissism, Freud turns with the same aim to some characteristics of human erotic life. His starting point is that children choose their sexual objects from their experiences of satisfaction, since their sexuality is autoerotic and can reach the world of objects only in connection with vital functions that serve the purpose of self-preservation. Although it follows as an analytic judgment from the theory itself, Freud considered this to be confirmed by observation in the study of the object choice of children, who "derived their sexual objects from their experiences of satisfaction" (1914, 87), since autoerotic satisfaction, where the source and the object coincide in the erotogenic zone, neither needs nor acknowledges the object. Hence "the sexual instincts are at the outset attached to the satisfaction of the ego-instincts" (1914, 87); Freud calls this process *Anlehnung*, "leaning-on." "The sexual instincts are at the outset attached to the satisfaction of the ego-instincts; only later do they become independent of these" (1914, 87). Strachey makes the point (1914, 87, n. 2) that the process refers to the instincts and not to the child and the mother. Freud calls this form of object choice *Anlehnungstypus*, which Strachey rendered in English as "anaclitic type," by analogy with the grammatical term "enclitic," used of particles that must be appended to the preceding word in the sentence to which they are joined.

Although Freud here for the first time gives a name to this type of object choice, the concept of autoerotism obviously goes hand in hand with this view of the relations of the child with the external world. If the sexual instinct, like Leibniz's monad, can remain totally enclosed within itself, the subject's connection with the world must come from elsewhere, from the ego-instincts. I believe that this is another reason Freud has to defend the "ego-instincts" at all costs; he fails to realize that by initially denying the sexual instinct the possibility of an object relation, he makes it forfeit much of its autonomy and importance. From this point of view, it seems that it was not only Jung who questioned the importance of infantile sexuality! Jung's argument is based precisely on the fact that libido has a supplementary character for Freud in that it is inevitably supported by the ego-instincts. "It is hardly to be assumed that the normal '*fonction du reel*' [Janet] is maintained only through affluxes of libido or erotic interest" (1916, 141–42).[7] The Spanish version, presumably amended by its author over the years, puts it more forcefully: "It is hardly to be assumed that the normal '*fonction du reel*' [Janet] is maintained only by supplementary duties, that is, by erotic interest" (*Simbolos de Transformacion*, 1982, 146). Ultimately, I consider it easier to refute Jung by the theory of object relations in psychoanalysis than by that of autoerotism and primary narcissism.

7. *Wandlungen und Symbole der Libido* was translated into English in 1916 as *Psychology of the Unconscious*.

In addition to anaclitic object choice, Freud discovers another, which he was not prepared to find; in this form the choice is made not on the model of the object but on that of the ego. This form is so surprising to Freud that he has no hesitation in saying that his observation was the main reason for his adoption of the hypothesis of narcissism.

In this way Freud finally distinguishes two types of object choice, anaclitic and narcissistic, which he regards as two paths the individual may follow. He here puts forward the relation to the object and narcissism as two equally valid alternatives open to the child, but he immediately afterward reaffirms his argument in favor of a primary narcissism:

> We have, however, not concluded that human beings are divided into two sharply differentiated groups, according as their object-choice conforms to the anaclitic or to the narcissistic type; we assume rather that both kinds of object-choice are open to each individual, though he may show a preference for one or the other. We say that a human being has originally two sexual objects—himself and the woman who nurses him—and in doing so we are postulating a primary narcissism in everyone which may in some cases manifest itself in a dominating fashion in his object-choice. (1914, 88)

The text is ambiguous, and this is why I have quoted it at length. I believe Freud means that the individual always has these two possibilities, but at first had only one, the narcissistic choice of object. I draw attention to this difficulty in the text because this is the point of divergence in psychoanalytic theory between those who believe that narcissism is primary, object relations coming only later, and those who maintain that mental life begins with the relation to the object, narcissism being only a turning back and therefore always secondary.

To illustrate these two types of object choice, Freud examines the erotic life of men and women. He finds a fundamental difference: only men are capable of attaining complete—that is, anaclitic—object love; women conform to the narcissistic type, loving themselves and needing to be loved before loving. Freud's distinctions between men and women in the matter of object choice are irrelevant for our present purposes; the subject is in any case polemical, as these ideas can be rejected without detracting from the hypothesis of a primary narcissism.

Freud ends this section by asserting that the primary narcissism of children is one of the postulates of the (new) libido theory, thereby opening the way to the final part of his essay, in which he discusses the ultimate fate of primary narcissism.

III

In the third section, after contrasting Adler's (1910) concept of masculine protest with that of castration anxiety, Freud considers what has happened to the megalomania of the child, from which the hypothesis of infantile primary narcissism had been deduced. He finds that a part of the ego-libido has been directed to the object while another has succumbed to the repression that proceeds from the self-respect of the ego. Freud now puts forward an idea that was to be important in the changes his theory of the mental apparatus was to undergo in the 1920s: he postulates that the necessary condition for repression is the construction of an ideal that becomes the target of the self-love whose object in childhood was the ego. The latter is constantly compared with this ideal, and this is the conditioning factor of repression. The love the real ego enjoyed in infancy is now directed toward this ideal ego. Incapable as always of giving up a satisfaction once enjoyed, man can forgo the pure perfection of childhood only by re-creating it in this ideal ego which replaces the lost narcissism of childhood.

Freud here rightly distinguishes between idealization and sublimation, which are radically different concepts because the former concerns the object and the latter the instinct. This distinction facilitates our understanding of Freud's idea of love: he repeats that sexual overvaluation of an object is an idealization of it. Love, whether narcissistic or anaclitic, is then necessarily connected with idealization of the object. As Freud was to say *Group Psychology and the Analysis of the Ego*, the loved object enjoys freedom from criticism, and its characteristics are valued more highly than their real worth (1921, 112). The tendency that falsifies judgment is idealization. In idealization, the object is treated in the same way as our own ego, so that when we are in love a considerable amount of narcissistic libido overflows onto the object. If this process continues, the object eventually attracts to itself the entire narcissistic love of the ego for itself. The object has, so to speak, consumed the ego: "*The object has been put in the place of the ego ideal*" (1921, 113; Freud's emphasis).

This view is highly controversial, and many analysts believe, on the contrary, that idealization is indicative of a failure of the capacity to love. And in any case, what kind of love is it that the greater its intensity the more it falsifies its object?

Freud now moves on firmly toward the structural theory of the 1920s, suggesting that it might be possible to find a special psychic agency responsible for ensuring the narcissistic satisfaction of the ideal ego, watching the actual ego and comparing the two. This agency would be what we call "conscience." Recognition of this agency explains the delusions of being watched (*Beobachtungswahn*) of paranoiacs and also some characteristics of normal individuals. By this solid reasoning, Freud has already given a full description of the superego, finally to be introduced into the theory in *The Ego and the Id* (1923). Although this agency arises from the lost narcissism of infancy, Freud has no doubt that the stimulus for its formation stems from the influence of parents on the child and subsequently that of the child's educators and society in general.

Since Freud maintains that a large amount of homosexual libido is mobilized to form this narcissistic ideal ego, in which it finds outlet and satisfaction, we must assume that this ideal is constructed on the basis of the parent figure of the same sex. This assumption is confirmed because Freud tells us immediately afterward that the revolt against this censoring agency is an attempt at liberation from the parental influence and withdrawal of homosexual libido from the relevant parent figure. The ideal must thus stem not only from the primary narcissism of the child but also from its relations with its parents. Many contemporary authors therefore consider the superego to be a two-part structure, made up of the superego proper and of the ego ideal.

Conscience serves introspection, fuels the philosophical attitude for the construction of speculative systems, conditions the symptoms of paranoia, and plays a fundamental part in a normal person's self-regard (*Selbstgefuhl*). Self-regard is indeed closely bound up with narcissistic libido, as is obvious from the fact that it increases in schizophrenia (in the form of megalomania) and decreases in the transference neuroses, varying in direct proportion to the narcissistic component of the subject's love life. Freud firmly believes that dependence on the loved object must necessarily reduce self-regard; this opinion will certainly not be shared by analysts who do not include idealization among the defining characteristics of love between the sexes.

By way of summing up, Freud tells us that the development of the ego consists in a departure from primary narcissism, which at the same time gives rise to a vigorous attempt to recover it. Primary narcissism is abandoned by displacement of libido onto an ego ideal imposed from without; at the same time the ego has sent out libidinal object cathexes. If the ego has become impoverished in this way, it enriches itself once more from its satisfactions in respect of the object and by fulfilling its ideal. Self-regard thus has three sources: the residue of infantile narcissism, fulfillment of the ideal, and satisfaction of object-libido. All analysts will agree with this summing up, although some (including myself) believe that megalomania and self-regard do not belong to the same class of psychological facts.

LIBIDO AND EGO INTERESTS

In the closing years of the nineteenth century, Freud wrote his first clinical works on the neuroses, in which he also examined some psychotic clinical pictures; later, however, his method became restricted to the former, and the psychoses were relegated to a marginal position.

Genuine interest in the subject was aroused when Jung published *Uber die Psychologie der Dementia Praecox* (*The Psychology of Dementia Praecox*). This famous work convincingly showed that the complexes described by Freud in the neuroses and in dreams are also found in dementia praecox when the psychoanalytic method is applied, as well as the word-association method introduced by Jung some time earlier.

Psychologically, the only difference between dementia praecox and the neuroses is that the complexes are much more powerful in the former, damaging the complex of the ego and its functions (Jung, 1907, 68). Sufferers from dementia praecox cannot free themselves from their complexes, so that their personalities are severely impaired (69).

Jung, however, does not say that this situation is the cause of the disease but inclines to the belief that toxic factors are also involved: "Nevertheless I must once again repeat the oft-mentioned proviso that between hysteria and dementia praecox there is only a *similarity* of psychological mechanism and not an *identity*. In dementia praecox these mechanisms go much deeper, perhaps because they are complicated by toxic effects" (77; Jung's emphasis). Jung concludes that, in dementia praecox, it is by no means clear whether the complex causes or precipitates the disease (97).

In the following year, Abraham suggested that the difference between hysteria and dementia praecox could be explained by the fact that, in the latter, the libido was irrevocably withdrawn from objects (1908, 70). Dementia praecox destroyed a person's capacity for object love because "the psychosexual characteristic of dementia praecox is the return of the patient to auto-erotism, and the symptoms of his illness are a form of auto-erotic sexual activity: (1908, 55, 73–74). Freud is right in saying that Abraham's paper contains almost all the essential views put forward in his study of Schreber (1911, 70, n. 1); I would say that it also contains many of those set out in "On Narcissism: An Introduction."

A year later, Ferenczi wrote "Introjection and Transference," distinguishing between neurosis, in which the world of objects is introjected, paranoia, in which libido is projected into the external world, and dementia praecox, in which libido is withdrawn from the object. All these works had a definite influence on Freud's study of the case of Schreber (1911), which includes many of the ideas we have examined. To explain Schreber's latent homosexuality, the starting point of his paranoia, Freud maintains that, during the narcissistic stage, when the individual takes himself as his object, the genitals already play an important part, so that narcissistic object choice is connected with homosexuality. After heterosexual object relations have been attained, the homosexual instincts are combined with the ego-instincts to form the social instincts. So it is sublimated homosexuality that helps establish the bonds of friendship, collaboration, and comradeship among men. Freud therefore believes that paranoia destroys the sublimations achieved by the dependence of the homosexual instincts on the ego-instincts; we may note in passing that this foreshadows the concept of *Anlehnung*, which, as we have seen, was developed in the 1914 essay. Homosexual libido is liberated and regresses to the narcissistic stage, where paranoiacs endeavor to defend against the (re)sexualization of their social instinctual cathexes (1911, 62).

After examining the etiopathogenesis of homosexuality and narcissism in Schreber's mental illness—a truly brilliant contribution—Freud turns to the characteristics of repression in paranoia, concentrating on the judge's experience of the end of the world. Following Abraham (1908), he explains it by the withdrawal of libidinal cathexes from the external world. The experience of the end of the world is a projection of an internal catastrophe: the subjective world has been destroyed when libidinal cathexes have been withdrawn from it, and the patient tries to reconstruct it through his delusional and hallucinatory symptoms. On the basis of the clinical evidence that traces of megalomania frequently occur in paranoia, Freud states that the decisive point in this illness is that the libido liberated from objects becomes attached to the ego and is used to aggrandize it, as at the stage of primary narcissism. The length of the paranoiac's step back from sublimated homosexuality to narcissism is a measure of the amount of regression characteristic of his illness (1911, 72).

Freud, however, points out that the clinical evidence does not favor his argument at all, for the delusions of persecution directed by Schreber against Flechsig appeared before the fantasy of the end of the world, which would mean that the return of the repressed actually preceded the repression; he tries to resolve this contradiction with the ad hoc hypothesis that the withdrawal of libido is partial, concerns only a single complex, and then attains its full development. In the case of Schreber, withdrawal of libido from the figure of Flechsig may have been the initial process, followed by the delusion of persecution that brought the libido back to Flechsig (though with a negative sign to mark the fact of repression); the battle now broke out anew, this time with more powerful weapons. The object of the conflict, Flechsig, has become more and more important, attracting to itself the entirety of the libido, just as the sum of resistances is mobilized. In this way the partial conflict becomes total, and the triumph of the forces of repression is expressed in the experience of the end of the world, the ego alone having survived.

This solution is indeed ingenious, but I find it unconvincing. Freud tries to place megalomania in the center of the phenomenon of psychosis because he believes that this will furnish irrefutable proof of his hypothesis of narcissistic libido. As we now know, thanks to the work of Money-Kyrle (1965), Meltzer (1966), and others, megalomania is an extremely complex phenomenon, and it is unlikely that it is due merely to the economic change resulting from the transfer of libido from the object to the ego. Abraham's simpler and more direct proposal satisfactorily explains the experience of the end of the world within libido theory, but Freud cannot fully accept it because it takes no account of primary narcissism. It should also be pointed out that the experience of the end of the world is proper not to paranoia but to schizophrenia, especially at the initial stages; this also calls into question one of the premises of Freud's theoretical edifice.

We must now inquire whether the withdrawal of libido is a sufficient explanation of the fantasy of the end of the world or whether the ego cathexes must also be taken into account. There are two possibilities: either libidinal cathexis coincides with ego interest or a profound disturbance of the distribution of libido may give rise to a corresponding alteration in the cathexes of the ego. Freud does not make a clear statement on this point and accepts that there may be both a reflex effect by the libidinal alterations on the ego cathexes and, conversely, a secondary and indirect disturbance of the libidinal processes owing to an abnormality of the ego, although he tends to believe that the paranoiac's altered relation to the world "is to be explained entirely or in the main by the loss of his libidinal interest" (1911, 75).

Of the two alternatives left open by Freud, Jung, as we have seen, leans toward the first: libido and ego interest are the same, and this is the only possible explanation for the alteration of the "fonction du reel" in psychosis. I also said that in my opinion Freud's hesitations and—why not?—his impatience are connected with a libido theory based on an autoerotism that dispenses with the object (reality), which is attained only when primary narcissism is overcome.

Another point totally neglected by Freud throughout his argument is the influence of aggression, which Adler had proposed as early as 1908 as an alternative to libido; this was to enter into Freud's theories only from 1920 on. Using other theoretical instruments and without herself having been harassed by Adler and Jung, Melanie Klein (1946) was able to support Freud's views by pointing to the splitting mechanisms in Schreber's illness. The experience of the end of the world is now explained not only by the withdrawal of libido from the object but also by the perception of the fragmentation of the ego, which is projected outward. In this sense, Klein was able to accept that the processes of ego fragmentation determine the libidinal alterations and the break with reality, without feeling herself to be involved in the polemic with Jung. Another author who thought along these lines and whose work has stood the test of time is Garma, who stated as early as 1931 that "the loss of contact with reality is a consequence of instinctual repression" (66): reality is repressed together with the id and not in order to satisfy it, as was thought at the time.

It remains only for me to say that, however much one may agree or disagree with Freud's paper, no analyst will deny that the introduction of narcissism to the theoretical corpus of psychoanalysis was a momentous event that continues to inspire our science.

REFERENCES

Abraham, K. (1908). The psycho-sexual differences between hysteria and dementia praecox. In *Selected Papers*. London: Hogarth Press, 1973, p. 64.

Adler, A. (1908). Der Aggressionstrieb in Leben und in der Neurose. *Fortschr. Med.*, 26:577 (quoted by Freud).

———. (1910). Der psychische Hermaphroditismus imd Leben und in der Neurose. *Fortschr. Med.*, 28:486.

Fairbairn, W. R. D. (1941). A revised psychopathology of the psychoses and psychoneuroses. *Int. J. Psycho-Anal.*, 22:250–79.

Ferenczi, S. (1909). Introjection and transference. In *First Contributions to Psycho-Analysis*. New York: Brunner-Mazel, 1952, p. 35.

———. (1917). Disease—or patho-neurosis. In *Further Contributions to the Theory and Technique of Psycho-Analysis*. New York: Brunner-Mazel, 1980, pp. 78–89.

Freud, S. (1895). On the grounds for detaching a particular syndrome from neurasthenia under the description "anxiety neurosis." *S.E.* 3:85.

———. (1905). *Three Essays on the Theory of Sexuality. S.E.* 7:123.

———. (1910a). *Leonardo da Vinci and a Memory of His Childhood. S.E.* 11:57.

———. (1910b). The psycho-analytic view of psychogenic disturbance of vision. *S.E.* 11:209.

———. (1911). Psycho-analytic notes on an autobiographical account of a case of paranoia (dementia paranoides). *S.E.* 12:1.

———. (1912a). Contributions to a discussion on masturbation. *S.E.* 12:239.

———. (1912b). Types of onset of neurosis. *S.E.* 12:227.

———. (1912–13). *Totem and Taboo. S.E.* 13:1.

———. (1914). On narcissism: An introduction. *S.E.* 14:67.

———. (1915). The unconscious. *S.E.* 14:159.

———. (1917). A metapsychological supplement to the theory of dreams. *S.E.* 14:217–35.

———. (1918). From the history of an infantile neurosis. *S.E.* 17:1.

———. (1920). *Beyond the Pleasure Principle. S.E.* 18:1.

———. (1921). *Group Psychology and the Analysis of the Ego. S.E.* 18:65.

———. (1923). *The Ego and the Id. S.E.* 19:1.

———. (1950 [1895]). A project for a scientific psychology. *S.E.* 1:281.

Freud, S., and Abraham, K. (1965). *A Psycho-Analytic Dialogue: The Letters of Sigmund Freud and Karl Abraham, 1907–1926*. London: Hogarth Press.

Garma, A. (1931). La realidad exterior y los instintos en la esquizofrenia. *Rev. Psicoanál.* 2 (1944): 56–82. (Originally published in the *Internationale Zeitschrift für Psychoanalyse* (1932): 183.)

Jones, E. (1953–57). *Sigmund Freud: Life and Works*. 3 vols. London: Hogarth Press.

Jung, C. G. (1907). Über die Psychologie der Dementia Praecox, *Halle* [trans.: *The Psychology of Dementia Praecox*, New York, 1909. Reprinted in C. G. Jung, *Collected Works*, vol. 3, ed. H. Read, M. Fordham, G. Adler; trans. R. F. C. Hull; Princeton, Princeton University Press, Bollingen Series, 1960.]

———. (1910). Psychic conflicts in a child. *Collected Works* 17:13.

———. (1912). *Wandlungen und Symbole der Libido*. Leipzig: Deuticke. (*Psychology of the Unconscious*. New York: Moffat, Yard, 1916. *Símbolos de Transformación*. Barcelona: Paidùs, 1982.)

Klein, M. (1928). Early stages of the Oedipus conflict. In *Love, Guilt and Reparation and Other Works*. London: Hogarth Press, pp. 186–98.

———. (1946). Notes on some schizoid mechanisms. In *Envy and Gratitude and Other Works*. London: Hogarth Press, pp. 1–24.

Kohut, H. (1971). *The Analysis of the Self*. New York: International Universities Press.

Meltzer, D. (1966). The relation of anal masturbation to projective identification. *Int. J. Psycho-Anal.*, 47:335–42.

Money-Kyrle, R. (1965). Megalomania. In *Collected Papers*. Strath Tay, Perthshire: Clunie Press, 1978, pp. 376–88.

Rank, O. (1911). *Ein Beitrag zum Narzissismus. J. Psychoan. Psychopath. Forsch.*, 3:401.

Rosenfeld, H. A. (1958). Some observations on the psychopathology of hypochondriacal states. *Int. J. Psycho-Anal.*, 39:121–24.

———. (1964). The psychopathology of hypochondriasis. In *Psychotic States: A Psycho-Analytical Approach*. New York: International Universities Press. 1965.

Stekel, W. (1908). *Estados nerviosos de angustia y su tratamiento. Buenos Aires: Imán, 1947*. (First published as *Nervose Angstzustände und ihre Behandlung*. Berlin and Vienna: Urban and Schwarzenberg.)

Introduction to "On Narcissism"

NIKOLAAS TREURNIET

INTRODUCTION TO AN INTRODUCTION

It is difficult to understand Freud's work without some idea of the scientific concepts on which he based his models. The physiologist Helmholtz had discovered that the laws of the conservation of energy apply to living organisms as well as to inorganic matter. Freud adopted Fechner's constancy principle as a physiological analogue to Helmholtz's discovery that the psychic apparatus tends to keep the quantity of excitation at the lowest possible level. The principle of constancy called for the discharge of quantities of energy if they became too large, as in the case of accumulated or "dammed-up" excitation from the outside (first phase) or the inside (second phase). Affects and impulses were conceived of as moving in a system of communicating vessels, a theory of affective and libidinal hydraulics.

Biology in the period of Freud's intellectual development was heavily weighted in favor of "purity" in laboratory experiments, in which the object of investigation was isolated as completely as possible and environmental conditions were assumed to be constant. There was as yet no appreciation of the dynamic relationships between the organism and the environment.

Another precondition for understanding the development of Freud's thinking is acknowledgment of his indifference to the rules of semantics. He used language according to his needs, as an artist uses his materials. Precise use of a term had little meaning for Freud; it was the context that mattered. It is thus essential for those who wish to master the subject to tolerate the ambiguities rather than try to eliminate them.

BEFORE 1914

Freud's thinking can be divided roughly into three phases. A grasp of the essential concepts of each phase is necessary in order to understand what developed later and the many inconsistencies that still exist in psychoanalytic psychology.

In the first phase, then, lasting till 1897, the pent-up unconscious forces giving rise to symptoms were thought of as affects or emotions that had been aroused by real traumatic experiences. The emphasis was on the influence of external reality. The quantity of stimulation impinging on the "mental apparatus" from the outside was considered to be very much greater than that from the inside, threatening to overwhelm the (at that time still purely conscious) ego in a painful fashion and thus leading to the unbearable feeling of helplessness or "trauma." The ego was equated with consciousness, both as a center of experience and as an agency that could perform the function of defense against the quantities of affect generated by the trauma. This quantity, called "mental energy," might be augmented or diminished, by stimulation or discharge respectively, rather like the workings of a reflex arc. This first phase is not merely of historical significance. Its main concepts, including trauma, quantities of affect, and defenses against painful experiences, have survived and have turned out to have great significance in recent decades for the problem of narcissism (see below).

This so-called affect-trauma phase ended abruptly with Freud's discovery that he had not distinguished between the recall of a past wish-fulfilling fantasy and the recovery of a repressed traumatic memory. It was the realization of this distinction and the discovery that the unconscious does not distinguish between truth and emotionally charged fiction that led to the developments of the second phase (1897–1926).

In this phase the concept of a "quantity of energy" pressing forward for discharge was transferred by Freud from the external to the internal world.

Attention shifted from conflict with an overwhelming external reality to conflict with overwhelming drive excitations. The fundamental function of the mental apparatus was now seen as harnessing the instinctual drives, with a relative neglect of external traumatic influences and their corresponding affects. Affects were seen almost entirely as drive-derivatives pressing for discharge and devoid of communicative function. These concepts were formed into the well-known systems Unconscious, Preconscious, and Conscious, the topographical frame of reference.

During the first half of the second phase Freud was intensely involved in protecting his revolutionary discoveries of the drives and infantile sexuality against bitter attacks from his colleagues and society. Only very gradually did he again turn his attention from the repressed to the repressing forces and from the internal sources to the external aspects of conflict, the love objects. This process was sharpened by his conflicts with Jung and Adler, who challenged Freud to give his views on the ego, power conflicts, and social influences.

In the beginning of the second period, analysis was conceived as a procedure in which the analyst observes the patient and his associations as a more or less isolated, neutral, scientific object. Freud's discoveries of the meaning of transference focused his attention more and more on the relation between self and object.

1914: FREUD'S NARCISSISM PAPER

Reading this paper is like witnessing the creation of a work of art. Here, out of all kinds of raw materials, Freud carved the contours of the important developments to come without much regard for the rules of conceptual clarity.

In the first part of the paper he claimed a place for narcissism not only in perversions and psychosis but in the normal course of development. Grandiose, omnipotent, and magical thoughts and feelings existed ubiquitously in the mental life of children. Consequently there must be an original libidinal cathexis of the ego of which some is later given off to objects, "much as the body of the amoeba is related to the pseudopodia which it puts out" (1914, 75). With this amoeba metaphor Freud betrayed his intuitive understanding of the role of emotional vulnerability in narcissistic phenomena, in remarkable contrast to the physical hydraulics of the libido theory.

Freud started on a rather complicated and obscure argument that disclosed his ambivalence. On the one hand, he wanted to preserve the familiar distinction between ego-instincts (of self-preservation) and libido; on the other hand, he had to "admit that the hypothesis of separate ego-instincts and sexual instincts . . . rests scarcely at all upon a psychological basis but derives its principal support from biology" (79). The contrast between ego-instincts and sexual instincts was replaced by another contrast, that between self-love (narcissism) and object-love. The first was a somatically based theory, the second a psychological theory.

In the second part of the paper Freud unfolded both his libido theory and his theory of object relations, interrelating them with the concepts of narcissism and object-love. He assumed that an individual had a fixed quantity of libido at his disposal. The more libido invested in the object, the less in the self, and vice versa. This distinction did not mean that the libido involved was qualitatively different but rather that its location differed. Ego-libido and object-libido, then, had a complementary relationship, like communicating vessels. The system was not completely closed because frustration could influence the quantity of libido. Frustration increased ego-libido as well as object-libido, and if it became too intense or lasted too long, a damming-up of both kinds of libido occurred. An overflow of libido then resulted in an anxiety attack ("actual neurosis") in the case of object-libido, or hypochondriacal panic in the case of ego-libido.

At that time Freud's ego concept was not used in the sense in which it was later employed in the structural model. It included the system Conscious as well as referring to the subject himself as distinct from the object. It is preferable to use the term "self" rather than "ego" if the second meaning is intended, because the meanings concern different conceptual realms connected with different ways of acquiring knowledge (see below). Libidinal cathexis of the object, then, is object-love, and libidinal cathexis of the self is narcissism.

Freud assumed that narcissism exists from the moment the infant has a rudimentary awareness of himself. This primitive self, however, is a product of the undivided pleasure principle in that the infant attempts to maintain all that is pleasurable as part of the self, in addition to the pleasurable aspects of the object. This fusion of the pleasurable aspects of the self and object is called primary identification and results in the "purified pleasure ego." The process of primary identification causes the state of primary narcissism.

When, through primary identification with a good object, the child has a strong enough "reservoir" of narcissism and consequently is able to endure some unpleasure, the object is gradually perceived as separate from the self. The libidinal investment of this now separate object ("object-love") is regarded as a consequence of displacement of some of the libidinal investment of the self, now extended like the pseudopodia of an amoeba to include the object. As object-love develops, a state of residual narcissistic investment of the self persists and coexists with it, forming a hydraulic balance. This object-love follows gradually from the child's discovery that the object is a source of pleasure and that he is dependent on the object for the fulfillment of his needs. This is the so-called need-satisfying, or anaclitic object.

Secondary narcissism concerns the libidinal reinvestment of the self that results from withdrawal of certain amounts of libido from the object. This happens especially in cases of disappointment with the object or in mourning for a lost object; further, it occurs as a normal developmental process in secondary identification[1] and where some of the libidinal investment of the admired or loved object is then transferred to the self as a consequence of this identification. Finally, it also happens when a person lives up to his ideals.

That Freud did not conceive of the boundary between self and object as fixed and rigid was clearly stated again in 1938, when he summed up the processes involved: "to begin with, the child does not distinguish between the breast and his own body; when the breast has to be separated from the body and shifted to the 'outside' because the child so often finds it absent, *it carried with it as an 'object' a part of the original narcissistic libidinal cathexis*" (188; italics added). This is a striking description of the origin of the narcissistic object relation. In loving what one is, what one was, what one would like to be, and what was once part of the self, one loves objects containing aspects of the self, one loves objects with "primary narcissistic libido." In contemporary terminology: one loves self-objects differently from the way one loves love-objects.

Let me now describe briefly what was harvested from this paper, which was a starting point for many of Freud's later lines of thought. The paper first of all constitutes a transitional point in the development of the ego concept. The development of the ego consists of a departure from primary narcissism, resulting in vigorous attempts to recover that state by narcissistic object choice, by identification, and by efforts to fulfill the ego-ideal, in

1. In contrast to primary identification, in which there is no clear subjective boundary between self and object, in secondary identification there is a definite boundary or subjective distinction between self and object.

that (developmental) order. Concepts such as object choice, identification, and ego-ideal paved the way for the later structural theory. The function of the later superego as guardian of the regulation of narcissistic value was recognized as rooted in identification with an idealized object. Its importance for group psychology was mentioned in passing. The connection between narcissism, idealization, and exhibitionism is implicit in Freud's emphasis on self-regard as an expression of the size of the ego and his description of the feeling of being watched. Finally, there is the beginning of a distinction between the experientially distant concept of ego as mental apparatus and the near concept of ego as self. Infantile narcissism, and with it infantile ego building, were at last seen as having an instinctual nature. For a long time to come this was to remain more important than the narcissistic aspects of sexual development.

The basis for an object-relations theory had been laid. There was a dawning access to the preoedipal emotional world and the importance of good object relations for "His Majesty the Baby" and his ego building. Nowadays this theory, involving the relatively simple notion of the distribution of libido between self and object, is seen to be grossly inadequate and clinically misleading.

In this so-called libido theory, affects were discharge products and completely isolated from their ideational content. Affects therefore could not have a communicative function, at least theoretically. In fact, Freud had observed the contagiousness of affects in groups and considered them the basis of empathy, but he could not acknowledge the communicative aspect of affect until 1926 because of his adherence to the libido theory. Although the amoeba metaphor harbored the notion of exquisite affective vulnerability, this intuitive insight could not be elaborated because of Freud's very strong emphasis on the role of constant internal forces. Frustration was not traumatic per se, as injury to the self, but because it resulted in a damming-up of ego- or object-libido with a consequent overflow of excitation. Pathological processes, which prompted a withdrawal of interest from objects and reality—that is, secondary narcissism—could not yet be a result of conflict, because the concept of a defense against objects and reality did not exist. Defense—that is, repression—existed only against internal forces. That affects were denied a communicative function and secondary narcissism a defensive function was probably due mostly to Freud's adherence to the libido theory and to the constancy principle.[2]

2. It is only Freud's notion of libido distribution between self and object, as part of the constancy principle, that I consider obsolete, not his ideas about instinctual drives in general.

That he had more ideas on the subject becomes clear in the opening statement of the third section: "the disturbances to which a child's original narcissism is exposed, the reactions with which he seeks to protect himself from them and that paths into which he is forced into doing so are an important field of work, which still awaits exploration." He did not live to witness these further explorations. Nevertheless, the similarity between Freud's types of narcissistic object choice and Kohut's idealizing and mirror transferences is striking; the distinction between narcissistic and anaclitic object choices returns in Winnicott's concepts of environment-mother and object-mother; and Freud's views about primary narcissism are clearly discernible in Margaret Mahler's description of the symbiotic phase.

FREUD AFTER 1914

After Freud's narcissism paper the process of internalization gained more and more weight, not as one of the ego functions but as the basic way of psychic functioning. Only by means of identification—according to Freud perhaps the sole condition under which the id can give up its objects—can the ego gain power over the id and mitigate its demands. Neuroses now had become disturbances of the ego.

In *Inhibitions, Symptoms and Anxiety* (1926) Freud acknowledged for the first time the communicative function of affects in his concept of anxiety as a signal of danger. Freud now distanced himself clearly from his former discharge theory, which viewed affects as arising within the interior of the mind, as if the mental apparatus were isolated from its environment, leading to a reification of the concept of mental energy.

With the establishment of his new theory of anxiety the second period in Freud's theory formation had come to an end, almost thirty years after he had shifted his attention from external influences to internal sources. Now that the economy and internal dependency relations of the agencies of the mind had been safeguarded by a systematic structural theory, Freud could direct his attention to the functions of adaptation to and integration of reality and object world. He never explored the influence of the external world as systematically as he had explored the internal forces in the mind, and he never changed his position vis-à-vis narcissism and object relations after 1914.

During his last years, however, he did focus his clinical interest on the oral phase, on the early mother-child interactions, on separation anxiety as a prototype for all other anxieties, and on the reconstruction of preoedipal traumatic experiences. Consequently he became interested in the problems of denial and splitting, defenses against reality and the object world. As the blows to our narcissism always come from reality, we can frequently observe a hatred of certain aspects of reality: what is hated is the evidence of the limitations of our omnipotence, the feeling of narcissistic mortification. By splitting and denial, which are part of each other, one can still maintain a belief in the efficacy of the pleasure principle in one portion of the conscious mind while in another portion fully recognizing the reality principle.

AFTER FREUD

Despite the fact that he introduced substantial changes in his theoretical views, Freud never changed his position about narcissism after 1914. It was a long time after his death before narcissism appeared as a central focus of interest in the psychoanalytic mainstream. The mind was a relatively closed system, maturation being equated with internalization. Clinically the emphasis was more on oedipal issues. Even in 1960 Hartmann held analysis to be a value-free enterprise (20–21), and Anna Freud's technical advice that there should be equidistance between the analyst and the agencies of the mind, without a role for the relationship of patient and analyst in the transference-countertransference universe, prevailed. Melanie Klein advanced an alternative theory, emphasizing preoedipal conflicts between self and object. Her concepts of internal objects, however, defined a similar closed system of internalized forces, without much room for interactional processes. In both groups, Freudian and Kleinian, there was little doubt about the resistance of internalized forces against pressures from outside—that is, about the degree of autonomy of structure.

Gradually this rigid picture changed. In England the "object-relation school" developed its ideas from Ferenczi's work, through Fairbairn and Balint, to Winnicott's fertile concepts of potential space, transitional phenomena, and true versus false self. On the Continent, the work of Lampl–de Groot and Grünberger paved the way for a better understanding of narcissism and its management in the psychoanalytic situation. In America, Stone, Gitelson, Loewald, Kernberg, and Modell tried to integrate Winnicott with classical analysis. Kohut distanced himself from any integration and developed his own school of self psychology, based exclusively on concepts about self and object. In child analysis, it was Margaret Mahler, with her description of the process of separation-individuation, and Anna Freud, with the concept of developmental lines, who added substantially to this trend of acknowledging the importance of object relations for ego development. The widening scope of psychoanalysis increased our knowledge substantially as borderline and narcissistic personality organizations became accessible to analysis. I shall treat the clinical, technical, and theoretical aspects of this development in that order.

Very vulnerable patients are characterized either by an extreme dependence on other persons or by an extreme defense against this dependence. Patients from the first group seek absolute fusion, merger, symbiosis. Alone they simply cease to exist; they disappear in a narcissistic hemorrhage without an object. There has to be someone there for them to feel alive. This search for the other is concerned less with desire than with the psychic economy of need that underlies addictive behavior and deviant sexual organization, in which sexuality is used as a drug. This is the borderline personality organization.

The other type of patient is characterized by withdrawal, noncommunication, and even negativism. Such patients are truly themselves only when they are alone. When they are with other people for too long, they become overstimulated and lose their boundaries. They disappear in a flood of unexpected catastrophic experiences in regard to an object. This is the narcissistic personality organization. Actually these patients are suffering from a serious depletion in their narcissistic reserves. Their sense of self is in danger of disappearing.

The *denial of separateness* from objects creates the illusion that the object is part of the self and cannot be lost or destroyed. The other person has to fulfill the function of (part of) the patient's structure. The *denial of connectedness*, the defense of noncommunication, on the other hand, means having to sustain the belief in a state of omnipotent self-sufficiency, side by side with an intense and overwhelming dependency, expressed as a craving for admiration. It is a striking paradox that in these defenses both the tie to the object and the separateness from the object can be denied. This means *the assumption that all the classical mechanisms of defense are intrapsychic* (that is, between the agencies of the mind) *is incorrect.*[3] The motive for

3. There is one exception. In 1936 Anna Freud published an object-related defense in her description of altruistic surrender as a denial of separateness. In 1951, during the IPA Congress on Mutual Influences in the Development of Ego and Id

defense here is directed outward. The danger that must be defended against has to do with the extreme vulnerability of the self. The defense is against the possibility that an unempathic response from the other will shatter the sense of self. So in addition to overwhelming intrapsychic conflicts, there is an important area of conflict between the person and his environment, which Freud once believed to be characteristic of the psychoses. These defenses can be called psychoticlike in that the locus of the defensive process is in the tie to the object. Affects are the medium through which defenses against objects occur.

Arrest and regression of drive and ego development are thought to be secondary to environmental failure with "narcissistic" patients. The developmental trauma of extreme helplessness, experienced in relation to former objects, elicits in the child a desperate attempt to remain hidden and unfound, a withdrawal of all "pseudopodia." Defensive narcissism, then, is almost always a reaction to actual helplessness. The child correctly perceives that the parents cannot protect him or her from the dangers of the real world.

The fact that we were faced with psychic organizations designed to seek or avoid the most primitive mode of love—fusion—on the one hand, and the fact that an extreme hatred of reality was displaced to the analyst and analysis, on the other hand, had important technical consequences. Narcissistic transferences and their management drew attention to the empathic dimension of the analyst's actions. What gives them this dimension is the overall context of his attitude, his purpose, his intent—that is, his "countertransference" in a broad sense. Elements of caretaking functions, implicit in the narcissistic tie of the patient to the analyst, are by now part of ordinary psychoanalytic technique. This implies that a not inconsiderable share of the analytic work consists of confronting the patient with the needs of his narcissistic transference and the defensive function of his narcissism vis-à-vis his rage. This includes, however, integrating failure with success through pointing out the constructive aspects of the patient's failure, discovering the strengths lying behind his weakness as a negative image of a growth-need, sometimes to be seen as a quest for cohesion, instead of envy or desire for affection. As far as the patient is concerned, this validation has been compared to the function of a mirror. It is central to the therapeutic action of

[*sic*], she read a paper about the denial of connectedness: "Negativism as a defense against emotional surrender" (1952). The mainstream of classical analysis, however, was not yet ready to appreciate the importance of this paper and of object-related defenses and conflicts.

psychoanalysis, in the sense that the analyst communicates to the patient an image of the person he can become instead of the drive-cathected monster he fears he is (Loewald, 1960). Interpretation "upward" is often necessary to correct the results of the parents' misnaming of affects. If the need for growth, initiative, and individuality and the wish to be "different" are interpreted as oedipal rivalry, the analyst degrades the quest for a healthy self-experience into a destructive part-impulse, thus attacking the patient's sense of the value of his self. This is often a repetition of the narcissistic rage of a parent who could not bear the child's individuality and thus promoted the child's development of a rigid, false self.

The paradigm for this technique comes not from Freud's metapsychology but from Winnicott's "holding environment," by which the necessary empathic atmosphere of the analytic setting and the narcissistic transferences could be presented and managed.

From this position the analytic setting itself is regarded as containing important elements of the mother-child relation. It is a view that sees the analytic setting as an open system. The holding environment is a world created and protected by the mother standing between the child and the "real reality" of facts, joined by the communication of genuine affects. Even if the analyst uses a pure and classical technique his responses still provide a new object relationship. In every analysis, but especially in narcissistic cases, it is essential that at certain well-controlled "moments of truth" the patient be aware that he is able to elicit genuine emotion from the analyst. And this brings us to the *passive* aspect of the analyst's sensitivity as opposed to the *active* quality of his empathy. Transference does not have to be restricted to the idea that the patient distorts his perception of the analyst; it should also be taken to include all those unconscious and subtle attempts to manipulate the analyst in the analytic situation, in order to evoke a particular type of response. It is a way of conveying and discharging emotion directly, with the intention of arousing reactions and affecting the other. "The other," the analyst, should not be afraid to let himself be responsive and aroused. In short, the analyst may perceive affects in either the active or the passive mode. The active mode corresponds to a process of empathy and carries with it a certain pleasurable recognition. In the passive mode the analyst is acted upon; this is a less pleasurable experience, less under conscious control, and may require some measure of self-analysis from the analyst in order to identify the source of affects. This latter mode is also known as projective identification. Here we have a further demonstration that the fundamental data of psychoanalysis consist of the perception of affects and that this perception corresponds to the visual and tactile perception used in other sciences.

The holding environment, then, envelops a space in which the psychoanalytic process has the potential to evolve. It creates a background that is safe as well as sufficiently pleasurable in which to work analytically. Its *interactive* processes create the right atmosphere for the evolution of *intrapsychic* processes—that is, a transference neurosis—to take place in the foreground. It also gives the psychoanalytically suspect concepts of interaction and support some dignity.

The fact that we have learned most about these phenomena from our sickest patients has cast a certain prejudicial pall over these issues. We have become accustomed to thinking of these phenomena as deeply regressive. Yet we know that all our patients, many of whom function extremely well, have the wish to merge, but fear that their sense of self may be totally fractured by an unempathic response. These people are in no sense psychotic or borderline.

Although the concept of internalization is indispensable, the very success of this theory may have carried it too far in one direction. Self-object differentiation and the associated need for affirmation of the self through mirroring are not linked to the preoedipal period, as if it were a separate archaeological stratum. We are less completely internalized vis-à-vis our human environment than structural theory and our pride would lead us to believe. The need for transitional relatedness—that is, for maintaining an illusion of connectedness with a protective object—is never ending.

Freud compared the narcissistic hurts that psychoanalysis, through painful insight, inflicted on humanity to those inflicted by Galileo's work. The discovery that man was not master in this own mind was added to the realization that the earth was not the center of the universe and that man was descended from animals. There is, however, a fourth narcissistic mortification that is undeniably connected with the discoveries made both in and outside analysis in recent decades: not only is man not master of his own mind; he is also far less "autonomous" in his social reality than he would like to believe. Man's social anxiety (and with it his corruptibility) is much greater than Freud thought—perhaps because he himself had such an immense reservoir of social courage.

All this has had a profound impact on our theory formation. There has always been controversy surrounding the question of how to conceptualize those forces that inspire the ego to activity. Ego functions operate not because they exist but because they become stimulated. In classical terminology, the ego disposes of a reservoir of libido and neutral energy. It makes use of a central decision-making function (Rangell, 1971), deriving its zest from a central driving force—narcissism—which inspires the investment of ideals and ambitions. Besides stirring the ego functions to action, this same narcissism can regard them with contempt and even endanger their survival, as in melancholia. This conflict between the "superego ideal" and the ego manifests itself in the field of depressions. In psychoses and borderlines the essence of the pathology was considered to be a defect in or the absence of an internalized superego ideal formation: where the agency supplying the ego with a sufficient feeling of self-value is grossly deficient and this vital source of narcissism is taken over by the environment, just as in the very small child. Thus in very vulnerable patients the ego becomes permanently reliant on an idealized object to take over the function of the missing superego ideal formation—to supply the ego or self with sufficient narcissism for it to execute its tasks. The vulnerability of the self should be viewed to a substantial extent as a consequence of primitive guilt about aggression: an object-related defense is often a protection against intense ambivalence, sadism, envy, rage, and hate, resulting in the vicious circle of insatiable narcissistic hunger because self-punitive aggression destroys realistic self-love (Kris, 1983). The controversy over these issues is not whether there is internalization of conflict; the real discussion is about the *degree* of internalization of conflict.

Freud's theory has guided us quite far, even in understanding the deficiencies of very vulnerable patients. As so often in psychoanalysis, fundamental insights in pathology resulted in later insights of a more general nature. The equation of maturation with internalization gradually broke down. The structure of the ego is less resistant to change and the superego more corruptible in compromises of integrity (Rangell, 1980) than we want to believe. Theoretically this has strained (Sandler, 1969) the classical concepts beyond their capacity to explain new data. Study of internal dependency relations had to be complemented by study of external dependency relations. For this, classical theory needed help from object-relations theory. The Ego now has to compete with the Self; the superego ideal formation with the self-object; libido and aggression with affect; transference with self-object relations; resistance with empathic failure. The paradox was that in this competition the Self, the weak spot in metapsychology, took over the most basic ego function, an internalized structure center of initiative, but remained at the same time an endopsychic perception, exquisitely dependent on the immediacy of the response of the other, affirming or negating objects or being affirmed or negated by objects. The affects are the medium through which these responses, conflicts, and defenses, as well as ties between self and objects, occur.

We have yet to establish a science of relationships that encompasses the intrapsychic, on the one hand, and the psychoanalytic dyad, on the other. This problem is related to a peculiarity in our way of collecting data. In essence, in the psychoanalytic situation there is an alternation between two different functions of the analyst: the subjective stance, the "inside view," the empathic immersion in the patient, alternates with the objective stance, the "outside view," the more distant observation. In recent decades the classical stress on structural aspects—on internalization, ego-id relations, the "outside view," the observational stance, the "I-it relationship" (Modell, 1984), on the intrapsychic—was complemented by and shifted toward the process aspect—external influences, self-object relations, the "inside view," the "I-thou relationships," the empathic introspective stance and interactional responsiveness. Or, to put it more succinctly, structural theory was complemented by object-relations theory.

Psychoanalysis, then, encompasses both forms of knowledge, and this continues to be its central paradox—it is a hermeneutic as well as a natural science. This is the same problem Freud struggled with when he stated, "I try in general to keep psychology clear from everything that is different in nature from it, even biological lines of thought. For that very reason I should like at this point expressly to admit that the hypothesis of separate ego-instincts and sexual instincts (that is to say the libido theory) rests scarcely at all upon a psychological basis, but derives its principal support from biology" (1914, 79–80). Freud then advocates that we pay more attention to the psychological phenomena instead of waiting for biology to solve our dilemma and arrives at his new dualism: instead of ego-instincts versus sexual instincts we now have to do with ego-libido versus object-libido; or, in more modern terminology, instead of ego-id relations we have arrived at self-object relations.

The difficulty is, however, that all efforts at integration of these two epistemological positions have been thwarted by the adamant theoretical nature of the dilemma. The most orthodox classical analysts have tried to solve it by depreciating the findings of object-relations theory. At the other extreme

Kohut did away with all of classical analysis, establishing the absolute supremacy of the self over the ego and denying any independent existence to drives as a motivating force, other than as disintegrative products of a fragmented self. Modell (1984), between the two extremes, accentuated the insolubility of the dilemma by accepting the device of complementarity in his recognition of two opposed and contradictory views, both of which are correct but incomplete. He justified his position by a comparison with quantum mechanics: Niels Bohr had proposed that both views regarding the nature of electromagnetic waves—that is, as particles and as waves—were correct if one took into consideration the position of the observer. In this way basic dualities could be accepted without straining for their mutual resolution, reduction, or integration. Modell quotes Bion (1970), who noted that a science of relationship has yet to be established—that is, a discipline that would relate one element in the structure of the subject to one element in the structure of the object. What is needed, according to Modell, is a structural psychology that moves beyond internalization, one that can also be applied to the psychoanalytic dyad.

This was the situation when, in 1983, Sandler and Sandler proposed their modification of the topographical frame of reference. They disconnected the close association between the tripartite model and the concept of internalization and agreed that even from a strictly classical point of view the division of ego, superego, and id leaves a fundamental question to some extent unanswered—namely, what are the pathways of communication among the three provinces of the personality? Freud himself never used the tripartite model exclusively, and Anna Freud stated in 1972 that she felt free to fall back on the topographical aspects whenever convenient. She strongly recommended her bad habit of moving between the topographical and the structural frames of reference because it simplified thinking enormously. As she openly acknowledged: "It is very interesting to look at the losses in psychoanalytic theory that occur under the name of progress. It is important to see that, with every step forward, we lose some very useful things."[4]

The vicissitudes of self-object relations, conflicts, and defenses, which cannot be represented in the experientially distant structural model, are much more at home in the topographical frame of reference, which has always been more suited to represent experientially near concepts. In the same way the preconscious is also suited to represent Winnicott's concept of a poten-

4. As quoted by H. Blum, 1985, 90.

tial space, in which transitional phenomena and movement can take place. The Sandler and Sandler model is an attempt to give our recent knowledge about narcissistic and self-object dependency in the here and now a theoretical representation in the concept of the "present unconscious," spatially pictured in a second box with a second censorship oriented toward the avoidance of shame, embarrassment, and humiliation and finely tuned toward well-being and safety in the here and now. The first box contains the "past unconscious" with all the internalized preoedipal, oedipal, and adolescent childhood conflicts, conflict solutions, and self-object relations. An advantage of this model is that it represents more satisfactorily the communication between different mental systems. There is also some resemblance to Winnicott's metaphors, true self being represented in the past unconscious and false self in the present unconscious.

Apart from its intrinsic value, I have mentioned this paper to demonstrate that the subject of narcissism, more than any other psychoanalytic topic, shows how useful earlier theoretical formulations of Freud still are. Besides the topographic frame of reference it is easy to detect elements of Freud's affect-trauma theory in our current views on narcissism. The very subject of narcissism, however, also softened the impact of Freud's most disturbing discovery—the drive—together with the economic point of view.

If we forget for a moment our daily psychoanalytic practice and approach the subject with "academic" sophistication, we will discover that modern biology teaches quite different things. Freud's concept of instinct, as something arising only from within the organism, does not apply to the observation that the formation of object relations is a process of caring involving two people. Modern biology tends to view an organizing principle like psychoanalytic instinct theory as an antiquated notion. At every stage of development the addition of something from the environment is genetically (that is, in the congenital, hereditary sense) provided for. This is as true for man as it is for other species. For example, human beings or animals raised in social isolation cannot perform the sexual act. On the other hand, ethologists, who noted that for a primate group affects are the medium through which vital motivational information is conveyed, observed the instinctual origin of the communicative aspects of affects. The concept of drives is under constant attack, as it always has been.

In his 1914 paper Freud tried to show that narcissism was just as sexual as object-love. Modern analytic literature on narcissism claims the opposite: oral, anal, phallic, oedipal wishes, and the guilt over them, all have a narcissistic core. The concept of drives has been eroded by many analysts; what is our stance vis-à-vis this internal struggle?

When we begin to look too closely at our concepts our theory breaks down. The effort to "define" our concepts rigorously involves the danger of reification: ego-id turns into a biochemical power station, self-object into a computer game, in which we find the attraction or repulsion of "representations." This was implicit in the following observation by Anna Freud. She was speaking about the concepts of defense, but her remarks are applicable to all psychoanalytic concepts: "The point is that one should not look at them microscopically, but macroscopically as big and separate mechanisms, structures, events, whatever you want to call them. . . . You have to take off your glasses to look at them, not put them on" (1965, 90). This applies equally to our drive theory. It is my conviction that regardless of the obvious inadequacy of psychoanalytic drive theory, such theories in some form or another cannot be eliminated from psychoanalysis. They should be used, however, as Freud used them: metaphorically.

What we experience in our daily practice is temperament, gusto, affect, emotion, passion, force, and movement from the most stubborn resistances via the most free associations to the most expressive enactments. What we observe further is that these temperaments, emotions, movements, and so on have strong roots in childhood and in the body. Psychoanalysis thus preserves metaphorically the notions of sanguine vitality, energy, life, and emotional power and keeps these notions paradoxically in an experiential context. In Freud's own words: "The power of the id expresses the true purpose of the individual organism's life. . . . *There can be no question of restricting one or the other of the basic instincts to one of the provinces of the mind*" (1940 [1938], 148–49; italics added). The superb paradox: affect, emotion, force, intensity—in other words, "drive"—is everywhere in the mind, not only in the id but also in the ego and the superego. With this, Freud did not mean that man is a possessed monster. One may call it affect —and many analysts do—as long as this does not mean "being affected" but designates a central driving force. Kohut called it something like the vigor of the self, thus readmitting some sort of drive concept.

Ego, superego, and id are metaphors expressing a strong emotional need and a search for safety, values, and pleasure in all the transactions between self and nonself. In these transactions sexuality, narcissism, and—last but certainly not least—aggression play a central motivating role. The drive concept is related to the temperament of the analyst as well as to traditions of Western intellectual development with its emphasis on the individual. Writing on the theory of ego autonomy Rapaport stated:

> Thus, while the ultimate guarantees of the ego's autonomy from the id are man's constitutionally given apparatuses of reality relatedness [that is, representations and objects as important factors in "neurotic," "ordinary," classical defenses], the ultimate guarantees of the ego's autonomy from the environment are man's constitutionally given drives [that is, the drive as an important factor in "psychotic," object-related defenses against the outside world; compare perversions]. . . . Man's constitutionally given drive-equipment appears to be the ultimate (primary) guarantee of the ego's autonomy from the environment, that is, its safeguard against stimulus-responsive slavery. (1958, 18)

Theory is in the last resort more than an anemic compilation of factual knowledge, especially if it touches on the most human of human rights: the right of the child to an understanding of his passions. Theory, then, is taste.

In May 1926, in a letter to Franz Alexander, Freud expressed his belief in the vitality of his creation in his expectation that psychoanalysis would outgrow him: "I do not believe that you and others should settle for elaborating and summarizing current analytic knowledge. You cannot guess what problems lie ahead of you, for whose solution you will think of me in friendly commemoration."[5]

REFERENCES

In tracing the development of Freud's theoretical thinking I consulted Sandler, Dare, and Holder (1972), "Frames of Reference in Psychoanalytic Psychology," nos. 1–7, 10; and Leupold-Löwenthal, *Handbuch der Psychoanalyse*. For the post-Freud period I used formulations by McDougall, *Theatres of the Mind*; Modell, *Psychoanalysis in a New Context*; Sandler, "The Background of Safety"; and Thiel, *Psychoanalytische Therapieen*.

Balint, M. (1968). *The Basic Fault: Therapeutic Aspects of Regression*. London: Tavistock.

Bion, W. (1970). *Attention and Interpretation*. New York: Basic Books.

Blum, H., ed. (1985). *Defense and Resistance*. New York: International Universities Press.

5. My translation from the original, as reproduced in Leupold-Löwenthal, 1986.

Freud, A. (1952). A connection between the state of negativism and of emotional surrender. *Int. J. Psycho-Anal.*, 33:265.

———. (1963). The concept of developmental lines. *Psychoanal. Study Child*, 18:245–65.

———. (1965). *Normality and Pathology in Childhood*. New York: International Universities Press.

Freud, S. (1914). On narcissism: An introduction. *S.E.* 14:67–102.

———. (1926). *Inhibitions, Symptoms and Anxiety. S.E.* 20:75–175.

———. (1940 [1938]). *An Outline of Psycho-Analysis. S.E.* 23:139–208.

Gitelson, M. (1962). The curative factors in psychoanalysis. *Int. J. Psycho-Anal.*, 43:194–206.

Grünberger, B. (1979). *Narcissism: Psychoanalytic Essays*. New York: International Universities Press.

Hartmann, H. (1960). *Psychoanalysis and Moral Values*. New York: International Universities Press.

Kernberg, O. (1975). *Borderline Conditions and Pathological Narcissism*. New York: Jason Aronson.

Kohut, H. (1978). The psychoanalytic treatment of narcissistic personality disorders: Outline of a systematic approach. In P. Ornstein, ed., *The Search for the Self*. New York: International Universities Press, pp. 477–509.

———. (1984). *How Does Analysis Cure?* Chicago: University of Chicago Press.

Kris, A. (1983). Determinants of free association in narcissistic phenomena. *Psychoanal. Study Child*, 38:439–58.

Lampl–de Groot, J. (1985). *Man and Mind*. New York: International Universities Press; Assen: Van Gorcum.

Leupold-Löwenthal, H. (1986). *Handbuch der Psychoanalyse*. Vienna: Orac.

Loewald, H. W. (1960). On the therapeutic action in psychoanalysis. *Int. J. Psycho-Anal.*, 41:1–18.

McDougall, J. (1982). *Theatres of the Mind*. New York: Basic Books, 1985.

Mahler, M., Pine, F., and Bergman, A. (1975). *The Psychological Birth of the Human Infant*. New York: Basic Books.

Modell, A. H. (1984). *Psychoanalysis in a New Context*. New York: International Universities Press.

Rangell, L. (1963). Structural problems in intrapsychic conflict. *Psychoanal. Study Child*, 18:103–38.

———. (1971). The decision-making process: A contribution from psychoanalysis. *Psychoanal. Study Child*, 26:425–452.

———. (1980). *The Mind of Watergate: An Exploration of the Compromise of Integrity*. New York: Norton.

Rapaport, D. (1958). The theory of ego autonomy: A generalization. *Bull. Menninger Clinic*, 22:13–35.

Sandler, J. (1960). The background of safety. *Int. J. Psycho-Anal.*, 41:352–56.

———. (1969). *On the Communication of Psychoanalytic Thought*. Leiden: University Press.

———. (1973). Frames of reference in psychoanalytic psychology. *Brit. J. Med. Psych.*, 46:29, 37, 143.

———. (1979). Frames of reference in psychoanalytic psychology. *Brit. J. Med. Psych.*, 49:267.

Sandler, J., Dare, C., and Holder, A. (1972). Frames of reference in psychoanalytic psychology. *Brit. J. Med. Psych.*, 45:127, 133, 143, 265.

Sandler, J., and Sandler, A.-M. (1983). The "second censorship," the "three box model," and some technical implications. *Int. J. Psycho-Anal.*, 64:413–25.

Thiel, J. H. (1986). Psychoanalyse en psychotherapie op analytische grondslag bij narcistische problematiek. In R. A. Pierloot and J. H. Thiel, *Psychoanalytische Therapieën*. Deventer: Van Loghum Slaterus.

Winnicott, D. W. (1958). *Through Paediatrics to Psychoanalysis*. London: Hogarth Press, 1982.

———. (1965). *The Maturational Processes and the Facilitating Environment*. London: Hogarth Press.

———. (1971). *Playing and Reality*. Harmondsworth: Penguin.

Letter to Sigmund Freud

LEÓN GRINBERG

Dear Sigmund Freud:

I have been asked to conduct a seminar on the subject of "On Narcissism: An Introduction," the paper you wrote in 1914. I realize that it may be presumptuous to invoke you personally for this purpose, but I am experiencing certain difficulties in approaching the task and believe I can make a better job of it if I can engage in a dialogue with you, as the interlocutor who can resolve my doubts, and with whom I can raise objections and offer alternative viewpoints.

My difficulties arise largely because I not only have to communicate concepts that continue to be fundamental to psychoanalytic theory but also feel bound to disagree with some of the considerations you put forward. Conscious of your love of truth and the honesty you have shown throughout your work, however, I shall proceed with these objections as homage to your scientific integrity and creative genius. Since only what could be measured and quantified was regarded as "scientific," many of your brilliant discoveries had to be forced into a mold in order to conform to the established canons. I assume, too, that your emotional reaction to your disagreements with Jung and Adler influenced your approach to some aspects of your theme.

Your paper is admirable and at the same time worrying. It contains fundamental innovations, such as the concept of the ego-ideal, the value of sublimation, self-regard, object choice, the self-observing agency, and conscience; but these are accompanied by certain contradictions and statements that are perhaps debatable, such as your uncompromising insistence on the importance of libidinal quantities in explaining the concept of narcissism, to the almost complete exclusion of object relations and their role in this concept.

Did you yourself not teach us to enter the complicated labyrinth of fantasies and wishes existing in the unconscious? Because you did, it is hard for us to recognize you in the Freud who insists on explaining love and illness to us by quantities of energy. Did you imagine that your valuable intuitions, which form the cornerstone of psychoanalytic theory, would be taken seriously only if you imposed this "scientific" character on them?

As a result, both the term and the concept of "narcissism" became confused and controversial, lending themselves to a variety of interpretations. Different authors have deduced from your paper that narcissism may be regarded variously as a sexual perversion, a phase of development, a libidinal cathexis of the ego, and a particular type of object choice.

I wonder why—and I put it to you—if narcissism was considered a phase of development, it was not acknowledged as such in your subsequent references to the theory of libidinal development. Could it be because, oddly enough, the concept of narcissism contains an implicit acknowledgment of the object relation, even if only through the intermediary of the id-ego relationship or because the ego takes itself as its object? Perhaps narcissism might constitute the object theory of autoerotism. How would you react to this idea?

I might perhaps have wished for a more explicit treatment of the principal function of narcissism in the life of the individual, its essential influence throughout the course of development, and the way infantile narcissism is transformed into the equally essential mature narcissism of the adult. Of course, this is directly bound up with the two types of narcissism—healthy narcissism, which is indispensable to life, and pathological narcissism, which appears to predominate in your discussion and which, significantly, is the type on which the subsequent psychoanalytic literature has tended to concentrate.

I shall now try to explain as clearly as possible how I have understood your concepts, the doubts to which they give rise, and my own views.

In the first part of your paper, you insist on explaining the occurrence of narcissism on the basis of libido theory, ascribing its origin to the libidinal cathexis of the ego. This definition introduces a complication into the theory of instincts that becomes more manifest when you make a fresh distinction between "ego-libido" (or narcissistic libido) and "object-libido," which cathects objects. It follows from this new hypothesis that the ego, previously characterized as the seat of the instinct of self-preservation, now has to be regarded, owing to its libidinal cathexis, as the seat of an important part of the sexual instinct—the narcissistic part. This change fueled criticism that you were tending toward a monistic, instinctual conception of the psyche, "reducing everything to sex." Although this criticism is unfounded since you have always been consistently dualistic in your approach, you certainly came up against a serious obstacle in the new conception of the theory of instincts. This aroused serious doubts in you, although it took you years to conclude that the separation between sexual and self-preservative instincts was unconvincing. Finally, you integrated them in the so-called life instinct, which you contrasted with the death instinct.

I believe that the instincts are closely bound up in the results of the dynamic interaction between the ego and the object and that the affects, which are at work from the beginning of life, are among the component parts of the instincts. The affects function as generators of meaning and carriers of the motivations underlying the search for the object.

In my view, the well-known model of the "container/contained," representing the dynamic relationship between something that is projected (that which is contained) and an object that contains it (container), is a working hypothesis that is extremely useful for an understanding of narcissism. In addition, it serves to facilitate our understanding of the possible vicissitudes of the mother-infant relationship. The infant needs to evacuate his anxieties and painful emotions into the breast. The normal mother, having a capacity for "reverie," acts as a container that receives the unpleasurable affects of the baby (contained) and manages to soothe his anxiety by successfully transforming his hunger into satisfaction, his pain into pleasure, his loneliness into companionship, and his fear of dying into tranquility. She also acts as a model for the child.

We could therefore regard narcissism in terms of a container/contained model whereby the child, who was first contained in the container of the mother's uterus and subsequently in that formed by her capacity for reverie and tolerance, converts his ego, shortly after birth, into a container for a vitally important affect, love (contained), which will be directed first toward himself (narcissistic love) and later toward objects, on the model of the mother.

The ego always wants something from the object (for example, satisfaction of a need, love, security) or to get rid of something (tension, insecurity, anxiety, depression, and so on), in accordance with the pleasure-unpleasure principle.

You say in your paper that autoerotism predates narcissism and the formation of the ego. You maintain that "something" must be added to autoerotism in order for narcissism to arise as such: this "something" is, of course, the ego. We may suppose, however, that ego formation is a gradual process that commences at the very beginning of life, so that a rudimentary ego related to an object must exist from the beginning. You yourself elsewhere interpreted thumb-sucking in babies as the pleasure derived from the experience at the mother's breast, now reproduced autoerotically.

Observations appear to confirm, however, that thumb-sucking predates contact with the breast. In this case, the explanation might be that it owes its existence to an innate prefiguration of the breast (or of something capable of satisfying the needs felt by the baby). Such prefigurations could correspond to the category of "protofantasies" you describe.

Hence any definition of narcissism is inseparable from a definition of the ego. The existence of the ego demands an object, and vice versa. Each is formed by interaction with the other.

You taught us that the ego arises as a modification of the surface of the id under the influence of the outside world. The ego perceives the stimuli from the surrounding environment. But this environment consists of objects—in particular, the mother who feeds the child and from whom he obtains his most important sensations. It is hard to say who takes the initiative in these first contacts. The answer may be that they both do, that there is a harmonious encounter between the baby who seeks and the mother who offers. At first, this interchange takes place by way of an object relationship that is undifferentiated from the point of view of the baby (primary narcissism). The successive introjections and projections between the baby and the mother encourage ego growth in the child, who eventually becomes able to distinguish the object as an autonomous entity (secondary narcissism).

The body plays an important part in this process of ego formation. As you yourself put it: "The ego is first and foremost a bodily ego." The encounter between the biological and affective needs of the child and the mother's erotic pleasure in satisfying these needs through her affection, caresses, and body contact is an essential factor in the development of the notion of the body.

There is no doubt that the mother-child relationship at the beginning of life constitutes a psychic unity in constant interaction, which lays down important foundations for the narcissistic model and its characteristics. In addition to her original and constant function as the agent for the satisfaction of the child's needs, the mother must respond to his affects and organize his responses. In this way, she lends meaning to the child's affects and behavior. If she responds appropriately, she can mitigate the persecutory intensity of the child's affects, encourage the growth of his mind and psychic organization, and facilitate the development of a healthy narcissism.

The identification in which the child is fused with his mother (primary identification) promotes the narcissistic perfection of childhood and plays a part in the establishment of the child's love for himself, thereby giving rise to the development of the ideal ego.

The feeling of omnipotence is one of the main characteristics of narcissism and finds its full expression in the most primitive state of the child's development, when he is most dependent and his ego is at its weakest and most immature. The child's omnipotence is reinforced by the fantasy of being fused with his mother. Consequently, each pleasurable experience will for him be a further proof of his omnipotence. Of course, this omnipotence and the feeling of narcissistic love will be threatened by the process of separation from the breast and from the mother.

In my opinion, primary identification constitutes a primary narcissistic state in which, by way of primitive identifications, the subject both takes part in and is the founder of an archaic, symbiotic, and undifferentiated object relation in which the child will receive from the object the contributions necessary for his ego to go on developing.

Consolidation of the ego will depend on the child's being able to direct sufficient love toward himself (narcissistic love) in a satisfactory form, as a result of his own achievements and of the mother's contributions. Where this does not occur, we have an alteration in the narcissistic equilibrium, which then proves to be fragile and in constant need of external contributions to make up for internal lacks. Such compensation is the principal objective of patients whose narcissism has undergone a pathological development: they seek relations with "narcissistic objects" capable of giving them the impression that they are alive and real. This search, however, also contains within itself an attempt to gain freedom from another form of narcissism, associated with the death instinct and characterized by the absence of a wish for a love relationship with the object, symbolizing the death of the world or the ego, or both. This narcissism of death, with its powerful destructive tendency, must be distinguished from the narcissism of life described above.

It has been said that when narcissistic love is not satisfied, the development of love is disturbed and cannot extend to object-love. This is similar to what occurs in mourning the loss of a loved object. In my view, this loss includes the loss of parts of the self and of ego functions that were formerly projected onto the object.

Object-loss, like the loss of the projected aspects of the ego, may carry with it a depressive feeling, causing failure in love for oneself, or narcissistic love, accompanied by feelings of lack and helplessness, and a reduction in self-regard, constituting a "narcissistic wound." When this happens, the development of love for the object is also disturbed. Narcissistic collapse, as a consequence of the loss of the valued image of the ego, gives rise to an extremely painful affect, sometimes experienced as a veritable depressive catastrophe.

I believe that in the game with the cotton-reel and its corollary, the mirror game, of which you gave us a masterly description in 1920 and which has remained a set-piece in the psychoanalytic literature, the child is expressing the relationship between the disappearance of the object and that of himself. The child's game with its two scenes, the reel scene and the mirror scene, for me represents a clear dramatization of what happens in every process of mourning: when confronted by object-loss, "the individual runs to the mirror" to see what has happened to his own image. For this reason, in every process of mourning an object, it is necessary to investigate the state of the individual's ego and his mourning for himself in order to gain an accurate impression of the nature of the mourning for the external object. Moreover, I consider that when the ego is capable of adequate self-reparation, it is in the best position to work through the mourning healthily and to repair satisfactorily the internal object thereby represented. This self-reparation corresponds to what we might call healthy or normal egoism, concerned both for the ego and for the object.

On this point, I note that you did not dwell on the concept of "ego interest." Indeed, with very few exceptions, this term henceforth disappears from your works. To indulge in a play on words, I would say that your excessive interest in defending the concept of libido displaced and diminished your interest in ego interest, which I consider to be of particular importance.

I believe that ego interest must be related to the vital issue of healthy egoism, just as altruism is related to the interest directed toward the object. Do you not agree that the more one feels filled, rich, capable of giving and of being enriched by giving, the more one is capable of loving the object?

The opposite is observed in patients who respond with a "negative therapeutic reaction." These patients' inaccessibility may be attributed to their excessive preoccupation with their damaged internal objects. They feel that they must care for and repair all their loved and hated objects before thinking about themselves. This preoccupation with their internalized objects, which they feel they have attacked with all the force of their envy and pathological egoism, gives rise to an unbearable unconscious guilt. They feel the need to sacrifice themselves for their internal objects, and it is this that makes their resistance to treatment so stubborn.

Pathological egoism may also be expressed in other ways, causing other kinds of disturbances, such as hypochondria, in which the individual withdraws libidinal interest from his love objects: he ceases to love. You yourself mention hypochondria as one of the routes by which to study narcissism, others being organic illness and the love life of the individual. You say that a damming-up of libido in the organ produces unpleasure, and you add that the decisive factor is not so much the absolute magnitude of this material process as a certain function of this absolute magnitude. I believe that, by this statement, you are implicitly moving toward a more qualitative view, in that you refer more to the function than to the magnitude itself. In using the word "qualitative," I mean to convey that you are not so much emphasizing an impersonal concept of energy, tension, and discharge here as inclining toward motivation and the search for meaning. The meaning of the hypochondria may be observation and control of the internal object within the organ, which is experienced as damaged and is therefore feared and hated at one and the same time.

At one point you compare hypochondria with the anxiety of the transference neuroses. Of course, there is a whole range of hypochondriacal states, extending from simple preoccupation with one's own person to hypochondriacal delusions. I would suggest that we might introduce the term "signal hypochondria," equivalent to "signal anxiety," which tends to preserve self-regard and the integrity of the bodily ego by the deployment of different defenses. The "hypochondriacal mini-reactions" arising in patients when particular areas of conflict are touched upon in the analysis are relatively frequent; it is significant that such patients then begin to complain of physical troubles.

I would include "self-regard," which you discussed so superbly in your paper, in the same group of concepts as "healthy egoism," "ego interest," and what I call "signal hypochondria."

Self-regard is a complex affective-cognitive state determined by a large number of factors. It is an ego function, which implies an active process of judging or assessing one's own self. In addition to your excellent description of the nature and qualities of this feeling, you say in your paper that self-regard depends very closely and particularly on narcissistic libido. This view again arouses doubts and disagreements. If self-regard is taken as an affective concept, how can you treat it as synonymous and interchangeable with narcissistic libido, which is an instinctual concept? If you explain self-regard as a libidinal cathexis of the self, it would have to diminish when the libido is cathected in objects; conversely, it ought to increase when it is withdrawn from objects and cathects the self. But our clinical observations will sometimes show otherwise. We see that people with high self-regard are those who are best able to take an interest in others, whereas those whose self-regard is very low are incapable of doing so and are preoccupied with themselves.

When self-regard is threatened, reduced, or impaired, narcissistic activities are undertaken to protect, restore, and stabilize it. This mobilization of narcissism for the purpose of regulating self-regard is not incompatible with a continuous object relation, which may perform the same function.

Regulation of self-regard is a continuous, active process. In order to examine it as such, we may resort to a model representing narcissism both "transversely" and "longitudinally." The former has the characteristics attributed to narcissism as a phase of development; it implies a particular type of object relation (narcissistic) and a system for the regulation of self-regard. The latter would relate to a constant in the regulation of self-regard, applicable to each individual stage of development. Narcissism would then be a component of all stages of development, and this might perhaps be more consistent with what is frequently observed in clinical practice.

Other parts of your paper also seem to me to be rich in content—for instance, your excellent study of the two forms of object choice and, in particular, the concept of the ego-ideal. Some of your observations on love are truly valuable—for example, the idea that people's object choice may conform to the anaclitic type (the woman who feeds or the man who protects) or the narcissistic type (where the self is sought as a love object). Some of your other conclusions, however, are not fully borne out by clinical experience. You state that a person who loves has sacrificed a part of his narcissism, leading to an impoverishment of the ego as a result of the withdrawal of libidinal cathexes. This loss to the benefit of the loved object does not always occur; we often find that the capacity to love considerably enhances self-regard and enriches the ego. Again, why do you place such emphasis on the difference in object choice between men and women? I do not believe this to be justified. Men, just like women, may seek to be loved in order to satisfy their narcissism, just as women may accede to the full love of the object onto which they transfer their narcissism, the state that you say predominates in men.

I feel that this section of your paper reflects a serious blind spot. I consider it is relevant to ask why you did not mention the other important affect, the opposite of love: hate. You include it in a subsequent paper, in explaining the vicissitudes of instinct. You say that love can have not just one but three antitheses: loving/hating, loving/being loved, and loving/indifference. You add that the ego loves itself and hates the outside world because it is a source of unpleasurable stimuli. In my opinion, love and hate coexist from the beginning of life and are directed just as much toward objects as to the ego. My point is that hatred and aggression, feelings that I miss in your paper, are essential for an understanding of pathological narcissism.

It is precisely this pathological narcissism that characterizes the category of the narcissistic neuroses, to which you attached so much importance in support of your concept of narcissism as based on the accumulation of libido in the ego.

In distinguishing between the transference neuroses and the narcissistic neuroses, your criterion was that sufferers from the latter did not form transference relationships. You continued to hold fast to this view despite your deeper convictions; elsewhere, notwithstanding your initial pessimism, you did not rule out the possibility that there might one day be some means of gaining access to narcissistic patients, for you made the significant statement that in many acute psychotic disturbances there is a normal person hidden in some corner of the patient's mind.

Since the time when you asserted that patients with narcissistic neuroses could not be analyzed, wide-ranging evidence has accrued to the effect that psychotics *do* form an intense transference relationship with their therapists, determined by their psychopathology and their traumatic childhood history. The transference in these cases is not formed only with whole objects. It also constitutes an archaic, infantile response, based on aspects of the primary process and directed toward part-objects, in consequence of these patients' characteristic dissociation.

I cannot help wondering, my dear Master, to what extent you might have changed your theory of narcissism if you had subsequently been able to see for yourself the analyzability of narcissistic patients and the intense transferences they can develop. Perhaps you might then have attached less importance to quantities of libido and instinctual factors and turned instead more toward unconscious motivations and fantasies and toward the far-reaching significance of such valuable discoveries as self-regard, the ego-ideal, and so on.

Idealization, the ideal ego, and the ego-ideal are exciting aspects of your paper. You state convincingly that the child cannot keep up the belief in his own perfection, owing partly to the admonitions of others and partly to his own critical judgment; he then tries to recover it by reestablishing within himself an ego-ideal that becomes the "heir to narcissism"—the lost narcissism of infancy. This ego-ideal stems from the idealized internal objects that have received projections of good feelings and the valued parts of the self.

I feel that your emphasis on the distinction between idealization and sublimation is important: the former has to do with the object, whereas the latter is related to an instinct that is diverted from its sexual aim and changes its object, without, however, succumbing to repression. I should like to emphasize this last point, as sublimatory activity not only implies the development of higher-level interests but also, because it is not subject to repression, helps to enrich and expand the ego.

The ego-ideal largely satisfies vitally important affective needs of the individual by stimulating and protecting self-regard, in accordance with narcissistic aims. But though you accept that it furnishes satisfaction, you say at the same time that its formation increases the demands of the ego and favors repression. You then refer to a psychic agency, the "conscience," which has the particular function of monitoring the actual ego and measuring it by that ideal. You also say that this agency, like the ego-ideal, arises from the critical influence of the parents and of society. The ego-ideal, which is nurtured by the conscience, then takes on the characteristics of the "superego," which you were to develop years later.

The problem arises of how to consider the relationship between the ego-ideal and the superego. In later writings you treat them as synonymous, but then you again distinguish them, describing the superego as the carrier or vehicle of the ego-ideal. Nowadays, many analysts tend to retain the theoretical and clinical distinction between the two concepts in describing their normal and pathological aspects. For example, attention has been directed to the cruelty of the early superego formations, owing to the introjection of objects invested with the sadism stemming from the child's projections of his oral-sadistic and anal-sadistic impulses. You yourself acknowledged that the severity of the superego not only was a consequence of the internalized aggression of the parents but also arose from the child's own hostility. The superego of more advanced states of development will become more mature and benevolent. For its part, the normal ego ideal determines the values and ideals to which the individual aspires; it helps to strengthen the feeling of identity, with appropriate discrimination between internal and external reality. The pathological ego-ideal, on the other hand, is tyrannical and persecutory, imposing extremely high and unattainable objectives: when the ego is unable to satisfy the demand for perfection and therefore to ensure its own esteem, it usually falls into a narcissistic depression; it feels that it loses the love and protection of the "ego-ideal object" having these characteristics.

Paradoxically, the perfection acquired by the ego-ideal is responsible for repressing "narcissistic perfection" and initiating the release of the self. You point out that ego development consists in a process of distancing from primary narcissism and that this takes place by displacement of libido onto an ego-ideal imposed from outside. You also stress that the ego-ideal has both an individual and a social component—the common ideal of a family or a nation, for example. You add that dissatisfaction owing to failure to live up to this ideal results in the release of homosexual libido, which is transformed into a sense of guilt or social anxiety.

It is a pity that this last point, which is so important, is treated so briefly at the end of your paper. It is frustrating not to be able to follow the development of these attractive ideas to which you were to return years later. Perhaps it is because of the desire for more aroused by your profound reflections and wise teachings.

This letter is already very long, but before ending it, I should like to give you a broad outline of the impact and subsequent development of your theory of narcissism.

Since you wrote your original paper a large number of publications have appeared containing interesting ideas about the application of the concept of narcissism to the theory and practice of psychoanalysis. The following ideas have had the greatest impact: conceptualization of narcissism as libidinal cathexis of the self and not of the ego; the repercussions of object-relations theory on the concept of narcissism; the importance of representations of self and object in narcissism; the redefinition of narcissism in noninstinctual terms as an "ideal state" of affective well-being; the clinical importance of narcissistic personalities; narcissism conceived as a structure or as a state; the influence of the ego-ideal in the maintenance and regulation of self-regard; the relationship between narcissism and the feeling of identity; and narcissism as a defense against affects.

In the past few years, a number of theories have attracted wide attention in the psychoanalytic community. One of these maintains that the concept of narcissism corresponds to primitive object relations in which omnipotence plays an important part, together with disavowal of the separation between self and object, with envy and aggression predominating. This pathological narcissism is distinguished from another kind, which is libidinal and positive. A second theory holds that narcissism is a privileged relational state representing man's tendency to return to his prenatal abode. According to a third theory, the child tends to replace the perfection of primary narcissism by two agencies: the grandiose self and the idealized parental imago; it emphasizes the development of the libidinal cathexes and takes no account of the vicissitudes of aggression. The fourth theory maintains that the grandiose self is not a libidinally cathected archaic configuration but a pathological condensation of the real self, the ideal self, and the ideal object; it takes account of both libidinal and aggressive instincts and holds that narcissistic and object cathexes occur simultaneously.

This dialogue with you, my dear Freud, my internal Freud, my old mentor, has cheered me. It has given me a better understanding of the essential points of your paper, leaving others in a useful penumbra of associations.

I do not know what you will think of everything I have written, nor am I sure that I have been able to convey to you clearly my admiration for the singular richness of content of the paper, my doubts, and also my objections to some of your views. At any rate, I intend to make this letter public, so that students, colleagues, and I can reflect together on your ideas and so that we can proceed further along the paths that your brilliant discoveries have opened up for us.

Sincerely yours,
León Grinberg

Narcissism in Freud

WILLY BARANGER

In psychoanalytic theorizing, the concept of narcissism occupies a position similar to that of identification: both led to a profound restructuring of psychoanalytic theory. Identification gave rise to a radically different view of psychic structure when it was discovered that psychic structure stemmed largely from the vicissitudes of the object relation by way of the structuring role of identification. Once introduced, narcissism completely overturned the theory of instincts; the ultimate root of psychological conflict now became situated in the struggle between libido and destructiveness, Eros and Thanatos.

The concept of narcissism has another aspect, however, which is highly relevant to our present subject. The theory of narcissism directly affects the concept of an object and that of psychic agencies (the ego and even the superego). It also raises some extremely complex problems. Only the most scrupulous examination of Freud's numerous references to narcissism can yield an idea of the multiplicity of meanings he assigned to the term, as well as the labyrinth of inherent theoretical problems. Even the exact sense in which he used the term is not simple. Freud introduced the concept into psychoanalytic theory in 1909 or 1910, but its use gradually increased until it eventually embraced phenomena apparently inconsistent with its original meaning. At the same time, as frequently occurs in the evolution of Freud's thought, the new concepts coexisted with formulations that they should logically have supplanted. Two questions must therefore be answered prior to any theoretical study: What made it necessary for Freud to introduce the concept of narcissism? What are the major stages in the evolution of this concept?

The first question can be answered quite easily. The need to introduce the concept stemmed first of all from the study of homosexuality in Freud's essay on Leonardo da Vinci. Another important factor was Freud's growing interest and that of some of his disciples in what we would nowadays call "psychotic states"—an interest that culminated in Freud's admirable analysis of Schreber's memoirs. The relevance of these two sources that necessitated the introduction of the concept persists.

The historical development of the concept involved a drastic change of direction, as was noted by Laplanche and Pontalis[1] and by Strachey.[2] In spite of these authors' efforts to resolve the contradictions introduced by Freud in *The Ego and the Id* (1923), which represented a far-reaching modification of the concept, they end with a question that leaves the problem unsolved. Again, what are we to make of the contradiction in Abraham's thinking,[3] with his unqualified espousal of the "simple" solution that there is an autoerotic phase in the development of the libido followed by a narcissistic phase characterized by oral incorporation of the object?

The concept of narcissism turns out to be one of the most problematic and obscure in all psychoanalytic theory. We must therefore begin with a purely semantic approach, examining individually the many meanings of the term in Freud's work and then considering the problems they raise.

THE NINE SENSES OF THE TERM "NARCISSISM"

Nine meanings of "narcissism" can be identified and classified in three groups of three. The first group relates essentially to narcissism as one of

1. *The Language of Psycho-Analysis* (London: Hogarth Press and Institute of Psycho-Analysis, 1973), 255.
2. *S.E.* 19:63–66.
3. Karl Abraham, "A Short Study of the Development of the Libido, Viewed in the Light of Mental Disorders," in *Selected Papers* (London, 1927), 496.

the forms or vicissitudes of libido. In the second group, the emphasis falls on the object in the narcissistic states, and the problems of narcissism come together with those of identification in its introjective form. The final group consists of extensions of the term to refer to attitudes, feelings, and character traits indicative of the valuation, devaluation, or overvaluation of some aspect of the person.

The following meanings are subsumed in the term "narcissism":

1. A developmental stage of the libido characterized by the concentration of all libido within or toward the ego. In this sense, it denotes an intermediate stage between a "phase" regarded as autoerotic and a phase of object choice (*S.E.* 14: 69). Thus all the stages in which the libidinal interest of the ego is detached from the external world—in particular, sleeping (*S.E.* 14:225), psychosis (*S.E.* 12:72), fetal life as it is assumed to be (*S.E.* 14:222)—will be described as narcissistic.
2. The processes that make this state possible. For instance, we speak of "primary narcissism," the concentration of libido within the ego (or, after Freud introduced the differentiation between the ego and the id, the concentration of the id's libido in the ego), or the withdrawal toward the ego of libido formerly directed toward external objects: "secondary narcissism."
3. The point of fixation corresponding to this stage of development, which is involved both in the predisposition to homosexuality and in the etiological equation of the "narcissistic neuroses" (psychoses in present-day terminology).
4. The term is used in a different sense in the phrase "narcissistic object choice," which means that the subject chooses his object on the basis of his own characteristics, in accordance with some actual feature of his own being (for example, his sex) or with what he has been or would have liked to be, and so on. (*S.E.* 11:100).
5. Similarly, the situation of narcissistic choice may be introjected ("narcissistic identification"; *S.E.* 14:250). Here, the "narcissism" refers not directly to the ego but to its ego-ideal (*S.E.* 14:94) or the idealized object, which it imitates and whose commands it obeys. The center of narcissism in this case consists not of the ego but of the superego or ego-ideal, to which it tries to adjust and which alone is truly admirable.
6. By extension, the term "narcissism" is used for a set of attitudes, states, and even character traits extending from simple self-regard to megaloma-

niacal omnipotence on the part of the subject (*S.E.* 12:72), by way of all degrees of self-evaluation or overvaluation of some characteristic of the subject or of himself as a whole. Narcissism thus refers here to the subject's pride in his or her beauty (*S.E.* 12:138), to the overvaluation by children and "primitives" of the power of their own thoughts (*S.E.* 13:89–90), to a characteristic of the psychology of women: the wish to be admired and loved (*S.E.* 14:253), the overvaluation of the penis by men, and so on. Freud even describes various forms of a character type whose dominant feature is the "narcissistic" nature of its libido.

7. Everything that reduces the self-regard of the ego or its feeling of being loved by valued objects is called a "narcissistic wound."
8. There is a reference to the "narcissism of small differences" and even to the "small differences" between man and woman (*S.E.* 11:199).
9. Finally, mention must be made of perverse narcissism, which gave its name to the other phenomena and consists in taking one's own body as an object of contemplation and love.

NARCISSISM AND AUTOEROTISM

It is interesting to note the chronological distance between the introduction of the concepts of autoerotism and narcissism. The former appears for the first time we know of in a letter from Freud to Fliess dating from 1899; the latter does not occur until 1909—five years before its official "introduction" into analytic theory. The first text suggests that the concepts of autoerotism and narcissism were originally undifferentiated and that it was only in 1909 that their differentiation became necessary in Freud's thought. As we shall see, he did not achieve this differentiation without confronting a number of difficulties:

> The lowest sexual stratum is auto-erotism, which does without any psychosexual aim and demands only local feelings of satisfaction. It is succeeded by allo-erotism (homo- and hetero-erotism); but it certainly also continues to exist as a separate current. . . . Paranoia dissolves the identification once more; it re-establishes all the figures loved in childhood which have been abandoned . . . and it dissolves the ego itself into extraneous figures. Thus I have come to regard paranoia as a forward surge of the auto-erotic current. (*S.E.* 1:280)

This passage is truly prophetic of a number of subjects developed fifteen years later in "On Narcissism: An Introduction"; it clearly implies, on the one hand, the concept of autoerotism as a phase of libidinal development and, on the other, the inclusion in the situations constituting this phase of certain relations with objects. This was to induce Freud years later to differentiate the concept of narcissism. From this point of view, narcissism is clearly separated from autoerotism when objects enter into the theory, in regard to the homosexuality of Leonardo da Vinci and Schreber's psychosis —that is, when the demand for clinical understanding arises at the point where the differentiation of the libidinal quality can no longer dispense with the relation to the object and its structure.

It might appear that the introduction of the concept of narcissism into analytic theory does not greatly disturb the theory and might on the contrary help clarify it. This is not the case. As the following quotations show, Freud oscillates among a number of conceptions of autoerotism, narcissism, and the relations between them without any clear sign of a chronological development (except perhaps a tendency to abandon autoerotism as a phase after 1929; as we shall see, however, this oscillation is replaced by another that is just as important). In some passages Freud considers autoerotism to be a phase of development of the libido prior to that state of narcissism. In others he regards it as a mode of satisfaction characteristic of the narcissistic phase. In some of his works he defines autoerotism as the absence of objects; in others he recognizes that it coexists with object relations, or even that it appears after these relations have been established.

Autoerotism as a Phase

This was Freud's first idea (see the letter to Fliess dated 1899 quoted above). He returned to it in 1910: "Since at this first phase of infantile sexual life satisfaction is obtained from the subject's own body and extraneous objects are disregarded, we term this phase (from a word coined by Havelock Ellis) that of *auto-erotism*" (*S.E.* 11:44).

He returned more systematically to this idea of development in his study of Schreber:

> Recent investigations have directed our attention to a stage in the development of the libido which it passes through on the way from autoerotism to object-love. This stage has been given the name of narcis-

> sism. . . . There comes a time in the development of the individual at which he unifies his sexual instincts (which have hitherto been engaged in auto-erotic activities) in order to obtain a love-object; and he begins by taking himself, his own body, as his love-object, and only subsequently proceeds from this to the choice of some person other than himself as his object. (*S.E.* 12:60–61)

Logically enough, he chooses an external object very similar to himself (of the same sex) and can only then move on to a heterosexual choice. Here Freud clearly delineates a development that breaks down into four phases: autoerotism, narcissism, homosexual object choice, and heterosexual object choice. The same picture is presented in *Totem and Taboo* (*S.E.* 13:88–90).

In "On Narcissism," Freud gives a clear statement of the need to distinguish autoerotism and narcissism as developmental stages: "A unity comparable to the ego cannot exist in the individual from the start; the ego has to be developed. The auto-erotic instincts, however, are there from the very first; so there must be something added to auto-erotism—a new psychical action—in order to bring about narcissism" (*S.E.* 14:77).

Autoerotism as a Type of Behavior Characteristic of Narcissism

Freud writes: "Originally, at the very beginning of mental life, the ego is cathected with instincts and is to some extent capable of satisfying them on itself. We call this condition 'narcissism' and this way of obtaining satisfaction 'auto-erotic.' At this time the external world is not cathected with interest (in a general sense) and is indifferent for purposes of satisfaction." (*S.E.* 14:134). The contradiction between this passage and those quoted above (dating from the same period) is flagrant. And the following passage makes matters even more complicated:

> We have become accustomed to call the early phase of the development of the ego, during which its sexual instincts find auto-erotic satisfaction, "narcissism," without at once entering on any discussion of the relation between auto-erotism and narcissism. It follows that the preliminary stage of the scopophilic instinct, in which the subject's own body is the object of the scopophilia, must be classed under narcissism, and that we must describe it as a narcissistic formation. (*S.E.* 14:132)

Here appears what gives rise to most of the difficulties in the elucidation of the relations between autoerotism and narcissism: the lack of definition of the concepts of the ego and of the subject's own body. Scopophilia here constitutes a link between two contradictory concepts: objectively, a neonate "has" a body and "does not have" (for Freud) an "ego" as an organized agency. The body is at first the seat of all satisfactions and all pains. The ego is structured only afterward. Scopophilia, the pleasure of looking at one's own body, represents—as Freud suggests and Jacques Lacan emphasizes (the "mirror stage")—a crucial moment in the structuring of the ego as an organized agency possessing (or accommodated in) a complete body of its own.

Later on, in the *Introductory Lectures on Psycho-Analysis*, Freud again adopts this second approach:

> This narcissism is the universal and original state of things, from which object-love is only later developed, without the narcissism necessarily disappearing on that account. . . . Many sexual instincts begin by finding satisfaction in the subject's own body—auto-erotically, as we say—and . . . this capacity for auto-erotism is the basis of the lagging-behind of sexuality in the process of education in the reality principle. Auto-erotism would thus be the sexual activity of the narcissistic stage of allocation of the libido. (*S.E.* 16:416)

Quite probably, some of these contradictions on Freud's part are due to an implicit change in his conceptual model. Autoerotism has a meaning within a purely "instinctual" framework; we might say that it is confined to a closed system: the body-ego with its instincts, conceived in an energetic form—that is, as processes of discharge taking place within the subject's own body. Freud writes: "In the auto-erotic instincts, the part played by the organic source is so decisive that, according to a plausible suggestion of Federn . . . and Jekels, . . . the form and function of the organ determine the activity or passivity of the instinctual aim" (*S.E.* 14:132–33). Narcissism now involves the object (it should not be forgotten that the concept itself stems from the study of object relations: homosexual choice/replacement of external objects by the ego as an object). For this reason, we should not be surprised by the oscillations in Freud's thought concerning the relations among autoerotism, narcissism, and the object.

On the one hand, autoerotism is defined as libido without an object. On the other, Freud allows the existence of *libidinal* sexual objects from the beginnings of postnatal life:

> At a time at which the first beginnings of sexual satisfaction are still linked with the taking of nourishment, the sexual instinct has a sexual object outside the infant's own body in the shape of his mother's breast. It is only later that the instinct loses that object, just at the time, perhaps, when the child is able to form a total idea of the person to whom the organ that is giving him satisfaction belongs. As a rule the sexual instinct then becomes auto-erotic. (*S.E.* 7:222)

In terms of genetic stages, we thus arrive at the paradoxical solution that an object stage precedes autoerotism.

Our problems do not end here, however. Logically, there is a third solution, and this too is to be found in Freud: autoerotism coexisting with object love: "Alongside these and other auto-erotic activities, we find in children at a very early age manifestations of those instinctual components of sexual pleasure (or, as we like to say, of libido) which presupposes the taking of an extraneous person as an object" (*S.E.* 11:44). Freud's formulations as to timing ("the very beginning of mental life," "the first beginnings of sexual satisfaction," "a very early age," and so on) are so vague that they afford no basis for an attempt at a coherent reordering that would be truly faithful to his thought. Freud is trying out solutions and formulating each of them by switching alternately from one scheme of reference to another.

But our tribulations continue. Freud's response to these thorny problems is to introduce new concepts and new discriminations: primary and secondary narcissism, narcissistic-libido and object-libido—all these complicate the concept of narcissism still further. The complication is made worse with the discovery of the death instincts. It was already difficult to formulate sadism in relation to the discovery of the narcissistic state; it is even more difficult to give a coherent formulation of the compatibility of these last concepts.

PRIMARY AND SECONDARY NARCISSISM

The distinction between primary and secondary narcissism, introduced by Freud in his first great work, actually followed from earlier writings. Schreber's megalomania had already induced Freud to think about the recovery of infantile omnipotence; it was also in connection with the latter (and possibly thinking of Schreber) that he coined the term "primary narcissism."

> [In megalomania] the libido that has been withdrawn from the external world has been directed to the ego and thus gives rise to an attitude

> which may be called narcissism. But the megalomania itself is no new creation; on the contrary, it is, as we know, a magnification and plainer manifestation of a condition which had already existed previously. This leads us to look upon the narcissism which arises through the drawing in of object-cathexes as a secondary one, superimposed upon a primary narcissism that is obscured by a number of different influences. (*S.E.* 14:75)

Freud was to return to this argument in the *Introductory Lectures*. In "On Narcissism: An Introduction," he investigates the vicissitudes of this primary narcissism more thoroughly:

> The development of the ego consists in a departure from primary narcissism and gives rise to a vigorous attempt to recover that state. This departure is brought about by means of the displacement of libido on to an ego ideal [*Ichideal*] imposed from without; and satisfaction is brought about from fulfilling this ideal.
>
> At the same time the ego has sent out the libidinal object-cathexes. It becomes impoverished in favour of these cathexes, just as it does in favour of the ego ideal, and it enriches itself once more from its satisfactions in respect of the object, just as it does by fulfilling its ideal.
>
> One part of self-regard [*Selbstgefuhl*] is primary—the residue of infantile narcissism; another part arises out of the omnipotence [*Allmacht*] which is corroborated by experience (the fulfillment of the ego ideal), whilst a third part proceeds from the satisfaction of object-libido. (*S.E.* 14:100)

This passage is very important indeed, not only because it shows very clearly the three vicissitudes of narcissistic libido but also because it accepts the narcissistic satisfaction that the subject may receive from the external world —which, as we shall see, was to lead to the distinction of two classes of libido and of object—and also because it introduces as a powerful (or all-powerful) source of narcissistic satisfactions another agency, the ego-ideal, which was to change its name and content in 1923 and become the superego.

In introducing narcissism, however, Freud came upon a theoretical difficulty, because at the time he assumed, on the one hand, the existence of two groups of opposing instincts (sexual instincts and ego-instincts)—an opposition he could not abandon without relinquishing the cornerstone of his entire edifice, psychic conflict—and, on the other hand, the existence of a libido whose seat was the ego and which for this very reason proved hard to distinguish from the ego-instincts. This could not but disturb the theory profoundly.

The following passage shows an attempt to escape from the impasse:

> Some of the sexual instincts are, as we know, capable of this auto-erotic satisfaction, and so are adapted to being the vehicle for the development under the dominance of the pleasure principle. . . . Those sexual instincts which from the outset require an object, and the needs of the ego-instincts, which are never capable of auto-erotic satisfaction, naturally disturb this state [of primal narcissism] and so pave the way for an advance from it. Indeed, the primal narcissistic state would not be able to follow the development . . . if it were not for the fact that every individual passes through a period during which he is helpless and has to be looked after. (*S.E.* 14:134)

This is a surprising conclusion: first, not all the libido can be narcissistic, but only a part of it requires an object from the outset; and, second, the ego-instincts are never capable of autoerotic satisfaction, so that they need an external object (maternal care in the state of helplessness of early infancy, as described by Freud). It is legitimate to wonder whether, in speaking of libido, which "from the outset requires an object," and ego-instincts, which require objects for the survival of the subject, Freud is not using the term "object" in two radically different senses. He is more specific on this point in other works. In any case, the idea of a total primary narcissistic state is discarded (because obviously no one could ever get out of it).

Abraham's model ("A Short Study of the Development of the Libido") is also rejected from the outset because it presupposes the existence of some autoerotic phase without objects and of a narcissistic phase characterized by a "total incorporation of the object." Now, in "On Narcissism: An Introduction," there are objects everywhere.

A Failed Revolution

Freud's difficulty in integrating narcissism within the opposition "ego-instincts versus libido," as well as his immersion in the study of the psychoses, of the role of guilt in normal development and in neuroses, of mourning, and so on, induced him to undertake a radical modification of the theory of instincts and at the same time brought about a revolution in which disorder was not lacking. The revolution began in 1920 with *Beyond the Pleasure Principle*, when Freud put together the ego-instincts and libido as two alternative forms of Eros, two life instincts: "We are venturing upon the further step of recognizing the sexual instinct as Eros, the preserver of all things, and of deriving the narcissistic libido of the ego from the stores of libido by means of which the cells of the soma are attached to one another" (*S.E.* 18:52). Apart from the confusion of levels (the biological and the psychological), which is much more frequent in this work of Freud's than in others, narcissistic libido is used in a deeper sense, arising directly from the origins of the soma, and in any case at a lower level than the ego. The revolution had begun and soon its principles were to be formulated in all their clarity, in *The Ego and the Id* (1923).

But in the same year, 1923, Freud published "Two Encyclopaedia Articles," in which he described the history of his ideas, and here conceptual confusion reigns:

> *Narcissism*. The most important theoretical advance has certainly been the application of the libido theory to the repressing ego. The ego itself came to be regarded as a reservoir of what was described as narcissistic libido, from which the libidinal cathexes of objects flowed out and into which they could be once more withdrawn. By the help of this conception it became possible to embark upon the analysis of the ego and to make a clinical distinction of the psychoneuroses into transference neuroses and narcissistic disorders. (*S.E.* 18:249)

In the second article, Freud refers implicitly to *Beyond the Pleasure Principle*, noting: "The libido of the self-preservative instincts was now described as narcissistic libido and it was recognized that a high degree of this self-love constituted the primary and normal state of things" (*S.E.* 18:257). Times and models are mixed up: the ego, as at the beginning of "On Narcissism: An Introduction," is the "reservoir" of this libido (and not something at a lower level than the ego, as in the previous quotation). The self-preservative instincts become "narcissistic libido" again, as Freud momentarily forgets the essential differences he had established between the ego-instincts, whose satisfaction can never be autoerotic and requires objects from the beginning, and narcissistic libido, which by definition can be satisfied autoerotically. Yet Freud's forgetfulness is not total, as he acknowledges only a "high degree" of self-love as the primitive stage of things, suggesting that a certain amount of the ego-instincts remains outside this situation or that a part of the initial libido is not narcissistic. We are in a tangle of contradictions.

It was legitimate to hope that they were temporary. Indeed, in the same year, 1923, in *The Ego and the Id*, Freud appears to have decided to take the discovery of 1920 to its ultimate conclusion—that is, to locate the "great reservoir" of narcissistic libido in the id, now instituted as an agency:

> This would seem to imply an important amplification of the theory of narcissism. At the very beginning, all the libido is accumulated in the id, while the ego is still in process of formation or is still feeble. The id sends part of this libido out into erotic object-cathexes, whereupon the ego, now grown stronger, tries to get hold of this object-libido and to force itself on the id as a love-object. The narcissism of the ego is thus a secondary one, which has been withdrawn from objects. (*S.E.* 19:46)

We thus arrive at a revolutionary but coherent conception: the ego is no longer the "great reservoir" of libido; this is now the id. It is the id that sends out the first and most important object cathexes.

The narcissism of the first kind, the narcissism of the ego, is no longer a primary narcissism but always a secondary narcissism. It stems from objects "cathected" by the id with which the ego identifies (which it introjects). The terminology is reversed: what Freud previously called "primary narcissism" is now necessarily "secondary narcissism."

Let us not rejoice too soon at this recovery of coherence, however. From 1923 to the end of his work, Freud returned to his first concept of narcissism, accommodating it basically in the ego and not in the id. This is confirmed by quotation after quotation: "the ego itself is cathected with libido. . . . the ego, indeed, is the libido's original home, and remains to some extent its headquarters. This narcissistic libido turns toward objects, and thus becomes object-libido; and it can change back into narcissistic libido once more" (*S.E.* 21:118). Again: "the ego is always the main reservoir of libido, from which libidinal cathexes of objects go out and into which they return again, while the major part of this libido remains permanently in the ego" (*S.E.* 22:103). Even in the *Outline* of 1938—admittedly an important work, but one that remained unfinished and was not revised conceptually as a whole by Freud—the most significant passage is the following:

> It is hard to say anything of the behaviour of the libido in the id and in the super-ego. All that we know about it relates to the ego, in which at

> first the whole available quota of libido is stored up. We call this state absolute, primary narcissism. It lasts till the ego begins to cathect the ideas of objects with libido, to transform narcissistic libido into object-libido. Throughout the whole of life the ego remains the great reservoir from which libidinal cathexes are sent out to objects and into which they are also once more withdrawn, just as an amoeba behaves with its pseudopodia. (*S.E.* 23:150)

Despite the clarification of 1923, the confusion remains unresolved. The revolution has left behind, side by side, mutually incompatible institutions (in this case, concepts). It may be that the great difficulty that prevented Freud from remaining true to his 1923 concepts was the idea that the id (because it lacked organization) could "cathect" objects. In order to love (or hate) an object, it is necessary to perceive it, to recognize it and to distinguish it from others. An entity that can do this is a subject endowed with an organized ego. Although the 1923 solution was more coherent, it came up against this problem of the subject, which we encounter upon each difficult change of direction in analytic theory.

The "Great Reservoir" and the "Amoeba"

The problem just raised—of Freud's contradictions in the theory of narcissism—did not escape the expert and perspicacious eye of James Strachey, who tackled it particularly in Appendix B to *The Ego and the Id*, where he referred to "apparently conflicting views." He ingeniously maintains that Freud, in his many descriptions of narcissism, resorts either concurrently or consecutively to two metaphors: that of the amoeba which sends out and draws in pseudopodia, and that of a reservoir which may empty itself of a content to fill something else and may at the same time take back the amount it has released, refilling itself with it. We have one biological model and one hydraulic model and this gives rise to contradictions. For this reason, it is difficult to accept Strachey's attempt to reconcile these contradictions. Let us see.

Strachey says that the analogy of the reservoir is ambiguous: it may mean either a storage tank for a liquid (or something similar) or a source of supply of this liquid or other substances. The id might be this source and the ego the tank in which its product accumulates. In the beginning, however, the ego and the id, the tank and the source, are not differentiated; this, according to Strachey, diminishes "the apparent contradiction in [Freud's] expression." I in turn should like to interpret Strachey. When he speaks of Freud's "apparently conflicting views," he may be referring to an obvious contradiction (and this is the case) or to an apparent contradiction, which, however, is not fundamental (which is what Strachey means). I do not in general believe in the utility of biological metaphors, and still less of hydraulic ones, in psychoanalysis. In this case, the metaphors become incoherent when it is a matter of a source of energy that at the same time sends out pseudopodia.

But as Strachey says (and I agree with him), this is a minor point. What is more important is that Freud sometimes maintains that the object cathexes emanate from the id, reaching the ego only secondarily and indirectly by way of "centripetal" (to avoid the term "introjective") identification; on other occasions he holds that the totality of the libido is conceived as going from the id toward the ego, reaching objects only indirectly.

Strachey's argument does not seem to be illuminating here. I cease to understand when immediately afterward he states that perhaps the two processes are not incompatible and that "it is possible that both may occur."

LIBIDO AND OBJECT IN NARCISSISM AND OBJECT RELATIONS

Of course, though Freud defines narcissism principally as a specific vicissitude of libido, it cannot be isolated from a concomitant vicissitude of objects and psychic agencies or structures. I have thus far concentrated on the former aspect, introducing the latter when necessary. I now propose to examine narcissism from the second point of view; here again, isolation is not feasible and repetition cannot be completely avoided.

The Two Types of Object Choice

As we have seen in connection with the opposition of ego-instincts and libido, Freud considers that the former require an object "from the beginning" and that the latter must also require one from the beginning in respect of a part of itself, while the other part is focused on the ego. The ego, thus converted into a repository of libido, sends out object "cathexes" that may subsequently be withdrawn toward the ego itself. There is, then, an opposition between the libido that is directed toward objects and that which is retained within the ego. There is a kind of balance between these libidinal forms, but never a strict equivalence, as a certain "amount" of narcissistic libido necessarily remains within the ego, and the libido directed toward objects may likewise qualitatively retain narcissistic features: "We see also, broadly speaking, an antithesis between ego-libido and object-libido. The more of the one is employed, the more the other becomes depleted" (*S.E.* 14:76).

This "simple" equivalence becomes complicated when Freud points out that the objects of the ego-instincts in turn become objects of the libido. In this case the libido becomes added to the ego-instincts, giving rise to a certain type of object choice: the "anaclitic," or "attachment" type (*Anlehnungstypus*); to this he opposes a narcissistic choice—that is, the choice of an object similar to the subject (or similar to what the subject was or would like to be, or to the form in which the subject has been loved or of the same sex as the subject, and so on). Note that the word *Anlehnung* refers not to the relation of the libido to an object to which it is "attached" but to the attachment of the libido to an ego-instinct which leads it toward a particular object:

> The sexual instincts are at the outset attached to the satisfaction of the ego-instincts; only later do they become independent of these, and even then we have an indication of that original attachment in the fact that the persons who are concerned with a child's feeding, care, and protection become his earliest sexual objects: that is to say, in the first instance his mother or a substitute for her. Side by side, however, with this type and source of object choice, which may be called the "anaclitic" or "attachment" type, psychoanalytic research has revealed a second type, which we were not prepared for finding. We have discovered, especially clearly in people whose libidinal development has suffered some disturbance, such as perverts and homosexuals, that in their later choice of love-objects they have taken as a model not their mother but their own selves. They are plainly seeking *themselves* as a love-object, and are exhibiting a type of object-choice which must be termed "narcissistic." In this observation we have the strongest of reasons which have led us to adopt the hypothesis of narcissism. (*S.E.* 14:87–88)

In these cases, "the path back to narcissism is made particularly easy" (*S.E.* 16:426).

Love obviously stems from the *Anlehnungstypus* and not from narcissistic choice. Freud shows the first type of choice is more characteristic of man than of woman, but this topic deserves to be treated in a different context.

In the case of the narcissistic choice (that is, the type of external object chosen) the narcissistic withdrawal is necessarily more pathogenic (and doubtless more complete); the amoeba puts out and draws in its pseudopodia, and so, metaphorically, does a human being normally, so that he can make new object choices when appropriate. In pathological mourning, in melancholia, in the "narcissistic" diseases, this ability for moving is lost and the withdrawal becomes irreversible. Freud opens here to psychological investigation an extremely fertile field. The structure of the narcissistic object still has many surprises in store for us.

Love and Narcissism

Freud's description of the state of being in love is of very great theoretical importance. This state implies a considerable involvement of narcissistic libido, which has been deposited in the object as a condition of its gratification. Love by the object for the subject becomes indispensable to the narcissism of the subject: "A person who loves has, so to speak, forfeited a part of his narcissism, and it can only be replaced by his being loved. In all these respects self-regard [*Selbstgefuhl*] seems to remain related to the narcissistic element in love" (*S.E.* 14:98).

There is a further step, in which something different occurs, similar to a change of center of the narcissistic libido; we might call this the depositing of valued aspects of the person in the object: "When we are in love a considerable amount of narcissistic libido overflows on to the object. It is even obvious, in many forms of love-choice, that the object serves as a substitute for some unattained ego ideal of our own. We love it on account of the perfections which we have striven to reach for our own ego, and which we should now like to procure in this roundabout way as a means of satisfying our narcissism" (*S.E.* 18:112–13).

Another case of being in love described by Freud takes matters even further, presupposing a much more complete structural transfer, in which the ego has become radically impoverished and the ego-ideal has taken up a position within the object, investing it with all perfections. "A worm in love with a star," as one of Victor Hugo's characters says. This implies complex structural processes that we can understand only on the basis of work subsequent to Freud's, such as that of Melanie Klein.

Freud shows his awareness of this complexity and of the impossibility of formulating it in exclusively instinctual terms in the following passage, to which I believe the greatest importance must be attached: "We might at a pinch say of an instinct that it "loves" the objects towards which it strives for purposes of satisfaction; but to say that an instinct "hates" an object strikes us as odd. Thus we become aware that the attitudes [*Beziehungen*] of love and hate cannot be made use of for the relations of instincts to their objects, but are reserved for the relations of the *total ego* to objects" (*S.E.* 14:137). Here is the solution to many of the difficulties we have been considering since the problem of the "great reservoir." The great reservoir neither loves nor hates. The entity that loves and hates is "an" ego, a person, a subject. This essential distinction in analytic technique does not escape Freud when he writes: "*Wo Es war, soll Ich werden*" (Where id was, there I shall be): "*Ich*" (I) and not "*das Ich*" (the ego). The distinction is pointed out by Lacan, contrary to the usual translations of the German phrase to date.

Being in love naturally leads us to the process of idealization mentioned by Freud in many passages. It is in a way comparable to the aggrandizement of the ego observed in the megalomaniacal aspect that commonly accompanies paranoia. It is also closely bound up with the formation of the ego-ideal: "The sexual ideal may enter into an interesting auxiliary relation to the ego ideal. It may be used for substitutive satisfaction where narcissistic satisfaction encounters real hindrances. In that case a person will love in conformity with the narcissistic type of object choice, will love what he once was and no longer is, or else what possesses the excellences which he never had at all" (*S.E.* 14:101).

The Structuring Function of Narcissism

Freud has no doubts about the close relationship between infantile narcissism and the formation of the ego-ideal. The ideal ego (that is, the idealized ego) of the narcissistic state is the prototype of the ego-ideal, resulting from a reincorporation of the former, previously projected on to an external object.

> This ideal ego is now the target of the self-love which was enjoyed in childhood by the actual ego. The subject's narcissism makes its appearance displaced on to this new ideal ego, which, like the infantile ego, finds itself possessed of every perfection that is of value. As always where the libido is concerned, man has here again shown himself inca-

> pable of giving up a satisfaction he had once enjoyed. He is not willing to forgo the narcissistic perfection of his childhood; and when, as he grows up, he is disturbed by the admonitions of others and by the awakening of his own critical judgement, so that he can no longer retain that perfection, he seeks to recover it in the new form of an ego ideal. What he projects before him as his ideal is the substitute for the lost narcissism of his childhood in which he was his own ideal. (*S.E.* 14:94)

This is the process of "narcissistic identification," which is "the older of the two" (*S.E.* 14:250). Freud is here hinting at a very important conclusion. Identifications ("introjective" identifications, in today's parlance) are more easily made at first with a narcissistic basis. We might say that the object that is introjected has first been modeled in accordance with infantile necessities and is reintrojected with only slight modifications. Although the terminology differs somewhat from Freud's, the idea is quite similar.

This ego-ideal in turn becomes the source of many satisfactions of a narcissistic character: the satisfaction of "being able to think oneself better than others" (*S.E.* 21:143), or "the consciousness of a difficulty overcome" (*S.E.* 23:118), even where this runs counter to the demands of the libido.

At this point the narcissistic state with its fantasized perfections converges with identification for the structuring of very important aspects of the personality.

NARCISSISM AND SADISM

Freud has convinced us of the validity and necessity of the concept of narcissism in order to cover a number of phenomena commonly observed in our practice. But considerable difficulty attaches to any attempt to reconcile the infantile narcissistic "perfection" and its convenient denial of a quite unpleasant real world with the internal or intrinsic existence—still more after 1920—of destructive instincts that are fundamentally incompatible with narcissistic felicity.

Freud was, of course, aware of the problem and solved it in different ways during the course of his development. All these solutions are interesting and surprise even the most assiduous reader of his work.

The subject is mentioned in "Instincts and Their Vicissitudes" (1915), where Freud compares the fates of scopophilia and sadism: "Similarly the transformation of sadism into masochism implies a return to the narcissistic object. And in both these cases [that is, in passive scopophilia and masochism] the narcissistic subject is, through identification, replaced by another, extraneous ego" (*S.E.* 14:132). Another quotation to the same effect is found in the same work:

> If we take into account our constructed preliminary narcissistic stage of sadism, we shall be approaching a more general realization—namely, that the instinctual vicissitudes which consist in the instinct's being turned round upon the subject's own ego and undergoing reversal from activity to passivity are dependent on the narcissistic organization of the ego and bear the stamp of that phase. They perhaps correspond to the attempts at defence which at high stages of the development of the ego are effected by other means. (*S.E.* 14:132)

This would suggest a narcissistic organization of sadism. How can these quotations be understood other than as an expression of primary masochism, which is, however, explicitly denied in the same work? "A primary masochism, not derived from sadism in the manner I have described, seems not to be met with" (*S.E.* 14:128). In the same work, Freud puts forward an easier solution, which has been used ad nauseum by certain present-day analytical schools: "Indeed, it may be asserted that the true prototypes of the relation of hate are derived not from sexual life, but from the ego's struggle to preserve and maintain itself" (*S.E.* 14:138). And again: "Hate, as a relation to objects, is older than love. It derives from the narcissistic ego's primordial repudiation of the external world" (*S.E.* 14:139).

Up to this point we have two alternative solutions: either there is a narcissistic organization of sadism, which implies a sadism directed toward the ego (that is, a primary masochism—a conception that is now rejected but that Freud was to arrive at later), or sadism has nothing to do with narcissism (which is essentially libidinal) and stems from the undeniable frustrations imposed by reality.

Fortunately, Freud does not content himself with the second (and easier) solution. It is only in *Civilization and Its Discontents* (1930) that we find another view of the matter:

> It is in sadism, where the death instinct twists the erotic aim in its own sense and yet at the same time fully satisfies the erotic urge, that we

> succeed in obtaining the clearest insight into its nature and its relation to Eros. But even where it emerges without any sexual purpose, in the blindest fury of destructiveness, we cannot fail to recognize that the satisfaction of the instinct is accompanied by an extraordinarily high degree of narcissistic enjoyment, owing to its presenting the ego with a fulfillment of the latter's old wishes for omnipotence. The instinct of destruction, moderated and tamed, and, as it were, inhibited in its aim, must, when it is directed toward objects, provide the ego with the satisfaction of its vital needs and with control over nature. (*S.E.* 21:121)

Not even this last quotation answers our original question, although it does approach an answer.

An entire line of Freud's thought tends toward allowing that there is "a sadistic organization" in narcissism. The id, with its "death instincts" (after 1920), is a source not only of destructiveness but also of self-destructiveness. This does not result, as Freud might at some point have thought, from the ego's need to defend itself from a more or less hostile world but from purely instinctual factors.

CONCLUSIONS

History of the Concept in Freud's Work

The concept of narcissism has an exceedingly complicated history in Freud's work; the line of development it follows is not straight but broken and full of fluctuations and even changes of meaning. Originally, what was subsequently to settle out as narcissism was mingled with the concept of autoerotism (1899). The process of settling out took place gradually between 1900 and 1914, by virtue of the need to take account of a number of phenomena including homosexual object choice and megalomania.

Autoerotism and narcissism then tended to become distinguished from each other. The former signified an objectless state prior to the formation of an ego and a mode of satisfaction of the libido with the subject's own body. The latter at first connoted a relation of the libido to the external choice in which it (the libido) gave up this object and turned back upon the ego itself, which recovered a former state in which it was the prototype of all future objects.

We thus have five terms, autoerotism as a stage of the libido, autoerotism as a mode of libidinal satisfaction, secondary narcissism, primary narcissism, and the ego-instincts, which are not capable of autoerotic satisfaction or distinguishable into phases or stages as the libido is. Freud oscillated among these five terms, sometimes partially reconciling them in one way and sometimes in another (for example, by maintaining that there were two phases, one autoerotic and the other narcissistic, contemporary with the ego instincts).

In 1923, with *The Ego and the Id* he appeared to arrive at a systematic conception. He now posited a primary narcissism, in which all the libido was concentrated in the id, while the ego was in the process of formation. The id cathected objects, and the ego's subsequent identification with these external objects (coupled with the corresponding orientation of the cathexis from the id toward the ego) constituted secondary narcissism; what had previously been called secondary narcissism was now referred to as primary narcissism. Autoerotism was nothing more than the mode of satisfaction of a structurally defined state, which was narcissism. At the same time, the concept of narcissism was progressively enriched, as narcissistic satisfaction could derive (1) from the id which loved the ego as it had loved external objects, (2) from the ego's feeling of being loved by the superego, or (3) from the approval of the superego congratulating the ego for obeying its commands. The id loved the ego; the superego loved the ego; the ego loved the id and the superego. Narcissism would then be the paradisiacal harmony rediscovered between the agencies—a kind of blessing by God the Father on the lovemaking of Adam and Eve in a paradise full of food, devoid of hate, and in which all fruits were permitted.

Freud was unable to sustain the formulation of *The Ego and the Id* on primary and secondary narcissism or this definition of autoerotism. For reasons connected with the theoretical frame of reference and the development of the theory of instincts, the entire problem of narcissism was raised once again: all the instincts—those of the ego—were no longer fundamentally different from the libido, and, on the other hand, both were radically opposed to another group of instincts, the death instincts, which now shook the existing order from top to bottom.

The problem then became insoluble, and Freud returned to earlier definitions of autoerotism and narcissism, even including a primitive narcissistic organization of sadism (which was absolutely logical but inconsistent with many other concepts). The historical examination shows that (1) the concept of narcissism is indispensable; (2) Freud never managed to harmonize it completely with the rest of the analytic theory (which was, moreover, continuously changing); and (3) we shall never know whether the great reservoir of libido was for Freud the ego or the id.

Results of Freud's Explorations into Narcissism

1. Paradoxically, the study of narcissism gives a fundamental boost to the study of object relations and the structure of the object.
2. A new chapter in Freudian "objectology" is opened, in particular as regards the perversions, states of being in love, groups, the psychoses, and normal development.
3. We begin to understand the relations between the structure of the object and the (specular or fanciful) characteristics of the subject himself and his agencies. Narcissism is structuring.
4. Any simplistic model of the developmental stages of the libido (Abraham) is eliminated from the beginning. Neither autoerotism nor narcissism can now be considered as other than relatively simple stages of a lineal evolution, (a) because Freud did not solve the problem of whether autoerotism should be defined as a developmental stage or as a mode of satisfaction; and (b) because a powerful antagonist of libido, Thanatos, appears after 1920, together with the inescapable idea of a "sadistic-narcissistic organization." Had due consideration been given to this point, subsequent analytic thought would have been saved from a number of errors and impasses (I say this in full recognition of Abraham's attempt at synthesis, which had its value, although it later became an obstacle to investigation owing to the obstinate decision of many analysts to stop thinking about it).
5. It is evident that Freud, in his last works, gradually abandoned the concept of autoerotism (except in the sense of a masturbatory mode of satisfaction).

Problems Raised by Freud

1. Freud's oscillations and contradictions give rise to a need to redefine narcissism, not now in terms of a libidinal or "thanatic" phase but in terms of object relations.
2. The metaphors of the reservoir and the amoeba do not facilitate this

redefinition. If they were eliminated, one of the bases of the contradictions in Freud's thought would disappear.

3. Freud's discovery of the two types of object relations (the attachment type and the narcissistic type) carries within itself the potential for extremely fruitful development provided that *Anlehnung* is regarded not exclusively as the attachment of one instinct to another but also as a type of relation to the object.
4. The concept of narcissism appears essentially to include a scopic element, as in the myth of Narcissus. The object of narcissism fluctuates between the body, the image of the body, the ego as an agency, and the person in some of his actual or imaginary characteristics or as a whole.

A Contemporary Reading of "On Narcissism"

OTTO F. KERNBERG

Freud's extraordinarily rich essay reveals several new developments in his thinking and introduces some of his most fundamental and permanent ideas. He explores narcissism as a phase of psychic development, as a crucial aspect of normal love life, as a central dynamic of several types of psychopathology (schizophrenia, perversion, homosexuality, hypochondriasis), in terms of the regulation of self-esteem, as the origin of the ego-ideal, and—by way of the ego-ideal—as an aspect of mass psychology. The only significant subjects related to narcissism that occupy contemporary clinical psychoanalysis not dealt with in his essay are pathological narcissism considered as a specific type or spectrum of character pathology and narcissistic resistances as an important factor in psychoanalytic technique. The theoretical and clinical observations that made these two subjects possible, however, are already implicit in this seminal essay.

In what follows I offer a critical reading of Freud's essay, focusing on the fate of the ideas it contains, especially on how these ideas have since been supplemented or modified.

When reading the Standard Edition version of Freud's essay (1914b), one must keep in mind that Strachey's "instinct" corresponds to Freud's

(1914a) *Trieb* (drive) and that Freud used the term as a purely psychological rather than a biological construct to denote a source of psychic motivation. It is also important to keep in mind that the translator's "ego" is not the ego of structural theory but the word Strachey chose to render Freud's *das Ich* (I), with its broader and more subjective connotations. When Freud describes, for example, how being in love can result in "impoverishment of the ego" (88), he is clearly referring to a sense of self and not to an impersonal psychic structure. In addition to making for conceptual ambiguity, Strachey's insistent use of "ego" has a deadening effect, somewhat redressed by the startling effect on us today of reading about "instincts" in a psychoanalytic context.

DRIVE THEORY AND EARLY PSYCHIC DEVELOPMENT

Bringing together indirect evidence from the study of human sexual development, schizophrenia, the neuroses, the perversions, and primitive cultures, Freud extends his libido theory. He proposes that libido evolves from a stage of primary narcissism to investment of objects with the tendency of later withdrawal of object-invested libido onto the ego in the form of secondary narcissism. This theoretical statement, sharply and concisely made near the beginning of his essay, immediately raises new questions in Freud's mind (which he deals with in the following pages) and also in our minds, questions that psychoanalytic theory is still dealing with.

Freud asks how primary narcissism relates to autoerotism and concludes that the latter is a primary manifestation of the libidinal drive that must exist from the beginning of life, whereas narcissism, the libidinal investment of the ego, requires first the development of the ego itself: autoerotism, therefore, must antedate primary narcissism. Second he asks how primary narcissism, as ego-invested libido, relates to the drive of self-preservation. The *Standard Edition* translation of this essay (1914b, 73–74) states: "narcissism in this sense would not be a perversion, but the libidinal complement to the egoism of the instinct of self-preservation." In the discussion that follows, one that has its polemical aspect—namely, Freud's critique of Jung's overarching new concept of "libido"—Freud defends the need to maintain, for the time being, the distinction between ego-instincts (self-preservation) and libido. He himself, as we know, abandoned the idea of ego drives later on when in 1920 he proposed the dual-drive theory of libido and aggression, the life and death drives.

The most remarkable aspect of the formulations on narcissism and object-libido in this essay is Freud's concept of the intimate relationship between libidinal investment in the self and in objects, and the central function of this dialectic relationship in normality and pathology—concepts that gave rise to the idea of normal and pathological narcissism. In contemporary language we might say that the investments of libido oscillating between self and objects, brought about by introjective and projective mechanisms, determine the mutual reinforcement of affective investment of the self and of significant others, the simultaneous buildup of an internal and an external world of object relations, which strengthen each other. There are, however, also problems derived from Freud's new formulations.

Even if we eliminate from consideration the outdated problem of whether or not self-preservation and narcissistic libido are the same, a major problem remains with the concept of primary narcissism itself. In light of what we now know about early development, it is legitimate to question Freud's implicit assumption that the psyche originates in what we would today call a closed system. Thus, the "autistic" phase of earliest development hypothesized by Mahler (Mahler and Furer, 1968) is currently being questioned (Stern, 1985). Whatever capacity for self-object differentiation exists in the first few weeks and months of life, the earliest stages of intrapsychic development would seem to be characterized by parallel, simultaneous developments of the symbolic structures reflecting self and object. In other words, I regard as highly questionable both the concept of autoerotism and that of a self or ego predating the psychic experience of the actual relation of the infant with the primary object.

Psychoanalysts are still debating whether, in the tradition of Melanie Klein (1945, 1946, 1952) and Fairbairn (1954), one may assume the existence of a differentiated self from earliest infancy; or whether, in the tradition of Jacobson (1964) and Mahler (Mahler and Furer, 1968), a symbiotic stage of development (lack of self and object differentiation) is the earliest organizing frame of psychic life; or whether, as Stern (1985) has suggested, an inborn capacity for differentiation of self and object is a fact that needs to be explored as regards its translation into intrapsychic experience. But all these theoretical currents point to the very early simultaneous development of self and object representations and question the notion of a state of autoerotism and of primary narcissism as well (unless primary narcissism is considered equivalent to primary object-love). In fact, Freud himself, in one of the final pages of the narcissism essay, as if in an afterthought, virtually equates primary narcissism and primary object-love! "The return of the object-libido to the ego and its transformation into narcissism represents, as it were, a happy love once more, and, on the other hand, it is also true that a real happy love corresponds to the primal condition in which object-libido and ego-libido cannot be distinguished" (Freud, 1914b, 100).

A parallel discussion has shaped the status of the concept of "primary masochism"—not referred to at all in this essay—which constitutes, in terms of Freud's later dual-drive theory of libido and aggression, the counterpart of primary narcissism. This discussion also points to the absence, in Freud's work—and a still unfinished task today—of a general integration of the developmental schemata of libido and aggression.

Although recent infant research is suggesting that infants are capable, in actual behavior, of extremely fine discrimination between objects in the first few weeks of life, one has to differentiate inborn behavior patterns from their psychic representations. It is also necessary to keep in mind the stage at which the capacity for symbolic manipulation of psychic experience develops. Following Jacobson and Mahler, I think that, from about the second to the fifth month of life, the baby begins to develop primitive representations of the self and of the object, but does not yet differentiate one from the other.

These self-object representations are of two kinds, depending on the experiences leading to their formation. If the experience is pleasurable (particularly in the context of pleasurable peak-affect-states), a "positive" self-object representation is established; if the experience is unpleasurable (particularly in the context of traumatic, painful peak-affect-states), a "negative" self-object representation is established. I believe that the libidinal investment of the positive or pleasurable self-object representations occurs in parallel with the aggressive investment of the corresponding painful self-object representations and that both libido and aggression are thus simultaneously invested in primary, undifferentiated, fused self and object representations. Simultaneously, however, under conditions of milder or moderate positive or negative affect-states, a more differentiated integration of experience may develop, with more reality-oriented perceptions of self and others that are only gradually integrated with the more "extreme" psychic structures constituted by the affectively overwhelming libidinally and aggressively invested self and object representations.

Returning to our starting point, I think that narcissistic libido and object-libido develop simultaneously, in affective investments that are not yet differentiated in terms of self and object, and that narcissistic libido and object-libido differentiate themselves only gradually from their common matrix in the undifferentiated, positive self-object representations. The same would be true for aggression, whether directed at the self or the object.

Using this developmental frame, I have introduced the concept of affects as intimately related to that of drives and of the development of drives as opposed to the presence of a differentiated drive from the beginning of life. The extent to which libido and aggression as overall drives are "ready-made" at the moment of birth and/or mature and develop throughout time, and the developmental relationship between affect and drive development, remain subjects of controversy and research in psychoanalysis as well as in other disciplines (Kernberg, 1984, 227–38).

SCHIZOPHRENIA, PARANOIA, AND HYPOCHONDRIASIS

Freud mentions various examples of the withdrawal of libido from objects onto the ego (or self) throughout the narcissism essay. He refers to the state of sleep, in which libido is withdrawn onto the self, the withdrawal of interests from the external world under conditions of physical pain and illness, and the case of hypochondriasis. He suggests that hypochondriasis reflects the withdrawal of object-libido onto the self and the body, in a way similar to the withdrawal of object-libido in other "actual neuroses" (neurasthenia and anxiety neurosis) onto "fantasied objects": object representations, as we would say. In contrast to hypochondriasis, schizophrenia ("paraphrenia" is Freud's effort to coin a term that encompasses schizophrenia and paranoia) would reflect the extreme of such withdrawal of object-libido onto the ego, in a parallel to the extreme withdrawal of object-libido onto fantasied objects, by the process of "introversion" in the psychoneuroses (the other actual neuroses would reflect more limited withdrawal of object-libido). Freud relates the extreme unpleasure associated with the withdrawal of object-libido onto the ego and the body to the intensified "damming-up" of libido. He proposes that all intensifications of tension are experienced as painful, all tension discharges as pleasurable. This proposal has been challenged by Jacobson (1953), who underlines the clinical observation that there are pleasurable tensions as well as discharges and unpleasurable discharges as well as tensions.

Based on his bold generalization regarding the effects of quantitative shifts in libido, Freud formulates a psychoanalytic theory of schizophrenia, postulating that, in the psychotic process, libido is withdrawn from objects onto the ego or self. The excessive damming-up of this libido brings about megalomania corresponding to a psychic mastering of the libido; a failure in this psychic function would give rise to the hypochondria of paraphrenia. Freud draws a parallel between this last outcome and the development of neurotic anxiety in the transference neuroses. He also refers to the restitutive phenomena in schizophrenia, which he later (1917a) describes as the psychotic reinvestments of objects in the hallucinations and delusions typical of that illness.

Even if the psychoanalytic exploration of schizophrenia and manic-depressive psychosis in the past forty years has generated understandings that have shifted psychoanalytic formulations in new directions, Freud's early hypotheses anticipated these directions and may be detected at the roots of contemporary psychoanalytic theories of psychosis. Thus, his concept of the withdrawal of libido from objects onto the self drew attention, first, to the "decathexis" of ego boundaries, then to the lack of differentiation between self and nonself, and eventually, to the lack of differentiation between self representations and object representations as the intrapsychic preconditions for loss of the capacity to differentiate between self and others. Jacobson's (1971) explorations of psychosis, her description of "psychotic introjection" (in which a regression occurs to undifferentiated or fused self and object representations), probably contributed more than anything else to the transformation of Freud's early, quantitative, energic formulation on psychosis to a qualitative, structural one.

Freud's study of mourning and melancholia (1917b) and his later development of the dual-drive theory of libido and aggression pointed to the importance of aggression in psychotic regression. Stimulated by this work, Fairbairn (1954) and Melanie Klein (1940, 1945, 1946) studied primitive object relations and primitive defensive mechanisms dealing with libidinal and aggressive investments. Following the same lead, Hartmann's work (1953) and American ego psychology in general focused on the failure to neutralize aggression in psychosis. In light of Mahler's (Mahler and Furer, 1968) and Jacobson's (1964) concepts of the symbiotic stage of development, I have proposed that, in schizophrenia, a fixation and/or regression to a pathologically activated state of refusion of self and object representations occurs under the impact of the dominance of aggressive over libidinal aspects of all early relations, with a corresponding predominance of the primitive defensive operations described by the British school (Kernberg, 1986, 1987).

Later in his narcissism essay, Freud refers to the importance of the ego-ideal in the determination of persecutory delusions in paranoia. The term "ego-ideal" here is used to cover functions he later incorporated in the concept of the superego. Freud traces the origin of the ego-ideal to the critical influence of the parents. It is not clear, however, whether he considers such persecutory delusions (and hallucinations) to be caused by the pathology of the ego-ideal or to be part of the restitutive phenomena that represent a psychotic effort to reinvest objects. In fact, Freud left open the major question of the extent to which narcissistic regressions in psychosis imply a libidinal abandonment of external objects and withdrawal onto the ego versus an abandonment of external objects with a regression toward internalized relations to primitive, pathological object representations.

Behind this question again lies the question of whether primary narcissism predates object relations or develops in parallel to the establishment of internalized object relations. When Freud proposes that the libidinal drive is inborn whereas the ego has to develop, it seems to me that he is tacitly assuming that such a drive has an object, even though the ego or self as an agency is not yet constituted. If this is so, is he implying that the objects of drives and the objects to which the self relate are of a different kind? Again, one of the crucial questions, then and now, involving the concept of narcissism is that of the intimate relation of the development of narcissism and object relations.

ANACLITIC TYPE AND NARCISSISTIC TYPE OF OBJECT CHOICE

The description of two types of selection of a love object is undoubtedly the central theme of Freud's narcissism essay and constitutes a basic contribution to the psychology of normal and pathological love relations. It is striking that, in contrast to the enormous recent literature on the psychology of sexuality, Freud's equally important observations on the psychology of love should have remained relatively neglected in psychoanalytic thinking over many years. Only the past two decades have witnessed a new outpouring of contributions to this subject, particularly in the French literature. I am thinking here of the work of Braunschweig and Fain (1971), David (1971), Aulagnier (1979), Gantheret (1984), Chasseguet-Smirgel (1985), and others.

Freud suggests that a person may love according to the narcissistic type: that is, what he himself is, was, or would like to be, or someone who was once part of himself. Or he may love according to the anaclitic, dependent, or attachment type: the woman who feeds him, or the man who protects him, and the succession of substitutes who take their place. Freud stresses that "both kinds of object-choice are open to each individual, though he may show a preference for one or the other," adding that "a human being has originally two sexual objects—himself and the woman who nurses him—and . . . we are postulating a primary narcissism in everyone, which may in some cases manifest itself in a dominating fashion in his object-choice" (88).

Freud proposes that men display predominantly the attachment type of love, and that the marked sexual overvaluation of the sexual object that characterizes the state of being in love derives from the transfer of the child's original narcissism to the sexual object. In contrast, the "purest and truest" type of woman evinces the narcissistic object choice, a love of herself reflected in the desire to be loved, so that the man who fulfills this condition is the one who finds favor with her. Freud's distinctions between male and female psychology have been seriously questioned in contemporary psychoanalytic literature on love relations, particularly the French literature mentioned above (Kernberg, in press a, in press b). Further, the distinctions Freud makes between narcissistic and anaclitic love become problematic throughout this essay, in which many observations seem to turn rapidly into their opposites, in the context of a dialectic relationship between narcissism and object-love.

For example, a woman who loves a man because he loves her is also choosing an anaclitic object because the man she chooses feeds her narcissistic needs and protects her, so that her object choice complements her narcissism. Or the man who anaclitically idealizes a woman whose sexual attractiveness he overvalues is also projecting his narcissistic overvaluation of himself onto her. Again, the original narcissism of the baby practically coincides with the projected narcissism of the parents who transfer their own infantile narcissism onto him. Particularly women, Freud tells us, project their own narcissism onto their baby, a road "which leads to complete object-love" (89). And "His Majesty the Baby" evolves in different directions according to whether the baby is male or female, thus pointing (implicitly) to the impact of infantile sexuality on the vicissitudes of narcissism and object-love in both sexes, a subject Freud touches upon only briefly in this essay.

As Laplanche (1976) has convincingly stated, what Freud here describes is really the intimate, indissoluble, and complex relationship between object-libido and narcissistic libido and the multiple transformations, integrations, and interactions of libidinal self and object investments in love relationships; this brings us to the transformation of narcissistic investment into the investment of the ego-ideal.

THE EGO-IDEAL

Freud now presents his first schema of what will later become the concept of the superego. When he describes the repression of significant aspects of infantile narcissism as motivated by the ego's "self-respect," the inadequacy of Strachey's "ego" as a term becomes apparent: it is hard to imagine an impersonal ego developing self-respect. Leaving aside the ambiguity of whether repression of infantile narcissism brings about its replacement or substitution by the ego-ideal or whether it is the ego-ideal that motivates the repression of infantile narcissism, this ego-ideal becomes the target of what was originally the self-love enjoyed in childhood. Infantile narcissism, the libidinal investment of the self, is replaced (at least to a significant degree) by the libidinal investment of the ego-ideal. Freud clarifies that the idealization involved in the process of formation of the ego-ideal has to be distinguished from sublimation, a process affecting object-libido, whereas idealization concerns the object, not the drive. Freud also postulates that another agency, "conscience," evaluates the relation between the demands of the ego-ideal and the actual achievements of the ego, regulating in the process the individual's self-esteem.

These formulations represent significant advances in Freud's move toward the theory of the tripartite structure. The demands for perfection, related to idealization processes in the ego-ideal, are implicitly linked to the self-attack and self-criticism derived from the prohibitive, punitive aspects of the superego. His comments on the functions of a "conscience" point to what we now call the sadistic precursors (Sandler, 1960; Jacobson, 1964) underlying the establishment of more mature integration of parental demands and prohibitions into the eventual superego. Freud explicitly links the normal self-criticism of conscience with the persecutory hallucinations and delusions of paranoia (95).

In light of Freud's discussion of the vicissitudes of object libidinal and ego (or self) libidinal strivings, it becomes evident that the ego-ideal, inheritor of primary narcissism, also represents the internalization of the idealized objects of infantile love, an idealization of the early objects that, in turn, reflects object libidinal strivings of the anaclitic type. Freud is hereby proposing a circular process in which, first, the hypothesized primary narcissism is projected onto objects that are idealized, and thus narcissism is transformed into object-libido simultaneously with the enactment of the anaclitic type of object choice. This process is followed by the internalization of idealized objects (reflecting object-libido) into the ego-ideal and the concomitant transformation of infantile narcissism into the narcissistic investment of the ego-ideal.

It seems to me that with time, the actual process of idealization is gradually transformed, together with the products of this process. Early idealizations, with their unrealistic character, and the strongly narcissistic implications of the early ego-ideal, gradually become transformed into processes of idealization that set up the complex value systems of early childhood. This, in turn, facilitates the development of the still more advanced or normal processes of adolescent idealization that are implied in the investment of aesthetic, ethical, and cultural values.

In this context, considering once more the vicissitudes of the development of aggression that a modern psychoanalytic conception based upon Freud's later, dual-drive theory would relate to that of libidinal transformations, one might add that the earliest idealization processes are also defenses against split-off persecutory tendencies related to projected aggression, and that later idealization processes have the characteristics of reaction formations against unconscious guilt (because of aggressive impulses) and of reparative and sublimatory libidinal strivings related to objects. Indeed, Freud (95–97) hints at this intimate relation between the vicissitudes of libidinal and aggressive strivings in his comments on conscience, its self-critical functions in normality and pathology, and its intimate link to censorship in dreams, although he has not yet taken the step of bringing together the ego-ideal and unconscious, infantile morality as the structure of the superego. The elements are there, however; their integration will follow, carried out not only by Freud but by a generation of psychoanalysts after him—for example, in Sandler's (1960) comprehensive analysis of the concept of the superego in Freud's work and Jacobson's (1964) systematic analysis of the structural development and integration of the superego.

The concept of the ego-ideal, that fundamental substitute/complement for infantile narcissism, provides Freud with a frame of reference to study the regulation of self-esteem, my next subject.

SELF-ESTEEM REGULATION

In the latter part of the essay, Freud turns to the clinical aspects of self-esteem regulation. After having established a theoretical framework—a metapsychology—for narcissism, he focuses on the most immediate clinical manifestation of narcissism—namely, fluctuations in self-esteem. These two basic aspects of the concept of narcissism also correspond, in effect, to the practical contemporary dual use of the term "narcissism" to refer both to the libidinal investment of the self (first spelled out thus by Hartmann, 1950) and to the clinical process of (normal or abnormal) self-esteem regulation.

At the level of metapsychological formulations, I prefer to think of the "self" as a substructure of the system ego reflecting the integration of the component self-images or self representations that develop throughout all the real and fantasied experiences of interactions with others—objects. The libidinal investment of the self evolves in parallel with the libidinal investment in objects and their psychic representations ("object representations"), which constitutes object-libido. I see object-libido and self-libido as intimately related to each other and also intimately related to the parallel investments of self and object representations by aggression. A healthy self is one that integrates not only libidinally invested but also aggressively invested self representations. In contrast, a pathological, grandiose self, which characterizes the narcissistic personality, implies a failure or incapacity for such an integration of aggressively invested self representations and a corresponding failure to integrate libidinally and aggressively invested object representations as well.

Returning now to the clinical use of the concept of narcissism as regulation of self-esteem, Freud begins by pointing out that self-regard, dependent on narcissistic libido, is in potential conflict with object-libido; that the investment of a love object tends to lower self-regard: "A person who loves has, so to speak, forfeited a part of his narcissism, and it can only be replaced by his being loved" (98). At several points Freud returns to this idea, one that has since been questioned in, for example, Chasseguet-Smirgel's (1985) comprehensive study on the ego ideal. In fact, Freud himself observes that it is unrequited love that ends up with reduced self-esteem while requited, mutual love increases it. Again, the increase of self-esteem in a satisfactory love relation points to the intimate connection between narcissistic and object-libido.

In my view, falling in love itself normally raises self-esteem, but only insofar as what is projected onto the love object is not a primitive type of ego-ideal but the sophisticated, developed ego-ideal of normal adolescence and adulthood, reflecting value judgments that transform aspects of the mature ego-ideal into a new reality created by the relation to the loved and idealized object. The actualization of the ego-ideal in the love relationship raises self-esteem. Neurotic falling in love, which involves more primitive aspects of idealization as well as many other sources of feelings of inferiority, differs from normal falling in love. And normal falling in love is gradually dissolved, if love is not requited, by a mourning process that, in turn, leads to further ego growth and not to lowering of self-esteem: the opposite holds true for the neurotic response to unrequited love. Normal mourning for the object of unrequited love enriches the experience of the self and opens new channels of sublimation.

Freud then examines the decrease of self-esteem that results from an inability to love: when, because of severe repressions, erotic love becomes impossible, self-esteem diminishes. If we accept the idea that the representations of loved objects are normally internalized in the ego, we might then say that the love received both from external objects and from their internalized object representations (including those that form part of the ego-ideal as well as those incorporated in the ego) increases self-esteem.

Elaborating on Freud's thinking in the light of the contributions to this subject by later generations of psychoanalysts, we might say that self-esteem fluctuates according to gratifying or frustrating experiences in relationships with others and a person's sense of being appreciated or rejected by others, as well as according to the evaluation by the ego-ideal of the distance between goals and aspirations, on the one hand, and achievements and success, on the other. Self-esteem also depends on the pressures that the superego exerts on the ego: the stricter the superego, the more self-esteem is lowered, and at bottom, such lowering of self-esteem would reflect a predominance of self-directed aggression (stemming from the superego) over the libidinal investment of the self. Self-esteem may also be lowered by lack of gratification of instinctual needs of both a libidinal and an aggressive nature, so that unconscious ego defenses that repress awareness and expression of such instinctual needs will impoverish the ego of gratifying experiences and thus "deplete" libidinal self-investment and diminish self-esteem. Finally, the internalization of libidinally invested objects in the form of libidinally invested object representations greatly reinforces the libidinal investment of the self; in other words, the images in our mind of those we love and by whom we feel loved strengthen our self-love. In contrast, when excessive conflicts around aggression override libidinal investment of others and, secondarily, their corresponding object representations, the libidinal investments of the self and self-love also suffer.

These observations regarding self-esteem regulation point once more to the intimate and complex relation between narcissistic and object-libido, and between libido and aggression. From that perspective, I believe we may question a certain tendency in Freud's essay to consider narcissistic libido and object-libido as adding up to a fixed total amount, in an inverse relationship with each other; I think self-invested libido and object-invested libido may actually strengthen and complement each other.

FREUD'S FINAL SUMMARY AND SOME FURTHER DEVELOPMENTS

The last section of the essay reformulates earlier thoughts and adds new topics, which hint at things to come. To begin, in summarizing the relation between self-regard and libidinal investment of objects, Freud not only repeats that unrequited loving reduces self-esteem whereas being loved increases it but also states that "a real happy love corresponds to the primal condition in which object-libido and ego-libido cannot be distinguished" (100). Again, primary narcissism is practically equated to primary object-libido.

Freud states that, though one part of self-regard is primary—"the residue of infantile narcissism"—another part arises out of the omnipotence derived from fulfillment of the ego-ideal, and "a third part proceeds from the satisfaction of object-libido" (100): again, narcissism and object-love flow into each other.

In an interesting if cryptic comment, Freud now states that being in love "consists of a flowing-over of ego-libido onto the object and has the power to remove repressions and reinstate perversions" (100). Freud then alludes to the importance of polymorphous perverse strivings as part of a normal love relation (a subject that has only recently begun to be explored further in psychoanalytic thinking [Kernberg, 1988]) and points to the intimate connection between perversion and idealization. He also refers to the narcissistic function of sexual love when a neurotic finds his or her sexual ideal by making a narcissistic object choice. This is the "cure by love" that Freud also mentions as a typical compromise formation in some patients whose initial incapacity for love, resulting from extensive repressions, is gradually resolved in the psychoanalytic treatment but who then, as an escape from the frustrations in the transference, select a substitute idealized sexual object to rationalize a premature disruption of the treatment. In his final paragraph, Freud briefly touches on the relation between narcissism and group psychology, a subject too complex to be explored in this discussion.

As I said at the beginning of this essay, one major subject related to narcissism that, for all practical purposes, Freud does not touch upon is narcissism as character pathology. He refers only to one type of character pathology linked to narcissism—namely, that of the narcissistic object choice of male homosexual patients. These patients may select another man who stands for themselves, while they identify with their own mother and love the other man as they would have wanted to be loved by her. In light of our present knowledge, this type of character is only one of several. I have described the following types (Kernberg, 1984, 192–96):

1. Normal adult narcissism, characterized by normal self-esteem regulation. It is dependent on a normal self-structure related to normally integrated or "total" internalized object representations, an integrated, largely individualized, and abstracted superego, and the gratification of instinctual needs within the context of stable object relations and value systems.
2. Normal infantile narcissism, of importance because fixation at or regression to infantile narcissistic goals (infantile mechanisms of self-esteem regulation) is an important characteristic of all character pathology. Normal infantile narcissism consists in the regulation of self-esteem by age-appropriate gratifications that include or imply a normal infantile "value system," demands, and/or prohibitions. A first type of pathological self-esteem regulation, reflecting the mildest type of narcissistic character pathology, consists precisely in fixation at or regression to this level of normal infantile narcissism This type is representated in *the* frequent cases

of personality or character disorders in which the regulation of self-esteem seems to be overdependent on the expression of or defenses against childish gratifications that are normally abandoned in adulthood. Here the problem is that the ego-ideal is controlled by infantile aspirations, values, and prohibitions. One might say that, in fact, when Freud described the neurotic lowering of self-esteem related to excessive repression of sexual drive, he was implicitly describing what later would be formulated as the structural characteristics of psychoneurosis and neurotic character pathology. This is a very frequent and—in light of our present knowledge of more severe narcissistic pathology—a relatively mild disturbance that is usually resolved in the course of ordinary psychoanalytic treatment.

3. A second, more severe, but relatively infrequent type of pathologic narcissism is precisely that described by Freud in his essay as an illustration of narcissistic object choice. Here, as in the case of male homosexual patients, the patient's self is identified with an object while, at the same time, the representation of the patient's infantile self is projected onto that object, thus creating a libidinal relation in which the functions of self and object have been interchanged. This, indeed, is found among some male and female homosexuals: they love another in the way they would have wished to be loved.
4. A third and most severe type of pathological narcissism is the narcissistic personality disorder proper, one of the most challenging syndromes in clinical psychiatry. Because of the intense study of its psychopathology and the psychoanalytic technique optimally geared to resolve it, it has now become one of the standard indications for psychoanalytic treatment. Freud's essay on narcissism stimulated later contributions to the understanding of the narcissistic personality, including those of Jones (1955), Abraham (1949), and Riviere (1936) during Freud's lifetime, and of Klein (1957), Reich (1960), Jacobson (1964), Van Der Waals (1965), and Tartakoff (1966) of a later generation. More recently, Grünberger (1979), Rosenfeld (1964, 1971, 1975), Kohut (1971, 1972, 1977), and I (1975, 1984) have attempted to develop new theoretical models as a frame of reference for the pathology of the narcissistic personality, as well as technical approaches specifically geared to deal with these patients.

It is my belief that pathological narcissism reflects a libidinal investment not in a normally integrated self-structure but in a pathological self-structure.

This structure, a pathologic grandiose self, condenses real self representations, ideal self representations, and ideal object representations, whereas devalued or aggressively determined self and object representations are split off or dissociated, repressed, or projected. In other words, in contrast to the normal integration of libidinal and aggressively determined self and object representations into the normal self, here what might be called a "purified pleasure ego" constitutes the pathological self-structure.

These patients typically project their own pathological grandiose self onto their temporary love objects, so that they are either idealizing others who unconsciously represent themselves or expecting admiration from others while identifying themselves with their own grandiose self-structure.

For these patients, the ordinary linkage of self to object is mostly lost and replaced by a grandiose "self-self" linkage underlying their frail object relations, a pathological development that truly constitutes a severe pathology of object relations with loss of both the investment in a normal self-structure and the capacity for normal object relations. The narcissistic personality has not replaced object-love by self-love but gives evidence, as Van Der Waals (1965) first pointed out, of a combination of pathological love of self and of others as well.

REFERENCES

Abraham, K. (1940). A particular form of neurotic resistance against the psychoanalytic method. In *Selected Papers on Psychoanalysis*. London: Hogarth Press

Aulagnier, P. (1979). *Les destins du plaisir*. Paris: Presses Universitaires de France.

Braunschweig, D., and Fain, M. (1971). *Eros et Anteros: Réflexions psychanalytiques sur la sexualité*. Paris: Payot.

Chasseguet-Smirgel, J. (1985). *The Ego Ideal: A Psychoanalytic Essay on the Malady of the Ideal*. New York: W. W. Norton.

David, C. (1971). *L'Etat amoureux: Essais psychanalytiques*. Paris: Payot.

Fairbairn, W. R. D. (1954). *An Object-Relations Theory of the Personality*. New York: Basic Books.

Freud, S. (1914a). *Zur Einfuhrung des Narzissmus: Gesammelte Werke*, 10:137–70. London: Imago, 1949.

———. (1914b). On narcissism: An introduction. *S.E.* 14:73–102.

———. (1917a). A metapsychological supplement to the theory of dreams. *S.E.* 14:217–35.

———. (1917b). Mourning and melancholia. *S.E.* 14:237–58.

———. (1920). *Beyond the Pleasure Principle*. *S.E.* 18:1–64.
Gantheret, F. (1984). *Incertitude d'Eros*. Paris: Gallimard.
Grünberger, B. (1979). *Narcissism: Psychoanalytic Essays*. New York: International Universities Press.
Hartmann, H. (1950). Comments on the psychoanalytic theory of the ego. In *Essays on Ego Psychology*. New York: International Universities Press, 1964, pp. 113–41.
———. (1953). Contributions to the metapsychology of schizophrenia. In *Essays on Ego Psychology*. New York: International Universities Press, 1964, pp. 182–206.
Jacobson, E. (1953). On the psychoanalytic theory of affects. In *Depression*. New York: International Universities Press, 1971, pp. 3–47.
———. (1964). *The Self and the Object World*. New York: International Universities Press.
———. (1971). *Depression: Comparative Studies of Normal Neurotic, and Psychotic Conditions*. New York: International Universities Press.
Jones, E. (1955). The God complex. In *Essays in Applied Psychoanalysis*. New York: International Universities Press.
Kernberg, O. (1975). *Borderline Conditions and Pathological Narcissism*. New York: Jason Aronson.
———. (1984). *Severe Personality Disorders: Psychotherapeutic Strategies*. New Haven: Yale University Press.
———. (1986). Identification and its vicissitudes as observed in psychosis. *Int. J. Psychoanal. Assn.*, 67:147–59.
———. (1987). Projection and projective identification: Developmental and clinical aspects. *J. Amer. Psychoanal. Assn.*, 4(35):795–819.
———. (1988). Between conventionality and aggression: The boundaries of passion. In W. Gaylin and E. Person, eds., *Passionate Attachments: Thinking about Love*. New York: Free Press, pp. 63–83.
———. (in press a). Sadomasochism, sexual excitement, and perversion. *J. Amer. Psychoanal. Assn.*
———. (in press b). Aggression and love in the relationship of the couple. *J. Amer. Psychoanal. Assn.*
Klein, M. (1940). Mourning and its relation to manic depressive states. In *Contributions to Psycho-Analysis, 1921–1945*. London: Hogarth Press, 1948, pp. 311–38.
———. (1945). The Oedipus complex in the light of early anxieties. In *Contributions to Psycho-Analysis, 1921–1945*. London: Hogarth Press, 1948, pp. 339–90.
———. (1946). Notes on some schizoid mechanisms. In J. Riviere, ed., *Developments in Psycho-Analysis*. London: Hogarth Press, 1952, pp. 292–320.
———. (1952). Some theoretical conclusions regarding the emotional life of the

infant. In J. Riviere, ed., *Developments in Psycho-Analysis*. London: Hogarth Press, pp. 198–236.

———. (1957). *Envy and Gratitude*. New York: Basic Books.

Kohut, H. (1971). *The Analysis of the Self*. New York: International Universities Press.

———. (1972). Thoughts on narcissism and narcissistic rage. *Psychoanal. Study Child*, 27:360–400.

———. (1977). *The Restoration of the Self*. New York: International Universities Press.

Laplanche, J. (1976). *Life and Death in Psychoanalysis*. Baltimore: John Hopkins University Press.

Mahler, M., and Furer, M. (1968). *On Human Symbiosis and the Vicissitudes of Individuation*. Vol. 1, *Infantile Psychosis*. New York: International Universities Press.

Reich, A. (1960). Pathological forms of self-esteem regulation. *Psychoanal. Study Child*, 15:215–32.

Riviere, J. A. (1936). A contribution to the analysis of the negative therapeutic reaction. *Int. J. Psycho-Anal.*, 17:304–20.

Rosenfeld, H. (1964). On the psychopathology of narcissism: A clinical approach. *Int. J. Psycho-Anal.*, 45:332–37.

———. (1971). A clinical approach to the psychoanalytic theory of the life and death instincts: An investigation into the aggressive aspects of narcissism. *Int. J. Psycho-Anal.*, 52:169–78.

———. (1975). Negative therapeutic reaction. In *Tactics and Techniques in Psychoanalytic Therapy*. Vol. 3, *Countertransference*, ed. P. L. Giovacchini. New York: Jason Aronson, pp. 217–28.

Sandler, J. (1960). On the concept of the superego. *Psychoanal. Study Child*, 15:128–62.

Stern, D. N. (1985). *The Interpersonal World of the Infant*. New York: Basic Books.

Tartakoff, H. H. (1966). The normal personality in our culture and the Nobel Prize complex. In R. M. Lowenstein, L. M. Newman, M. Schur, et al., eds., *Psychoanalysis: A General Psychology, Essays in Honor of Heinz Hartmann*. New York: International Universities Press.

Van Der Waals, H. G. (1965). Problems of narcissism. *Bull. Menninger Clinic*, 29:293–311.

The Theory of Narcissism in the Work of Freud and Klein

HANNA SEGAL

&

DAVID BELL

FREUD'S THEORY OF NARCISSISM

Freud's paper on narcissism marks a watershed in the development of his thought. By 1913 the theoretical model laid out in chapter 7 of *The Interpretation of Dreams* (1900) had been steadily developed and expanded. The paper "On Narcissism," however, caused a "disagreeable jolt" and "some bewilderment" (Jones, 1958). This paper saw the first revision of Freud's instinct theory and marked the beginning of a major return to theoretical questions that received their fullest exposition in the "Papers on Metapsychology" (1915). Reading the paper, one has a palpable sense of Freud's uneasiness with it. He wrote to Abraham, "The narcissism paper was a difficult labour and bears all the marks of a corresponding deformation" (Jones, 1955).

In the first phase of the development of his theory Freud's principal object was to trace the vicissitudes of the libido through an examination of the perversions. But by the beginning of the next phase, ushered in by the narcissism paper, he was becoming increasingly preoccupied with the functioning of the ego. Only four years before the narcissism paper Freud had coined the term "self-preservative instincts" (1910b).

Although much of Freud's theoretical work is couched in instinctual terms, his writings convey a vivid awareness of an internal world. Until the theory of identification was established, however, there was no way of conceptualizing this. Reading Freud, one often gets the impression that his two sides —the literary and the scientific—live uneasily with each other. The theory of identification provided a means by which these two ways of conceptualizing could be linked. In 1916, only a year after writing "Mourning and Melancholia," he wrote eloquently on the issue of character and the internal world in "Some Character Types Met with in Psycho-Analytic Work," in which he discusses Shakespeare's *Richard III* and Ibsen's *Rosmersholm*. In 1914, however, he attempted to conceptualize some very important observations in connection with homosexuality and the psychoses without any explicit theory of internalization or identification.

The paper "On Narcissism" is, as Freud said, "deformed" by the lack of an adequate conceptual apparatus to contain the important observations he wished to consider. It is one of the marks of his genius that, even when there was no adequate theory to deal with certain psychoanalytic observations, he would not abandon the observations. But in the narcissism paper the theory is stretched to the breaking point. These strains were to be brilliantly resolved in three key papers, all foreshadowed in the paper under discussion. These are "Mourning and Melancholia" (1915), which introduced, in a more coherent way, the theory of an internal world based on identification; *The Ego and the Id* (1923), which saw the founding of the structural model; and *Beyond the Pleasure Principle* (1920), which contained the second and final revision of instinct theory. Later in this chapter we will take these papers as starting points in examining the development of the theory of narcissism in the work of Melanie Klein.

Freud's main motives for writing the paper on narcissism were, broadly, clinical and theoretical, on the one hand, and political, on the other. The principal psychopathological problems that occupied him in this period were homosexuality and paranoid psychoses. The theory of narcissism provided the conceptual tool that linked these two psychopathological states. The principal works dealing with these problems are the Leonardo book (1910a) and the Schreber case (1911). As these works are based on speculations from biographical or autobiographical data, we will first examine some elements of the clinical case that Freud had been treating before the publication of the narcissism paper—namely, the case of the Wolf Man (1918). Although the Wolf Man case was written and published after the narcissism paper, all the clinical work was carried out during the four years that preceded it (1910–14).

In his elaboration of the case, Freud paid particular attention to the relation of narcissism to identification. The Wolf Man, after having been rebuffed by his dearly beloved "Nanya," turned his affections toward his father. According to Freud (1918, 27), he was "in this way able to renew his first and most primitive object choice which, in conformity with a small child's narcissism, had taken place along the path of identification." Freud at this time conceptualized identification as a narcissistic act, and such identifications occurred prior to the more mature situation involving object choice. The Wolf Man subsequently developed a passive sexual aim toward his father: "his father was now his object once more; in conformity with his higher stage of development, identification was replaced by object choice." The case of the Wolf Man thus presents a study of these crucial trends in the patient's personality—the passive (masochistic)[1] attitude, which was central to his repressed homosexuality, and his narcissistic identifications.

The Wolf Man is, of course, the study of a severe perverse character disorder, and it is clear that, as well as studying the vicissitudes of the libido, Freud is examining the whole question of character development in relation to the various predominant instinctual trends and identifications. The Wolf Man shared with Schreber preoccupations with defecation, religion, and identification with a passive figure in a violent intercourse. Although at the time of his analysis with Freud his symptoms were understood as essentially neurotic, his later breakdown revealed that these fantasies formed part of a psychotic core.

Freud conceptualized the repudiation of the passive (feminine)[2] currents in terms of the ego's need to defend itself. He states, "The ego has only an interest in self-protection and preservation of its narcissism." A key difficulty arises here, which has remained the subject of some controversy—namely, the relation of narcissism to perversion. Freud, in the Wolf Man case, clearly links them but also makes narcissism a part of the ego's need to protect itself—an activity that is hard to see as perverse.

In this case study one gains a real impression of the internal representation of a scene (a couple in intercourse and an observer) with a cast of characters in which there are shifting identifications (Meltzer, 1978). The

1. The masochistic identification with a damaged mother was extensively explored in this paper.

2. For Freud at this time, passivity and femininity were synonymous.

representation (or misrepresentation?) of the parental intercourse as a sadistic act has profound implications for character development. In the Wolf Man case, then, Freud gave his first account of an internalized primal scene with shifting identifications, which enter into narcissistic character formation.

It was, however, in the Leonardo work that Freud made his first statement on narcissism.[3] This paper also marks Freud's increasing preoccupation with character, for here he examines a person's whole life and work in terms of early experience and psychopathology.

Freud (1910a, 100) writes in connection with Leonardo's homosexuality: "The boy represses his love for his mother: he puts himself in her place, identifies himself with her, and takes his own person as a model in whose likeness he chooses new objects of his love. . . . He finds the objects of his love along the path of narcissism." Freud points out that in this identificatory process the boy "preserves his love for his mother." Nevertheless, he rather ambiguously states, "What he [Leonardo] has in fact done is to slip back to auto-erotism." This poses another conceptual difficulty because, for Freud, autoerotism implied a state preceding object-love. Yet in his statement, he describes what is clearly an object relationship. We will return to this complicated question later.

A common theme runs through the Wolf Man, Leonardo, and Schreber papers—namely, the relation of homosexuality to narcissism, and the relation of narcissism to psychosis. There is insufficient space here to address the many details of the Schreber case, but it will be remembered that, after an hypochondriacal illness, Schreber developed a psychotic state in which he built a grandiose delusional system in order to restore omnipotently a world destroyed by a catastrophe. The key features of this system were that "in order to restore the world" Schreber had to achieve "a divine relation" to God, this being effected through his transformation into a woman. Freud demonstrates that the end-of-the-world delusion was a projection of an internal catastrophe—that is, the end of the inner world owing to a withdrawal of "interest"[4] from it. He explains that, in the psychoses, the libido is withdrawn from objects (that is, the external world) and is turned onto the ego. In this way he links paranoia, narcissism, and megalomania. He goes on to say that paranoiacs are "fixated" at the stage of narcissism. Here he is using the

3. Although there is a footnote concerning narcissism in *Three Essays on the Theory of Sexuality*, this was added in 1910, the date of the publication of the Leonardo case.

4. It was in the Schreber case that Freud for the first time used the more general word "interest" rather than "libidinal investment."

language of the *Three Essays on the Theory of Sexuality* (1905), where the libidinal organization can become fixated at various stages of development.

When Freud writes of the withdrawal of libido (or rather "interest") from the world, it sounds like a very passive, quiet procedure. Indeed, he saw all the "noise" of the paranoid patient as being a result of the patient's attempts to reconstruct the inner world. Meltzer (1978) has noted that at the very point where Freud talks of the withdrawal of the libido, he quotes Goethe's Faust: "Woe, woe, thou hast destroyed a beautiful world, with powerful fist, in ruins it is hurled, by the blow of the demi-god shattered!" Thus Freud shows his intuitive understanding that the destruction of the inner world is not such a quiet procedure after all but is brought about by a "demi-god with powerful fist."

The Schreber case must have been what Freud had in mind when he wrote in the narcissism paper: "just as the transference neuroses have enabled us to trace the libidinal instinctual impulses, so dementia praecox and paranoia will give us insight into the psychology of the ego." Freud goes on to say that Schreber's delusions are in a certain sense true and, what is more, are consistent with Freud's evolving theory of narcissism—namely, that when all the libidinal "interest" is withdrawn from the external world the result is an internal catastrophe, the end of the inner world.

Richard Wollheim (1971) has pointed out that psychoanalytic theory not only offers models of mental functions but also describes how these mental functions are represented in the mind. He makes the point that although this is implicit in Freud's theory it was not explored further until Melanie Klein. In the Schreber case, however, Freud (1911, 75) gives an explicit statement of this: "It remains for the future to decide whether there is more delusion to my theory than I should like to admit or whether there is more truth in Schreber's delusion than other people may, as yet, be prepared to believe." For Freud, Schreber's delusions were concrete representations of those very mechanisms that constitute the psychosis.

The Schreber case provided Freud with fertile soil for his speculations on the nature of psychosis and, in particular, the relationship of paranoia, narcissism, and megalomania. Schreber's delusional system thus provided Freud with the model of the ego and object-libido later to be elaborated in the narcissism paper.

As for Freud's political motives for writing the narcissism paper, Strachey points out in his introduction that the concept of narcissism was to provide an alternative to Adler's "masculine protest" and Jung's "nonsexual libido." We think that these major theoretical difficulties were not really resolved until Freud wrote *Beyond the Pleasure Principle*—in which the duality of instincts was restored with the theory of life and death instincts. Adler's aggressive drive could then also be accommodated in a way more consistent with Freud's theoretical structure.

The narcissism paper is difficult to read because it contains a mixture of two different models of mental life—namely, libido theory and an implicit theory of internal object relations. In struggling with the issues raised in the paper Freud uses terms from the former theory in such a way that they lose their original meaning. For example, the term "ego-instinct" implies a very different use of the word "instinct."[5]

"On Narcissism" starts with a statement of the method that bore so much fruit in Freud's first phase—that psychopathology is a study of developmental arrest, and so the study of psychopathology gives rise to theories of development. The paper is concerned with an account of the phenomenology and dynamics of the "narcissistic neuroses" and also explores why this newly gained knowledge necessitates a different model of the mind.

In the paper the term "narcissism" is first used to describe the relationship in which a person takes his own body as his sexual object. In line with the method of the *Three Essays*, this situation—a perversion—represents a fixation of the libido at an earlier stage of development. It is, however, immediately clear that Freud realized that he was dealing with something more basic than the other perversions, as he goes on to point out that this "narcissistic attitude" is one of the limits of susceptibility of the individual to psychoanalysis.

Freud then looks for evidence of this primary state recapitulated in the perversion. He obtains this from three sources, all of them rather indirect as they are not based on clinical data. They come from the written reports of a psychotic man (Schreber), the observation of children, and accounts of primitive peoples. Freud states, "the hypothesis of separate ego and object instincts rests scarcely at all on any psychological basis."

As we have said, Schreber's delusions provided Freud with important evidence for the existence of primary narcissism. Freud links two important phenomenological features of the psychosis—the turning away from the external world and the presence of megalomania—and assumes that these must have some dynamic relation to each other. The statement that the psychotic turns his interest away from the external world and does not replace

5. This marks a move away from the concept of instincts as having a source, aim, and object toward a more exclusive interest in the aim of an instinct. Indeed, it is hard to say what would constitute the source of an ego instinct (see Wollheim, 1971).

this with internal fantasies must strike us as strange and requires further elaboration.

As Sandler and his colleagues (1976) pointed out, when Freud talks of the relation to the external world we must assume he means the relation to the mental representation of external reality.[6] Freud, however, speaks of "real objects" and "imaginary objects," the latter replacing the former as objects of interest in the neuroses. "Real objects" must therefore be accurate mental representations of external reality, whereas "imaginary objects," presumably, are distortions of external reality (by both fantasies and memories). In effect, Freud is saying that psychotics differ from neurotics in the relationship of the ego to the representations of internal and external reality.[7]

The connection between these two characteristic features of psychosis (withdrawal from reality and the presence of grandiosity) is described in terms of the vicissitudes of the libido. The libido withdraws from objects and cathects the person's own ego. Freud, in line with this theoretical model, assumes that this phenomenon must recapitulate a previous stage of development in which the libido primarily cathected the ego. This again gives rise to the concept of primary narcissism. Freud thus deduces (on theoretical grounds) the presence of a primary stage of narcissism that precedes object-love.

Wollheim (1971) has pointed out that the differentiation of autoerotism from narcissism gets perfunctory treatment in the paper. To some extent, it depends on whether the "self" or "the body" is taken as the love object. But as the ego is "first and foremost a bodily ego" (Freud, 1923), this distinction remains unsatisfactory. The debate becomes so theoretical because of the lack of clinical evidence, and Freud's great dissatisfaction with it is clear. The references to the omnipotence of thought of children and of primitive peoples are more illustrative than supportive.

The extent of Freud's dissatisfaction with the theory as now postulated —namely, of primary narcissism, object-libido, and ego-libido—is clear in the next part of the paper. One of the central difficulties is that he recognizes

6. Given that the withdrawal from reality really means withdrawal from the mental representation of reality, it becomes clear how this withdrawal leads to an *internal* catastrophe.

7. As mentioned above, Freud understood the withdrawal of interest from external reality as a passive procedure. One year later, however, he stated in "Instincts and Their Vicissitudes" that the apparent indifference of the ego to the external world in primary narcissism is, in reality, hatred of it. He says, "Indifference falls into place as a special form of hate or dislike."

he is very near to postulating a single kind of psychic energy. This problem is not only political (as it brings him close to Jung) but also theoretical, for Freud's model entailed a necessary dualism. Without this, it is difficult to account for repression. Freud states that the notion of ego-libido is not "rich in content," by which we assume he means that it lacks clinical supportive data—always the acid test for Freud. He shows his awareness of the problem by saying that there is a "total absence of any theory of instincts which can help us find our bearings" (78). Freud appeals to biological distinctions (between hunger and love) and, though tempted by this, states clearly that psychological facts must be kept distinct from biological ones. He argues himself round full circle and ends up by saying, "Let us face the possibility of error . . . [and be] consistent enough (with my general rule) to drop this hypothesis if psycho-analytic work should itself produce some other, more serviceable hypothesis" (79). Such evidence did, in fact, come later from psychoanalytic work. The questions of masochism and repetition compulsion led to the formulation of a new instinct theory—the theory of the life and death instincts.

The question of hypochondriasis raises problems of a similar nature. Freud has again shown his great clinical intuition in locating the hypochondriacal states closer to the psychoses than to the neuroses (as seen in the Wolf Man and Schreber cases). These states must, therefore, be understood in terms of the functioning of the ego. Freud's later formulation of a bodily ego links hypochondriasis to deeply unconscious fantasies about the body. In this context, however, he had to deal with the question of hypochondriacal anxiety within the ambit of the first anxiety theory. He suggests that the "dammed-up libido" (the cause of anxiety) is located in the ego. He points out pertinently, however, that it is not easy to explain why this should be unpleasurable, since increased quantities of libido located in the ego should lead to feelings of pleasurable omnipotence. Indeed, as he goes on to say, the more interesting question is why libido should leave the ego in the first place—in other words, why infantile narcissism, and the omnipotence associated with it, should ever be abandoned.

Here Freud turns again to literature and finds an answer in purely psychological terms in Heine's poetic and insightful statement that we need to create in order to be healthy. The whole question of the capacity for object-love (as opposed to self-love) becomes central to mental health. Freud, however, again turns to libido theory in saying that one needs to release libido in order not to suffer neurosis; thus he robs this notion of its central psychological impact.

When Freud turns from the psychoses and the attendant difficult theoretical questions to the whole question of the erotic life, he seems to be much more comfortable. He says that it is in the study of erotic life that we have the "strongest reasons for the hypothesis of narcissism." The reasons are strong because they are based on clinical data. It is worth pointing out, however, that all the examples given refer to secondary narcissism. He clearly has in mind the Leonardo case, supported by clinical work, when he talks of the man who looks for his own (projected) self in the object of his love. In postulating two different types of love, the anaclitic (love of the object that nourishes) and narcissistic, or self-love, Freud is struggling to define a type of love relation that is not narcissistic. In his description of "complete object-love" of the attachment (therefore nonnarcissistic) type, Freud describes what amounts to enslavement to an idealized object. To our minds, this type of relation, though it contains an acknowledgment of the need for the object, still bears strong narcissistic features. As we will discuss later, such enslavement is brought about through projection of aspects of the self into the object.

Some of the difficulties in this section of the paper arise from Freud's use of the term "object" in the sense of external objects. Elsewhere, however, he makes it clear that the external object obtains its character from what has been projected onto it. Earlier in the paper he calls this a "transfer of narcissism" to the sexual object, by which he means a projection of the idealized self. He makes further use of this idea in his discussion of the idealization of children.

When we move on to Freud's first elaboration of the ego-ideal we find him talking more explicitly about an internal world where identifications and projections take place—this being a necessary prior step to external projection (for example, of the ego-ideal) onto external objects. Here he differentiates an internal object that is not in the ego; thus, in effect, he distinguishes self and ego. The ego-ideal, a relic of infantile development, "he projects before him as his ideal." So Freud shows that an internal scenario in which ideal aspects of the self can be projected underlies the narcissistic object relation so clearly described in the Leonardo case. The capacity for forming an ego-ideal and for projecting it onto other objects clearly has important implications for object choice that are not fully explored in the paper.

Toward the end Freud again comes up against the limitations of instinct theory when he tries to delineate the features of nonnarcissistic love. When he talks of the "return of love" from the object, this seems to be closer to the hydraulic model. He is, as yet, unable to discuss what sort of internal preconditions must exist in order for the ego to obtain the enrichment ensuing from the capacity to love. The question becomes increasingly confusing when Freud writes of the normal happy state of being loved as a return to the primal condition in which object and ego cannot be distinguished—that is, to primary narcissism. When, at the end of the paper, Freud writes of the patient's preference for cure by love over cure by analysis, he is presumably talking of the patient's preference for an overwhelmingly narcissistic love, destined to failure as it takes so little account of reality.

The narcissism paper, then, comes at the point where the limits of Freud's first model have been reached. Implicit in the paper is an object-relations theory of development and a growing interest in the question of character and the internal world. These are, however, not developed further. We suggest that the paper has a number of theoretical problems: (1) the model of the ego- and object-libido, (2) the question of primary narcissism, and (3) the nature and function of the ego.

The model of ego- and object-libido threatened the duality vital to Freud's system, because the principal mental conflict, as presented, is now between instinctual forces that have the same origin. As Wollheim (1971) put it, "remove the duality and the whole theory of psychoneurosis would surely crumble. . . . It was precisely this duality that the discovery of primary narcissism appeared to threaten." The question continued to preoccupy Freud and finds its final resolution in *Beyond the Pleasure Principle*, where the proposition of the life and death instincts reinstates the duality. The idea of a primary destructive force was taken up most emphatically by Melanie Klein. Its relation to narcissism was explored by Herbert Rosenfeld (to be discussed below).

Primary narcissism—a state that precedes both the formation of the ego and object relations—remains in our view a most unsatisfactory concept. The difficulties with this theory are, to some extent, demonstrated by the different meanings Freud and various authors have given it. For example, it is sometimes referred to as a state between autoerotism and object choice, or an objectless undifferentiated state, that is, preceding autoerotism—a state assumed to be close to the intrauterine state. Here we would agree with the objections raised by Laplanche and Pontalis (1983)—that if one is to accept the existence of an objectless state, then it would be incorrect to call this narcissism, as Narcissus from his point of view perceived an object with whom he fell in love. Phenomenologically this is a state of object relations in which parts of the self are felt to be in the object.

The last section of the narcissism paper boldly presents the beginnings of the structural model. The ego and its functions became an increasingly important preoccupation for Freud after he had written the narcissism paper. In "Mourning and Melancholia" (1915) he was able, for the first time, to give a full account of an internal object relationship that involved projection and identification. This paved the way for the theory, expounded more fully in *The Ego and the Id*, of an ego built up from "abandoned object cathexes." This is really the point of departure for Melanie Klein, who went on to explore the constant interplay between projection and introjection in creating an inner world. As we have said, the proposition of the ego-ideal and the observing agency both foreshadowed the structural model with the formulation of the superego. Freud was later to acknowledge Klein (Freud, 1930) when he agreed that the murderousness of the superego bears no resemblance to the reality of the actual parents and must be based on the projection of murderous impulses arising from within. Toward the latter part of his life Freud became increasingly preoccupied with the role of aggression and gave it a much more prominent position.

THE DEVELOPMENT OF THE THEORY OF NARCISSISM IN THE WORK OF MELANIE KLEIN

Although some of the contradictions present in the narcissism paper were partially resolved by Freud's later work, he still maintained his belief in a primary narcissistic stage that precedes object relations. Klein, in one of her few explicit references to primary narcissism, clearly demarcates herself from Freud. She states:

> The hypothesis that a stage extending over several months precedes object relations implies that—except for the libido attached to the infant's own body—impulses, phantasies, anxieties and defences are not present in him, or are not related to an object, that is to say they would operate [in a vacuum]. . . . *there is no anxiety situation, no mental process which does not involve objects external or internal.* . . . furthermore, love and hatred, phantasies, anxieties and defences are indivisibly linked to object relations. (Klein, 1952; italics added)

In the same paper she goes on to say that states of "narcissistic withdrawal" are actually states in which there is a withdrawal to internalized objects. She thus explicitly departs from Freud's notion of an autoerotic and narcissistic stage that precedes object relations. We have already said that Freud is by no means unambiguous on this matter.

Klein believed that from the beginning there is a rudimentary ego that alternates between states of relative cohesion and states of unintegration and disintegration. This rudimentary ego forms intense relations to objects and uses defense mechanisms. At first these objects are primitive "part" objects, but with further development these become more integrated. The importance of this is not only theoretical but also clinical, for from this perspective there is no mental state, no matter how regressed a patient may be, that is objectless and conflict-free.

Klein emphasized the constant interplay of projection and introjection in the building up of an internal world of objects to which the ego relates and which are also experienced as relating to each other. It was in her painstaking study of these processes that she demonstrated the rapid oscillations that can occur in the state of the ego and of the internal objects.

Following Freud in the last phases of his work, Klein put great emphasis on the anxiety consequent on the infant's perception of his own violently destructive impulses toward his objects. She was much impressed by the archaic, murderous qualities of the infantile superego, which bore so little relation to external reality, and saw this situation as based on the projection of the infant's own destructive impulses—ultimately derived from the death instinct.

A major innovation was her concept of "positions" rather than stages of development. This concept refers to states of the ego, the anxieties that are present, the defenses against these anxieties, and the internal object relations. She described two positions that represent two phenomenologically distinct states: the paranoid/schizoid and the depressive positions.

As we will discuss later, narcissistic object relations are characteristic of the paranoid/schizoid position. In this state the world is deeply split between good and bad objects; this splitting takes place internally and is also projected externally. The dominant anxieties are of a paranoid nature, and the defenses are aimed at protecting the self and the idealized objects from the murderous objects that contain split-off and projected aggression originating in the infant's self. The defenses of denial, splitting, and projection are characteristic of this position. The basic developmental task is the building up of a secure enough good object in order for further integration to occur. If this is achieved the infant will be better equipped to face and cope with the anxieties inherent in the depressive position in which the infant develops a relation to "whole" objects.

In recognizing that the "good" and the "bad" objects are not in reality separate, the infant requires the inner strength to bear separation, fear of loss, and the guilt ensuing from the recognition of the damage felt to have been inflicted on the good object. The capacity to bear this guilt enormously strengthens the ego. The concern for the internally damaged objects leads to a wish to repair them rather than to deny their existence, and so the infant enters the ethical world. The successful negotiation of these depressive anxieties leads to a much firmer relation to internal and external reality and the capacity to differentiate self from object.

Klein used the term "positions" to emphasize that these are not only developmental stages but two different ways of relating to inner and outer reality, which, to some extent, are always present. Traumatic situations can cause some regression from the depressive to the paranoid/schizoid position, but if there is a secure enough inner good object, such a regression is temporary.

"Notes on Some Schizoid Mechanisms" (1946) is the key paper in which Klein presented her understanding of narcissism. The schizoid object relations she describes are of the type that would today be termed "narcissistic." In the paranoid/schizoid position the capacity for accurate perception of inner and outer reality is obscured through the mechanisms of denial, splitting, and projection. Internal and external reality are constantly in danger of collapsing into each other, and when they do, the outcome is psychosis. It is for this reason that Klein asserted that the "fixation point" for psychosis is located at a phase of development that precedes the negotiation of the depressive position. Like Freud, she considered that narcissism and psychosis are rooted in a stage of development preceding mature object relationships, but, unlike Freud, she describes this state not as objectless but as involving more primitive object relationships.

In this important paper Klein gave her first detailed description of the mechanism of projective identification. In projective identification aspects of the self are omnipotently denied and projected into the object, which then becomes identified with these projected aspects of the self. When aspects of the self that are felt to be good are projected, this leads to idealization of the object, while the hostile destructive impulses are split off and projected elsewhere. Because of the splitting, paranoia and idealization always coexist, the idealization often being used as a defense against paranoia. Such processes underlie the defense mechanisms of "reversal" and "reaction formation." It is because the object becomes identified with aspects of the self, to the extent that its real properties are obscured, that this mechanism is the basis of narcissistic object relations. It is a familiar clinical finding that narcissistic or "borderline" patients are equally prone to idealize or denigrate their objects. One relation can quickly change into the other. In both situations the subject has a profound incapacity to see his objects as they "really are." From the subjective point of view, of course, the objects that become identified with the self are not experienced as part of the self. When Narcissus gazes at his reflection in the water he does not know that what he sees is himself.

Patients who make excessive use of projective identification are trapped in a world made up of projected aspects of themselves. The profound denial and projection lead to a weakening of the ego, which becomes less able to cope with anxiety, leading to further splitting and projection: a truly malignant vicious circle. As well as exploring the basis of these narcissistic object relations, Klein examined what she called "narcissistic states" in which there is a withdrawal from reality toward an idealized internal object. If we recall Freud's description of Leonardo, it could be said that Leonardo identified himself with his idealized object (mother), while he projected another aspect of himself (the needy, dependent self) into the young men he pursued.

Projective identification of a more extreme type is frequently seen in psychotic patients. The process can be so massive that the patient loses his whole identity and takes over the features of his object (such as delusional beliefs that he is another person, usually someone powerful and famous).

To illustrate, Mrs. A, a psychotic patient, lay rigidly on the couch in an attitude of frozen terror for much of the first year of her analysis. She was later able to explain that when she walked behind the analyst on the way to the consulting room she found herself forced to stare at his behind. She experienced this as a violent assault on him and felt terrified of him. This patient felt she had made a violent intrusive attack with her eyes. The result was that she felt that the violent and intrusive aspects of herself were now present in the analyst, so she felt trapped with a terrifying object from whom she expected retaliation. It was characteristic of this patient that she often needed to hear the analyst talk so that she could determine from the sound of his voice whether he was the terrifying object she took him to be.

Such a situation is common in less ill patients and often underlies acute claustrophobic anxiety. These patients have a deeply held conviction that the attacked object can only retaliate. In this sense all the objects are felt to be as incapable of coping with the situation as they feel themselves to be. Patients who use projective identification to this extent are overwhelmingly preoccupied with the state of their objects. They listen to interpretations attentively, not in terms of what they communicate in words but as revelatory statements about the state of mind of the analyst.

In the latter part of her 1946 paper Klein gives a detailed phenomenology of schizoid object relations. These patients often feel themselves to be unreal or artificial. They can appear remote, having to keep a distance from their objects, which they feel contain terrifying projected aspects of themselves. Alternatively, they develop clinging compulsive ties to their objects, feeling that the loss of the object amounts to an annihilation of parts of the self. It is because projective identification leads to a depletion of the ego that these patients so often complain of feelings of emptiness.

There are many patients who experience love as a threat, fearing that it will deplete them. Male patients sometimes experience this concretely and have theories about becoming incapacitated by the loss of semen. Such patients, in fact, believe themselves to function in a way that corresponds to Freud's first hydraulic model of the libido. They feel that love is a substance of which they have a finite amount, and so they have to prevent themselves from losing it into their objects. In a certain sense they are correct, because in the love relation they fear, they do lose part of themselves through projective identification. Freud attributes some of these features to anaclitic love. It is for this reason that we have said that anaclitic love, as he describes it, has a strong narcissistic component.

To illustrate, Mr. B led a very limited life marked by profound sexual inhibitions. Although he did well educationally, he had been unable to use his abilities and worked in a rather menial job. Once in his life he had a girlfriend whom he desired. He became madly preoccupied with her and couldn't bear her being out of his sight. He felt he was breaking down. Following the end of this relationship he lived in a withdrawn, remote way. He proclaimed his self-sufficiency and maintained that he could not understand why anyone should allow another person to become important to him, that such a thing wasted one's time. Essentially he believed that all objects should be replaceable, and he attempted to live his life accordingly.

Sometimes he would describe situations in which he perceived two people who had a real interest and enthusiasm for each other. Such a perception was accompanied by intense pain, with a feeling that something was lacking in him. This momentary awareness, however, was quickly replaced by a state of arrogant superiority in which he would mock such people as being "very infantile."

He was late for practically every session of the first eighteen months of his analysis, intent on not "wasting time in the waiting room." He had a long-standing relationship with a black woman whom he saw as being totally dependent on him and for whom he often felt a great deal of contempt. He projected into her all the hated dependent parts of himself. He often experienced his analyst in a similar way, as someone dependent on him. Although Mr. B tried to be self-sufficient, at times he experienced a devastating sense of having wasted his life, accompanied by a terror of "growing old and being alone." A very envious man, he was always preoccupied with who was better off or worse off than himself. He constantly dreaded discovering that someone he had decided was "no good" was, in fact, more able than he.

The session reported below followed a period in which he was making some steps toward integration and moving away from his narcissistic attitude. He was beginning to feel that his analysis was of some importance to him. The session took place a few days before a break.

He was late for the session and after a brief apology went on to talk of something that had happened the previous evening. He had seen a car behind him which, "from the configuration of the headlamps," he realized was the same model as his analyst's. (It was also the same as his own, for a few weeks after starting his analysis, he had purchased a car of the same type and model.) He became intensely preoccupied with the need to know if it was the analyst's car. Some features of the car were different, and the driver was a woman (the analyst was a man). He felt that his need to establish to whom the car belonged was driving him mad.

An interpretation was made along the lines that he wanted to take a really good look inside his analyst to see what sort of a person he was, in particular to see if he was different from himself—something he had previously thought unlikely. He seemed relieved and also interested in this interpretation and went on to discuss a situation he had described before but never so vividly. He said that whenever he saw someone he believed to have certain valued qualities that he himself did not possess, he felt an immediate need to merge with or get inside this person. He called this process "colonization." He described the urge to get inside the object as unbearable. In such situations he had an intense urge to masturbate, but he tried to resist it as he felt it wasted something. He also explained that this often happened when he suddenly saw someone he had thought was "no good" in a new light.

This material gives a vivid description of this patient's difficulties and of how he coped with them. Because he functioned so much through projective identification (for example, by projecting the needy aspects of himself into his girlfriend and into the analyst who waited for him), his life was dull and repetitive. All his objects appeared similar because, in reality, they were containers for the projected aspects of himself. In this session he seems to have been very struck by the interpretation that was made, which he thought was new and which allowed him to see his analyst in a new light, as someone with qualities that were valuable and important to him. In this situation the analyst was experienced as being separate from him and not controlled by him. This time he did not, as he often did, quickly mock the interpretation and render it meaningless, nor did he take it over and make it his own (in the same way that he had made the analyst's car his car). He felt separate from the analyst and was immediately faced with unbearable feelings of desire for an object that he did not possess. The wish to get inside the object through "colonization" was a wish to wipe out the separation from the object and to possess it quickly and greedily. It is likely that he also projected good aspects of himself into his object and was desperate to maintain contact with them, through "colonization."

This material represented an important move forward in which he could retain the capacity to see a desired object that was separate from himself. But this was immediately followed by a wish to repossess it in masturbatory fantasy.

An important aspect of this material is the question of envy—Mr. B's preoccupation with establishing whether people were better off or worse off than he. He moved with remarkable facility from seeing a good esteemed object to representing the same object as worthless. This procedure seemed to be brought about by unbearable envy and it also defended him against envy.

The role of envy in narcissistic disorders has received increasing attention from Kleinian authors. The question of primitive envy received its first full treatment in the short book *Envy and Gratitude* (Klein, 1957). In this work Klein shows that envy is a psychological manifestation of the most destructive human impulses. She quotes Chaucer: "It is certain that envy is the worst sin that is; for all the other sins are sins only against one virtue, whereas envy is against all virtue and against all goodness." The envious person cannot accept things from the object, for to do so means to acknowledge its worth and separateness. Such people quickly devalue anything that is potentially useful to them (as Mr. B often did). They "bite the very hand that feeds them." Envy is fundamentally so incapacitating because it is the very goodness of the object that is hated, so that nothing useful can be obtained from it. Beyond this, however, an envious person is also constantly persecuted, for when he enviously attacks his objects, they turn, through projection, from loving objects into envious persecuting ones. Such patients are often extremely anxious about their own possessions, as they constantly feel that others will be envious and rob them.

In *Envy and Gratitude* Klein shows the close connection between envy and projective identification. The attack on the object is motivated by envy but also defends the subject against envy. She emphasizes that primitive envy is often hidden, split off, and silent. In the transference situation such envy often severely limits the patient's ability to use any analytical work and underlies severe negative therapeutic reactions.

The difficulties associated with excessive envy, and therefore excessive use of projective identification, are characteristic of the paranoid/schizoid position. Freud, in the paper under discussion, recognizes that the narcissistic attitude limits the individual's susceptibility to psychoanalytic treatment. From our point of view, this is because such patients have great difficulty in allowing themselves to receive anything of worth from their objects; instead of seeing and making use of it, out of envy they destroy the object and also their own capacity to recognize it as separate from themselves. In "Instincts and Their Vissicitudes" (1915) Freud, discussing primary narcissism, talks of a state in which the infant feels himself to be the source of all satisfaction: "When during the stage of primary narcissism the object makes its appearance, the second opposite to loving, namely hating, also attains its development" (136). He states in the same paper that "hate, as a relation to objects, is older than love. It derives from the narcissistic ego's primordial repudiation of the external world" (139). If one holds with the theory of primary narcissism, the discovery of the goodness of the external object comes relatively late and leads to narcissistic rage. If, with Klein, one holds that from birth there is a capacity for awareness of the external object, this narcissistic rage is an expression of envy.

So, for Klein, envy is a fundamental attitude and part of the paranoid/schizoid position. As the title of her book suggests, the polar opposite of this attitude is gratitude. The person who can be genuinely grateful to his objects and who can acknowledge the fact that he is separate from them can develop the capacity for genuine creativity. Because he is less envious he is less persecuted by envious objects and has a more secure relation to a good internal object and therefore can learn from experience. In other words, his object relations are predominantly those of the depressive position. Inherent in this move from the paranoid/schizoid to the depressive position is the lessening of narcissistic omnipotence. The patient's need to control and take over the analysis lessens with his increasing ability to tolerate his awareness of the analyst as a separate person who can be of use to him.

For Klein, envy is intimately related to the primary destructiveness of the death instinct. The struggle between the life and death instincts is seen as a continuous conflict in development and is represented psychologically by the struggle between love and gratitude, on the one hand, and hate and envy, on the other. These issues have been further considered by Rosenfeld (1971), who made explicit the link between envy and the death instinct. He explored the deep split that exists in some patients between the libidinal or needy part of the self, which wishes to be understood and helped, and the violent, destructive, envious part of the self, which seeks to dominate and triumph over the object and the hated dependent self. Such patients tend to keep their external objects in a devalued state, enviously undermining them while idealizing their own omnipotent destructiveness. To acknowledge a need for help is to put themselves in an unbearably humiliating situation. Whenever the analyst talks to them of anything needy in themselves, they experience this as an attempt to make them dependent—that is, to forcefully reproject dependency into them. Rosenfeld describes these patients as in the grip of a "powerful gang" that seeks to control them and that advertises itself as superior to the analyst. Such patients, if they do allow themselves to be helped, often feel that they are in terrible danger from this powerful gang.

A schizophrenic patient, Mr. C, spent many sessions in a state of blissful, mocking serenity, silently staring at his analyst. Occasionally, he would giggle at something that was said to him or would respond with a superior and patronizing comment. He seemed to be self-sufficient, to be narcissistic omnipotence personified. In one session, however, he informed his analyst that he was in communication with a group of people called "the Scientists" who advised him not to "talk to Dr. Bell [the analyst], who is quite mad." They told him that dying would be a good thing, for if he were to die, he could live forever. That the patient brought this up was obviously of enormous importance: he wished to escape from the grip of this powerful gang.

Shortly after this session he became acutely distressed and threatened to throw himself under a train. He felt in enormous danger, as he had betrayed the secrets of "the Scientists." His suicidal impulses were based on his terror of "the Scientists" but also on a painful state of confusion; he was no longer sure who was mad and who was sane. This also illustrates the closeness of envy to the death instinct.

It is possible to see this process in a less florid form in many patients who are less ill. Miss D, though clearly often experiencing desperate states of anxiety, would constantly talk about them in a superior way, inviting the analyst to join her in contempt for her own needy self. For example, she would talk of feeling terrible anxiety associated with a fear of dying. She would punctuate these accounts by remarking, in a sarcastic and superior voice, "how peculiar." She experienced any interpretations aimed at understanding her fears as attempts by the analyst to force her to be dependent and so make her inferior. She would bring letters to her session that she had written at home, which contained long accounts of her desperate need for help. She behaved as if she were not allowed to bring this extremely needy aspect of herself into the analytic situation and could only, so to speak, slip it in as a secret message. She seemed able to believe only in those relationships in which "one person is up and the other person is down." In line with this, when she actually did feel in great need—for example, before breaks that affected her deeply—she felt that she was with an analyst who was secretly triumphant and mocking, which meant that she had no one who could help her. It was a long time before she could even contemplate the idea that her analyst could be anything else but triumphant if he was leaving her in a dependent and needy state. In this sense she had a deep conviction that her analyst was identical to herself.

Rosenfeld thought that the "narcissistic organization" is both an expression of and defense against envy. He makes the point that awareness of separateness from objects, an awareness that causes frustration, inevitably leads to envy. He goes on to say that "aggressiveness toward objects therefore seems inevitable in giving up the narcissistic position and it appears that the strength and persistence of omnipotent narcissistic object relations is closely related to the strength of the envious destructive impulses."

The narcissistic omnipotent aspects of the self often exert a powerful and seductive influence that makes it increasingly difficult to make any contact with the sane, needy aspects of the patient. This is particularly so in patients who are more psychotic, who often hate life and idealize death as a solution to all problems. It is as if they are being lured toward death as a state in which they will be free of all need and frustration. These patients often feel that the analyst is burdening them with the will to live, which they hate. Technically, this is, of course, an extremely difficult situation. Rosenfeld says, "Clinically it is essential to find and rescue the sane dependent part of the patient from its trapped position."

Mrs. A, whose case was presented earlier, had pursued a career in which she looked after psychiatric patients. In this situation she identified all the patients with the hated dependent parts of herself. She started analysis for "help with some problems," but she later explained that she believed she was having analysis in order to become a psychoanalyst. This matter was further complicated by the fact that she knew her analyst was undergoing analysis as part of his psychoanalytic training. One year after starting her analysis she had an acute breakdown and was admitted to the hospital, where her analysis was continued. From the patient's point of view this represented the enactment of her wish to enter the analyst and return to an idealized intrauterine state in which she could surrender all the burdens of living.

So this patient offered two alternatives in order to be able to continue to live. In one, she abolished all separateness and lived inside the analyst, "the psychoanalytic hospital," a state that was idealized but, in fact, represented helpless invalidism. The alternative to this was to take over omnipotently all the capacities of her analyst and become him, so mitigating her dependency and envy of the good object. This patient had taken many overdoses and was often in the grip of a delusional belief that the best solution to her difficulties was death, which she felt was an ideal state, promising complete freedom from frustration and the burdens of living. This apparently represented unconsciously the longed-for return to the intrauterine state. To achieve this, however, she had to die.

Segal (1983, 1984) has further explored the idealization of death in these patients. Freud (1924) used the term "nirvana" to describe the seductive pull of the death instinct. Again, to quote Laplanche and Pontalis (1983), "'nirvana' evokes a profound link between pleasure and annihilation." One of the most difficult technical problems with such patients is to distinguish the sane part of the patient, the part that genuinely wishes the analyst's help, from the destructive part, which construes help as total possession and control.

Six months after leaving the hospital, Mrs. A made some important steps in arranging to get herself looked after by attending a day-center (something she had previously refused to do) rather than, as she put it, "lying in bed all day," as she felt tempted to do. Attending a day-center meant to her cooperating with her analyst, but to do this also put her in great danger. In a session shortly before a break, she said after a prolonged silence, "I think I don't want you to know that I need you." When asked what had happened that had led her to say this, she replied that she had imagined herself in the hospital having a fight with a big powerful patient who suddenly turned on her and pinned her down. She then imagined a particular nurse (someone to whom she had previously turned for assistance and whose help she had appreciated) asking her if she was okay. She imagined herself replying that she was all right. It was this fantasy that had led her to say that she did not want the analyst to know that she needed him.

This material illustrates the constant difficulty such patients present, for when the patient has cooperated and felt helped in a realistic sense, she suddenly feels overpowered by an envious, ruthless, violent part of herself, against which she is helpless and which silences her wish for assistance. This material also illustrates how important it is that the helpful object be active in trying to get access to the silenced, needy part of the patient and not be bought off by the patient's statement that "everything is okay."

Further work in this session revealed that the patient believed—or as she put it, told herself—that if she spoke to the analyst about her fear of the break and her feeling that she really needed him, she would be accused of wanting to possess him and not permit him to go away. In this sense she was saying that the analyst would be unable to distinguish the sane, needy parts of herself from those aspects that sought ruthlessly to possess her objects.

The question of the "narcissistic gang" or "pathological organizations" that form the core of these narcissistic difficulties has received increased attention from Kleinian authors during the past fifteen years. Basically, all of them agree that there is a profound split between the sane, dependent parts of the self and a narcissistic, destructive organization that attempts to dominate it. Such patients often feel they can omnipotently take over various aspects of their objects and possess them to avoid dependence and envy. Sohn (1985) describes this as the formation of the "identificate." These authors agree, too, that the split is also a split between a psychotic and nonpsychotic part of the personality, which is present in all of us (see especially Bion, 1957). Steiner (1979) has emphasized the relative stability that some of these patients achieve; they remain stuck "on a border" between the paranoid/schizoid and the depressive positive. He has also illustrated (1982) how the more perverse parts of the personality try to seduce and corrupt the patient's sanity. Sometimes these patients feel they have to "do deals" with the destructive parts of themselves. Mrs. A, for example, often had to engage in obsessive counting rituals at various points in the session to ward off "catastrophe," which usually meant her death, the analyst's death, or her parents' death. She felt that if she attended to these procedures for a given amount of time the omnipotent force would be placated and she might then be allowed to turn toward her analyst and listen to him. Sometimes, however, she became identified with this destructive omnipotent organization and in this state violently attacked the analyst's words, breaking them up into syllables that went round and round in her mind until they became meaningless. This procedure was associated with considerable triumphant excitement.

CONCLUSION

In this essay we have followed the various threads that Freud brought together in his narcissism paper. We have tried to show that it is only with his later formulations, in "Mourning and Melancholia" and *Beyond the Pleasure Principle*, that he resolved some of the theoretical difficulties inherent in this paper. With the restoration of a dualistic theory of life and death instincts and his increasing realization of the importance of aggression, the whole question of narcissism took on a different complexion. To quote Wollheim (1971) again: "It is only in *Beyond the Pleasure Principle* that the problem raised by primary narcissism receives its dramatic resolution. From the evident relief with which Freud presented his new position, we can infer the strain under which he and his theory had been placed these last few years."

Freud did not abandon the notion of ego and object instincts but grouped them together as part of the life instincts now seen as together opposing the death instinct (Freud, 1940); and, although he accepted at certain times that the first erotic object is the mother's breast, he continued to assert the existence of a primary narcissistic stage preceding object relations. We have contended that we find this concept clinically not useful and theoretically ambiguous. To quote again from Laplanche and Pontalis (1983): "From a topographical point of view it is difficult to see just *what* is supposed to be cathected in primary narcissism."

Some writers have suggested that self-esteem is a healthy remnant of primary narcissism. To our way of thinking, however, healthy feelings of self-esteem have more to do with an internal situation in which there is a secure relation to a good internal object rather than an ideal one.

We have also elaborated Freud's more intuitive notion of the destructiveness of narcissism. This is seen in his linking of narcissism to a fundamental resistance to analytic work, his recognition that the narcissistic attitude is opposed to all creativity, and last, but perhaps most important, his understanding of the close link between narcissism and psychosis. These issues have been further explored within the Kleinian school.

From this perspective, stable nonnarcissistic object relations can be achieved only when the depressive position has been negotiated, for it is in this process that there is a differentiation of the self from object. The move toward the depressive position is a move in the direction of a situation in which love and gratitude toward the external and internal good object can oppose the hatred and envy of anything that is good and is felt to be external to the self. The increasing integration and separation resulting from a withdrawal of projections allow love for an object to be objectively perceived. It also means allowing the object to be out of the subject's control and acknowledging it in relation to other objects. So, by definition, the capacity to negotiate the depressive position also involves a capacity to negotiate the Oedipus complex and allow an identification with a creative parental couple.

In the work of Rosenfeld, Sohn, Segal, and Steiner, the relationship between the narcissistic and nonnarcissistic parts of the self becomes a central focus of the analytic work not only with psychotic patients but also with the less disturbed. The sane awareness of the need for nourishment from an external object that cannot be controlled by the self is the basis of libidinal love, and this bears some relation to Freud's description of anaclitic love. The narcissistic aspects of the personality do all they can to deny this reality (the reality of dependence) and advertise a superior state of narcissistic self-sufficiency. In some patients this idealization of narcissism takes the form of an idealization of death and a hatred of life.

To conclude, we would like to return to the original Narcissus myth. Narcissus is trapped, gazing at something that he subjectively believes is a lost loved object but that objectively is the idealized aspect of his own self. He believes himself to be in love. He dies of starvation, however, because he cannot turn away toward a real object from whom he might have been able to get what he really needed.

REFERENCES

Bion, W. (1957). Differentiation of the psychotic from the non-psychotic personalities. *Int. J. Psycho-Anal.*, 39:266–75.

Freud, S. (1900). *The Interpretation of Dreams. S.E.* 4 and 5.

———. (1905). *Three Essays on the Theory of Sexuality. S.E.* 7.

———. (1910a). *Leonardo da Vinci and a Memory of His Childhood. S.E.* 11.

———. (1910b). The psycho-analytic view of psychogenic disturbances of vision. *S.E.* 11.

———. (1911). Psycho-analytic notes on an autobiographical account of a case of paranoia (dementia paranoides). *S.E.* 12.

———. (1915). Instincts and their vicissitudes. *S.E.* 14.

———. (1916). Some character-types met with in psycho-analytic work. *S.E.* 14.

———. (1918). From the history of an infantile neurosis. *S.E.* 17.

———. (1920). *Beyond the Pleasure Principle. S.E.* 18.

———. (1923). *The Ego and the Id. S.E.* 19.

———. (1924). The economic problem of masochism. *S.E.* 19.

———. (1930). *Civilization and Its Discontents. S.E.* 21.

———. (1940). *An Outline of Psycho-Analysis. S.E.* 23.

Jones, E. (1955). *Sigmund Freud: Life and Works*. Vol. 2. London: Hogarth Press.

Klein, M. (1946). Notes on some schizoid mechanisms. In *The Writings of Melanie Klein*. Vol. 3, *Envy and Gratitude and Other Works*. London: Hogarth Press.

———. (1952). The origins of transference. In *The Writings of Melanie Klein*. Vol. 3, *Envy and Gratitude and Other Works*. London: Hogarth Press.

———. (1957). Envy and gratitude. In *The Writings of Melanie Klein*. Vol. 3, *Envy and Gratitude and Other Works*. London: Hogarth Press.

Laplanche, J., and Pontalis, J. B. (1983). *The Language of Psycho-Analysis*. London: Hogarth Press.

Meltzer, D. (1978). *The Kleinian Development*. Strath Tay, Perthshire: Clunie Press.

Rosenfeld, H. A. (1971). Clinical approach to the psycho-analytical theory of the life and death instincts: An investigation into the aggressive aspects of narcissism. *Int. J. Psycho-Anal.*, 59:215–21.

Sandler, J., Holder, A., and Dare, C. (1976). Narcissism and object love in the second phase of psychoanalysis. *Brit. J. Med. Psychol.* 49:267–74.

Segal, H. (1983). Some clinical implications of Melanie Klein's work: Emergence from narcissism. *Int. J. Psycho-Anal.*, 64:269–76.

———. (1984). De l'unité clinique du concept d'instinct de mort. In *La pulsion de mort*. Paris: Press Universitaire de France.

Sohn, L. (1985). Narcissistic organization, projective identification and the formation of the identificate. *Int. J. Psycho-Anal.* 66:201–13.

Steiner, J. (1979). The border between the paranoid schizoid and depressive positions. *Brit. J. Med. Psychol.*, 52:385–91.

———. (1982). Perverse relationships between parts of the self: A clinical illustration. *Int. J. Psycho-Anal.*, 63:241–51.

Wollheim, R. (1971). *Freud*. Glasgow: Fontana.

From Narcissism to Ego Psychology to Self Psychology

PAUL H. ORNSTEIN

By the mid-1960s clinical practice in psychoanalysis had once more forced the issue of narcissism to center stage. This first happened in 1914, when, after several smaller but significant steps, Freud was compelled to introduce narcissism as a broader concept. In so doing he revised his libido theory—then the conceptual foundation of psychoanalysis—and prepared for major clinical and theoretical changes ahead, which gave this work its pivotal importance.

Both the original introduction of the concept and its more recent reemergence shook the foundations of psychoanalytic theory and practice, apparently for similar reasons. The new theories, Freud's own and later Kohut's, threatened the existing central conflict theory of psychoanalysis (Ornstein, 1983; Wallerstein, 1983). Narcissism thus became embroiled in heated controversy, both historically and more recently. No wonder Gay characterized the 1914 essay as "subversive" of Freud's own previous theories (Gay, 1988, 338). Subversive it was. According to a careful and incisive study of the literature of that period (1914–22) by May-Tolzmann (1988), it was for this very reason that most analysts of the time reacted to it negatively, with bewilderment and confusion. Few could embrace even some elements enthusiastically, and most disregarded it, not knowing how to integrate these new ideas within the existing conflict theory. We also learn from Jones (1955, 302–06) that he and some of the others around Freud found the essay "disturbing." Jones's explanation is worth recounting: "It gave a disagreeable jolt to the theory of instincts on which psychoanalysis had hitherto worked. The observations on which the new conception of narcissism was founded were so unmistakable and easily confirmed that we had to accept it unreservedly, *but it was at once plain that something would have to be done about the theory to which we were accustomed*" (1955, 303; italics added).

Something was indeed done about the theory a few years later: further revisions were made to the libido theory (Freud, 1915, 1920, 1923), followed by a drastic reformulation of the basic model of psychoanalysis (Freud, 1923, 1926). Few would challenge the assessment today that it was a revolutionary move on Freud's part to replace the topographic model of the mind with the tripartite structural model, to exchange the paradigm of id psychology with the new paradigm of ego psychology—which led also to a marked shift in psychoanalytic technique. These changes were foreshadowed in the new theory of narcissism. Our current interest in it is heightened by the fact that we can now discover in it the nuclei not only of ego psychology (in which it culminated) but also of object-relations theory and self psychology.

Thus there can be no question that the ideas expressed by Freud in "On Narcissism" were fundamental for the subsequent development of psychoanalysis. It is necessary for our present purpose to examine Freud's essay in order to assess his 1914 and later ideas on narcissism in relation to their historical impact on the evolution of psychoanalysis and their current theoretical position in our field (Bing et al., 1959; Pulver, 1970; Moore, 1975). This will also permit us to put Kohut's contributions into their proper perspective.

Rereading "On Narcissism," registering retrospectively the transitional nature of its propositions, and following their subsequent fate should enable us to use psychoanalytic theories more freely as discardable tools of observation. A rereading provides all of us with a corrective emotional experience.

Before turning to the specific lessons of this essay, we should cast a quick glance at the circumstances under which it was written. Freud had reacted strongly to the recent defections of Adler (1911) and Jung (1913) and responded to their respective challenges in the two essays he worked on simultaneously in 1914, the paper on the history of the psychoanalytic movement and the paper on narcissism. In "On Narcissism" his response is considered more "objective" and more "scientific," albeit at times he gives the appearance of being bent on demolishing his opponents' arguments, giving them no recognition for the legitimate questions they have raised. Freud was at pains to repudiate Jung's assertion that the libido theory failed to account for certain psychotic phenomena in the Schreber case (Freud, 1911). But—as Jones saw it—at this point Freud "was hard put to it to demonstrate one side of the conflict, to define any non-narcissistic components of the ego. His scientific career received an apparent check" (1955, 303). So, for Freud, this was a serious matter, and it is understandable that in striking back he mobilized all his emotional and intellectual capacities. In the second paper, "On the History of the Psychoanalytic Movement," he attacks his opponents more openly and is, according to his own description, "fuming with rage."

These circumstances undoubtedly contributed to both the form and the content of the essay on narcissism. Nevertheless, it would be misleading to focus unduly on the precipitating events and see this essay primarily as a defensive effort on Freud's part. After all, some of the themes he now wove into a grand design of the theory of narcissism had already preoccupied him for some time and had slowly emerged from within, albeit frequently stimulated by external pressures. It is this emergence from within, the inner logic of the evolution of psychoanalysis, that we are interested in pursuing. In doing so, we shall discover that "On Narcissism" is rightly considered one of Freud's most important works. Although it stands at the transitional point between id psychology and ego psychology—and hence will soon be eclipsed by newer ideas—nevertheless it contains all those elements of Freud's thinking that propelled him toward his momentous paradigmatic change within a decade or so (Freud, 1923, 1926).

KEY ELEMENTS IN FREUD'S THEORY OF NARCISSISM: THE ROAD TO EGO PSYCHOLOGY

A proper entry into this complex and multilayered work for a brief historical and conceptual exploration demands that we place ourselves into the framework of the psychoanalysis of the time. Freud himself makes it easy for us to know where psychoanalysis stood in 1914. In order to distance himself from Adler as well as from Jung, Freud carefully delineated the field, to show that his opponents worked outside it (Freud, 1914a).

The theory of psychoanalysis, he said, was based on the clinical "facts" of transference and resistance. These were then accounted for with the theories of repression, the unconscious, and infantile sexuality. These facts and ideas determined the analyst's clinical focus. In his explorations the analyst searched for the patient's unconscious, infantile sexual wishes and fantasies (the manifestations of the sexual instincts), which were in conflict with his self-preservative needs (manifestations of the ego-instincts, which instigate their repression). It was the conflict that characterized the core activities of the analyst. So important and central was this theory of conflict that analysis was often referred to as a "conflict psychology par excellence" and this epoch in psychoanalysis as one of "id psychology."

Nevertheless, all along, Freud also concerned himself with the other side of the conflict: the ego (of ego-instincts), repression, censorship, the secondary process, and so on. He began to form the conviction that it was the development not only of the libido but also of the ego that contributed to the formation of neurotic as well as psychotic disturbances.

This was the psychoanalysis around 1914 into which the concept of narcissism was introduced. The theory evolved slowly over time, with several notable developments en route prior to 1914. All of them have been referred to by Strachey, Jones, and many others, so a brief mention here will suffice.

The Observational Referents and Pre-1914 Threads of the Concept of Narcissism

The term "narcissism" had been around since the turn of the century, inspired by the Greek myth of Narcissus. It referred, narrowly, to a perverse form of self-love, in which a person's own body was his love object. Freud first enlarged on this narrow conception in connection with Sadger's view on narcissistic object choice in some forms of homosexuality (Nunberg and Federn, 1967, 303–14). Freud remarked that "this [narcissism] is not an isolated phenomenon but a necessary developmental stage in the transition from auto-erotism to object-love. Being enamoured of oneself (of one's own genitals) is an indispensable stage of development" (312).

Freud then elaborated further on the issue of narcissistic object choice in some homosexual patients (Freud, 1909 [2nd edition of Freud, 1905], 1910) and made two additional contributions to narcissism. The first observation was in relation to the analysis of Schreber's paranoia (Freud, 1911); the second in relation to the analysis of animism and magic in *Totem and Taboo* (Freud, 1913).

In the 1911 paper, in attempting to understand the role of a repressed homosexual wish in paranoia, Freud made use of the concept of narcissism as he had recently enunciated it in his paper on Leonardo (Freud, 1910). He spelled out here, more clearly, what happened in this developmental stage between autoerotism and object-love: "There comes a time in the development of the individual at which he unifies his sexual instincts (which have hitherto been engaged in auto-erotic activities) in order to obtain a love-object; and he begins by taking himself, his own body, as his love-object, and only subsequently proceeds from this to the choice of some person other than himself as his object" (1911, 60–61). "This half-way phase," says Freud cautiously, "may perhaps be indispensable normally; but it appears that many people linger unusually long in this condition, and that many of its features are carried over by them into the later stages of their development. What is of chief importance in the subject's self thus chosen as a love-object may already be the genitals" (612). His psychoeconomic concept of the distribution of the libido (sending it out to invest objects and withdrawing it to reinvest the ego) enables Freud to interpret Schreber's "megalomania" as well as his withdrawal from the outside world, which culminates in the end-of-the-world delusion. In megalomania the withdrawal of the libido from objects is reinvested in the ego (secondary narcissism), and this investment is added to the original, infantile, "omnipotence of thought" (primary narcissism). The withdrawal of libido from objects leads to the endopsychic perception of the collapse of the patient's inner world, represented in the externalized end-of-the-world delusion.

Freud's second additional contribution to narcissism is found in *Totem and Taboo* (1913). Here the idea of the omnipotence of thought (the ideational component of primary narcissism) attains a larger role, since it opens the way for Freud to interpret the dynamic mechanism operative in animism and magic.

The Observational Referents and Main Constituents of the 1914 Theory of Narcissism

Perhaps the most impressive aspect of the theory woven together from these threads is its grand design: the large variety of clinical and theoretical issues that Freud brought under the umbrella of the widened concept of narcissism. With this expanded theory the explanatory power of narcissism increased considerably. No wonder we are able to trace most later significant concepts in psychoanalysis to this pivotal work.

1. Extreme or severe forms of narcissism. Freud begins his synthesis by focusing on the clinically observable pathological forms: autoerotism and perversion; schizophrenic megalomania and withdrawal from the external world (end-of-the-world delusion).
2. Milder and more widespread forms of narcissism. He then immediately introduces the idea that individual, milder features of extreme narcissistic attitudes are also observable in other clinical contexts—for example, in homosexual patients, whose object choice is narcissistic in nature. Freud remarks here that the more severe as well as the milder forms of narcissism constitute one of the limits of their susceptibility to analytic influence.
3. Ubiquitously present, normal forms of narcissism. The recognition of severe and mild forms of narcissism in various neurotic conditions led Freud to assume that narcissism "might claim a place in the regular course of human sexual development" (1914b, 73). Freud's basic definition of narcissism now emerges: he considers it to be fundamentally "not a perversion [that is, pathology], but the libidinal complement to the egoism of the instinct of self-preservation" (73–74), hence a part of normal development.

Freud buttresses these ideas by elaborating on what he had already said regarding schizophrenic megalomania and delusions. He adds his observations on the mental life of children and primitive peoples (whose behavior is governed by their belief in the "omnipotence of thought") as well as observations on people in love, which support his concept of the normal developmental significance of narcissism. His famous amoeba image (75) depicts his (psychoeconomic) notion about the distribution of the libido: the more is invested in the ego, the less becomes available for the cathexis of objects, and vice versa. He adds organic disease, hypochondria, and the erotic life of men and women to the observational data already referred to and sheds light on them from the vantage point of the distribution of the libido.

Hand in hand with this expansion of the libido theory went the expansion of his still rudimentary ego psychology; the two are inevitably intertwined in their development to a considerable extent. They influence each other: any change in the libido distribution appears to change the ego, and vice versa. Freud had already portrayed the ego as secondary process, as censor, as instigator of repression, resistance, reality testing; now he clearly saw it as the seat of the ego instincts, the reservoir of the libido, as well as the agency of its distribution.

But Freud went much further than this. Having thus far established the main observational and theoretical points of his new and encompassing theory of narcissism, he immediately put its explanatory power to further tests with unexpected, heuristically significant, and far-reaching results. As the high point of this essay, he introduced the ego-ideal (and in conjunction with it defined sublimation and idealization); further elaborated on the origin and development of conscience (and in conjunction with it explained the delusion of being watched, as well as its normal equivalents: self-observation, self-criticism, and "endopsychic research"—Freud's phrase for introspection); specified the ego (more precisely the self-regard of the ego) as the instigator of repression; considered the consequences of repression for the distribution of the libido; and finally discussed in detail the sources and functions of self-regard—all of which derive from narcissism and are accounted for in this new theory.

In the process of identifying the many vicissitudes of infantile (primary) narcissism, Freud wonders about the ultimate fate of ego-libido in normal adults. Could it be, he asks, that all of it becomes transformed into object-libido? That is not the case. He proceeds to describe how and under what circumstances this new agency, the ego-ideal, becomes set up within the ego. It develops in response to that internal watchman we call conscience, which itself arose in response to parental criticism and the criticism of a whole host of others, including society at large. In response to these criticisms and because of his own awakening critical judgment, the growing child can no longer retain the image of his actual ego as perfect. He seeks to recover this lost perfection in his ego-ideal; this absorbs and binds a considerable amount of his narcissistic and homosexual libido—which is thus turned back onto his ego, enriching it once more. Henceforth his satisfactions will come from living up to this ideal. The agency of "conscience" will measure the distance between the actual ego and the ego-ideal and will see to it that living up to the ego-ideal will afford the needed satisfaction.

The satisfaction will come from heightened self-regard (self-respect, self-esteem). This self-regard depends on the "size of the ego" and comes from various sources. It is in part primary (the residue of infantile narcissism); another part originates from omnipotence corroborated by experience (fulfillment of the ego-ideal); and the third part derives from satisfaction in love (the successful deployment of object-libido).

Having surveyed the 1914 essay in its broadest outlines, let us reflect for a moment on Freud's key propositions before we turn to the question of what happened to them in the years that followed.

Freud considered narcissism as the libidinal complement to the egoism of the instinct of self-preservation—lodged in the ego as its reservoir. As part of normal development narcissism is a stage between autoerotism and object-love, hence, an aspect of the libido theory. On that account it is governed by the "law" of the distribution of the libido from a fixed amount in its reservoir. This means the more that is invested in objects, the less remains in the ego, and vice versa. Here "self-love" is in opposition to "object-love." There are additional aspects to narcissism, however, that were of great importance to Freud. "Narcissistic object choice" and the "omnipotence of thoughts" cannot easily be fitted into the libido theory (especially its psychoeconomic aspects), although Freud used both of these as evidence for his theory of narcissism. In their narcissistic object choice, people "plainly seek themselves as love objects," says Freud. But the four different variations of those "love objects" indicate not the seeking of libidinal gratifications but the enhancement, strengthening, and completion of the self. In the omnipotence of their thoughts people have the aspect of their narcissism, which is the nidus of their ego development. (Ferenczi's developmental theory of the ego belongs here.) In this instance, too, it is hard to imagine the central relevance of the libido distribution. (Ferenczi did not place his theory of the development of the sense of reality into the libido theory.) Then there is one more significant component of narcissism, the aspect that is part of the formation of the ego-ideal, which is only partially understood from the vantage point of the libido theory. In what follows we should examine the fate of these ideas.

All in all it appears (retrospectively) that the single-axis theory of narcissism was already too narrow at its inception and could not easily accommodate these two apparently different trends of narcissism (see May-Tolzmann, 1988). Many of the complications of both theory and technique that appeared later seem to be related to these very issues.

THE FATE OF FREUD'S KEY IDEAS ON NARCISSISM IN HIS SUBSEQUENT WRITINGS

1. The centerpiece of the concept of narcissism, its psychoeconomic aspect, and the fact that it placed the core psychic conflict between the sexual instincts, on the one hand, and the ego-instincts, on the other, were already a significant departure from earlier formations, where the sexual instinct was opposed by the ego. Freud continued to reassess his libido theory (1915, 1917, but especially 1920 and 1923). One of the results of this reassessment was that after 1914 he located the aggressive drive within the ego instincts. With the introduction of the tripartite model of the mind, a further and perhaps even more drastic revision became necessary. Freud now considered that there were two kinds of basic drives, the sexual and the aggressive. The self-preservative drives were now subsumed under self-preservative ego-interests (and no longer considered drives), in the context of the new organization of the ego.
2. In this new ego psychology—which became the leading paradigm of psychoanalysis—the conflict was once more clearly formulated as between the drives (sexuality and aggression) and the controlling structures of the ego. The drives were organized in the "id," which was now seen as the original reservoir of the libido, replacing the ego in this respect. The ego obtained its narcissistic cathexis only secondarily, as it was withdrawn from object cathexes. There was a special agency within the new ego, the "superego"—the ultimate heir to the ego-ideal—which exerted its influence on the drives via the ego's defensive operations.
3. The concept of the ego-ideal went through a number of changes between 1914 and 1923, when it was essentially replaced by the superego in Freud's own writings. The development of the ego-ideal also involved "identifications," later to be called "narcissistic identifications" (Freud, 1917). Hence, this was (along with related mechanisms such as "projection" and "introjection") a point of departure not only for the concept of the superego but also, even more broadly, for object-relations theory in general. In other words, through these concepts Freud also laid the groundwork for an object-relations theory. But because object relations were seen as so tightly connected to the libido in most formulations, object-relations theory never emerged as a separate, full-fledged paradigm in Freud's own work. The same applies to self psychology, although it is

> less easy to pinpoint its precursors because Freud used *das Ich* (as ego) interchangeably with *das Selbst* (one's own person, the self). But as he began to give the ego (as an agency of the mind) a more precise definition as a system, this interchangeability—as Strachey traces it carefully—no longer worked well; it became confusing. Yet the self never attained a metapsychologic position in Freud's writings. The need for such a psychoanalytic conception of the self is evident in "On Narcissism," and Strachey does, indeed, slip up (deliberately) on a couple of occasions and translates *das Ich*: "The ego ideal also became a more clearly recognized bridge to the external world, to society, just as its successor, the superego, has become. But for a psychoanalytic understanding of group formation and group disintegration the superego appears to be no substitute for the ego ideal" (Freud, 1921).

After this cursory glance at where his ideas on narcissism led Freud, we may now step outside of his own frame of reference and look at his key concepts from the vantage point of a few selected later contributors who redirected our thinking on these subjects, without necessarily altering Freud's basic paradigm of ego psychology, and only (implicitly or explicitly, as the case may be) modifying (or in practice actually abandoning) his libido theory.

THE FATE OF THE CONCEPT OF NARCISSISM IN THE POST-FREUDIAN LITERATURE

The first major advance beyond Freud's definition of narcissism was undoubtedly Hartmann's "small" step of redefining it "as the libidinal cathexis not of the ego but of the self" (Hartmann, 1950, 85; 1956, 433). With this Hartmann accorded the self a significant position in psychoanalytic theory, albeit still only as a content of the tripartite mental apparatus. He also corrected the interchangeable use of the terms "ego," "self," and "one's own person." This change was necessary to bring the concept of narcissism into the structural framework and to place it within the tripartite model. It was also necessary because, in relation to narcissism, we are dealing with two very different issues in the different usages of *das Ich*: one in which we refer to functions and cathexes of the ego (as distinct from cathexes of different parts of the personality) and one in which we refer to the opposition of the cathexis of one's own person (self) to that of other persons (objects). Hartmann retained Freud's 1914 and 1923 psychoeconomic notion of the distribution of the libido and added to it aggression (without fully integrating it with the concept of narcissism). With the changes he did introduce, he opened the way for others to pursue further refinements of many psychoanalytic concepts. Important among these are the various efforts to establish a psychology of the self side by side with the well-established psychology of objects (for example, Jacobson, 1954, 1964; Lichtenstein, 1965). Kernberg dealt most extensively and penetratingly with narcissism from the standpoint of the dual-drive theory and ego psychology (1975 and later writings).

Among the many examples of the consequences of Hartmann's conceptual separation of self from ego is the successful reclaiming and redefinition of the ego-ideal and the definition of the ideal self (Sandler, Holder, and Meers, 1963). Freud's new concept of the superego did not fully cover the functions assigned to the ego-ideal in its various interim formulations; and a certain ambiguity remained in Freud's own writings regarding the relationship between the two. Sandler and his colleagues did delineate Freud's changing definition of the ego ideal between 1914 and 1923 and were able to expand the concept and make it clinically relevant.

Another fundamental corrective effort involves the psychoeconomic principle of the distribution of the libido (Joffe and Sandler, 1968). As we have seen, Freud was able to use this idea to explain a large variety of psychotic, neurotic, and normal phenomena, at the same time demonstrating the encompassing usefulness of his newly revised libido theory. But this view was essentially quantitative, and what is needed in clinical psychoanalysis is a qualitative approach. It is here that Joffe and Sandler showed us the limitations of the concept of libido distribution with the aid of brief, but highly evocative clinical vignettes (1968, 57–58). They redirected our search for the understanding of narcissistic disturbances to ego-states or affect-states:

> The states which are important in any consideration of narcissism are not only determined by the state of the drives nor can they be more than partially understood in terms of the hypothetical distribution of energic cathexes. . . . The clinical understanding of narcissism and its disorders should be explicitly oriented towards a conceptualization in terms of a metapsychology of affects, attitudes, values and the ideational contents associated with these, from the standpoint of both present function and genetic development. (63)

Their idea of focusing on affect-states, rather than on drive discharge (without neglecting the latter) and its economics, is a major shift in psychoanalysis. This shift appears to narrow the applicability of the libido theory in general and in narcissistic disturbances in particular.

Since this is such a crucial shift, let us look at the review by Joffe and Sandler of the relevant literature (1968, 60–62), which points in the same direction. They noted that Freud himself, in his definition of narcissism, referred to it as the libidinal complement to egoism and that Freud's "descriptions in this connection always involved statements referring to attitudes of what later came to be called the ego" (59). Jacobson also takes the view that attempts to link such concepts as affects, values, self-esteem, and self-devaluation to quantities of energy make for extreme complication (1954, 1964). Fenichel spoke of "narcissistic needs" and "narcissistic supplies" without linking them to quantities of energy (1945, 40–41). He also defined self-esteem and self-love as connected with infantile omnipotent feelings, rather than drive-related experiences (39). Finally A. Reich's focus on ego-states, ego-attitudes, and defensive formations and their mode of regulation also indicates that these are paramount in narcissistic disturbances (1960).

Joffe and Sandler proceeded to formulate the nature of narcissistic pathology in terms of its underlying painful affect and the patient's symptomatology and behavior as efforts to deal with it (1968, 65). One of the many advantages of their proposition is that affects and attitudes not only capture the quality of subjective experiences but also become available to the empathic observer for use in the interpretive process.

We should take a quick look at one of their clinical images in transition to Kohut's self psychology: "we may assess a child who has problems over exhibitionism from the point of view of neurotic conflict over the discharge of exhibitionistic drive impulses." In this assessment, they say, "we also include the consideration of the function of exhibitionism in connection with the maintenance by the child of a particular type of object-relationship, and its function as a possible technique for gaining admiration and praise in order to do away with underlying feelings of unworthiness, inadequacy and guilt" (56).

We would have to raise the following questions: Could these two views of the psychopathology of that particular child be held simultaneously? Are they complementary or antithetical? If complementary, which should be interpreted first? Does the sequence matter? If antithetical, how would we decide which view is the relevant one in this case? We will leave these questions unanswered for the moment and return to them after we have surveyed Kohut's contributions to the issue of narcissism and self psychology.

In addition to these specific questions, however (which may be viewed as reflecting the core clinical problems in our field in connection with the issues of narcissism), we should add some observations about what we were left with in the mid-1960s to all that had already been contributed to the topic of narcissism since 1914.

The theoretical advances are easier to recognize and appreciate. They are substantial, even if still confusing (Moore, 1975). But what about the clinical issues? It is here that we run into more difficulties and sharper controversies. To put it in a nutshell: the idea of narcissism as basically normal has been stated clearly from 1914 on. But its replacement within the single-axis (autoerotism, narcissism, object-love) theory of the development of the libido (Ornstein, 1974) caused it to be viewed as something pathological to be overcome, in spite of repeated claims to the contrary. Remnants of narcissism within the ego were fixations to be loosened and transformed into object-love. A part of the original narcissism was "saved" in the structure of the ego-ideal. Self-esteem (now linked to the function of the ego-ideal) as a carrier of normal narcissism did not come fully into its own in the treatment process. This is because in analysis the focus largely remained on the conflicts emanating from the sexual and aggressive drives and the superego-inspired defenses of the ego, even when embedded in an object-relations theory. And here is another aspect of the definition that stood in the way of clinical therapeutic progress: narcissism—that is, the "narcissistic attitude" of patients (as it was conceived)—seriously limited the extent to which the patient could be influenced through psychoanalysis.

These particular handicaps (built into the theory of narcissism) retarded further progress both in theory and in practice for some time. This was inevitable, as I see it, because essentially all new formulations retained the single-axis theory of narcissism, thereby continuing to view narcissistic manifestations primarily as defenses and resistances (Ornstein, 1974). Joffe and Sandler (1968), however, show that they are hovering over a significant advance. In the way they present their ideas regarding their patient's exhibitionism, they are implicitly searching for a second line of development, because they do not necessarily consider the narcissistic issues in their example as defensive against the primary drive-related conflicts. Although this is significant, in the end it does not lead them to the step of breaking with the single-axis theory.

Where in all this are the transferences? Considering them as central guiding principles to diagnosis ultimately breaks the logjam.

KEY ELEMENTS IN KOHUT'S THEORY OF NARCISSISM: THE ROAD TO SELF PSYCHOLOGY

Kohut linked his own work to one of Freud's statements: "The disturbances to which a child's original narcissism is exposed, the reactions with which he seeks to protect himself from them and the paths into which he is forced in doing so—these are the themes which I propose to leave on one side, as an important field of work which still awaits exploration" (Freud, 1914b, 92). Kohut's writings detail these explorations extensively (1966, 1968, 1971).

But Kohut did not begin by sorting out the theory of narcissism, although he found Hartmann's definition helpful and considered narcissism (at first) to be the libidinal investment of the body-mind-self. Rather, he began his work with the psychoanalytic exploration of patients with narcissistic personality disturbances and gave detailed descriptions of their transference. It was from the study of the working-through process of these (then called narcissistic) transferences that Kohut derived his basic clinical and metapsychologic concepts. A thumbnail sketch of these transferences should serve as a background for the ensuing reflections on some of the concepts that constituted the building blocks of his theory of the self.

What Kohut found in the analyses of his patients was that their expectations, needs, demands, and fantasies clustered around two main issues (to which he later added a third). First, the patients expressed their need for someone to serve as an echo, and for affirmation, approval, admiration, and the bolstering of their self-esteem. The analyst mattered only to the extent that he could or could not be experienced by the patient as available to perform these needed functions. This "mirror transference," once established, effected an improvement in the patient's functioning—as if the analyst served as the necessary "psychic glue." Whenever the patient was disappointed in his expectations, as was inevitable, the disruptions in the transference were reflected either in the return of disturbed functioning or in outright fragmentation. Therefore the analytic efforts had to be focused on the immediate precipitating cause of the disruption (commonly related to some form of "unempathic" response by the analyst). Thus the reconstructions of the intra-analytic precipitants (and with it, often, the genetic precursors for the patient's vulnerability and proneness to fragmentation) would restore the cohesiveness of the transference.

The second cluster of experiences, which Kohut called an "idealizing transference," is expressed in the need of some patients to attach themselves to the analyst by putting him on a pedestal and experiencing him as all-knowing, all-powerful, and perfect so that they might partake of that greatness and perfection. These expectations and needs, when experienced as having been met, also lend the patient a modicum of cohesiveness and vitality as well as inner calm. But here, too, disappointments are inevitable, and once the patient's proneness to fragmentation is traumatically touched on, narcissistic rage ensues, and the other well-known consequences of a disrupted idealizing transference may follow. And here, too, the analyst's response has to be given in the form of reconstructive interpretations.

The details of these transference experiences and their working through, their felicitous or unfavorable outcome, permitted Kohut to reconstruct the infantile and childhood traumas that left the psyche with insufficient structure or with excessive defensive structures—those characteristic manifestations of "narcissistic pathology" that he observed and described in depth. Kohut postulated that the two transferences, briefly sketched above, arose in relation to the infantile "grandiose self" (mobilizing a mirror transference) and the "idealized parent imago" (mobilizing an idealizing transference). In this respect Kohut's theory of transference as arising on the basis of repressed and/or disavowed infantile needs and wishes was not different from Freud's postulation of the Oedipus complex as the basis for the transference neurosis. The clinical and theoretical equivalence of these three infantile structures is of significance because now patients with narcissistic personality disorders could also be considered analyzable. That is, not only their defensive narcissism but also (and more important) their narcissistic defects or deficits (expressions of fixations on one or another, or both of these archaic narcissistic constellations) could now be the central focus of their analyses. The assumption of two separate lines of development for narcissism and object-love was Kohut's first theoretical innovation. It was based on the observation that the working through of these transferences led to the transformation of archaic narcissism to more mature forms, without the mobilization of an oedipal transference neurosis. Thus he opted for separating out the narcissistic attitudes and ego-states from classical libido theory (while retaining the idea of the libidinal nature of narcissism).

The clinical and technical implications of this highly unpopular change were of fundamental importance. The analyst was no longer to expect (and subtly push) the patient to give up a narcissistic position in favor of object-love. He had to conduct the analysis in such a climate and in such a manner as to facilitate the transformation of archaic to more mature forms of narcissism. In the mirror transference this meant the attainment of a more stable self-esteem regulation; an increased capacity for the pursuit of one's goals and purposes; and an increased ability to enjoy the functions of one's body and mind. In the idealizing transference this transformation meant the acquisition of self-soothing, self-calming, self-controlling, and drive-channeling capacities, based on the firming up of the matrix of the ego and on "transmuting internalization" of values and ideals.

We should point here to a few of the most significant differences among Freud, most of the post-Freudian literature, and Kohut's formulations. The first issue concerns the quality of the libido. (We should remember here that when Kohut speaks of libido, he means "abstractions referring to the *psychological* meaning of the essential experience" [1971, 39; italics added].) For Kohut the target or direction (whether toward the object or the self) of the libidinal investment was not the determining factor of the quality of the libido. He assumed two different qualities to begin with, the narcissistic and object-libido. In this manner he emphasized the qualitative (affective) aspects of human experience. By recognizing narcissistic (later self-object) transference, he could demonstrate that "the other" could be invested with narcissistic libido—that is, could be experienced as part of the patient's self. For Kohut object-instinctual libido could occasionally invest the self—for example, during objective self-assessment or in incipient schizophrenia. This qualitative differentiation is important since for Freud the object was either invested with libido or not, which led to a variety of inaccurate clinical observations. For instance, having one or two friends might mean intense object cathexis, and an abundance of them might still mean a narcissistic one.

Kohut considered narcissism per se as the normal "fuel" for structure building. Pathology in this context is not a pathology of narcissism but a pathology of the structures of the self (deficiencies, defects, or defensive structures), owing to inadequate narcissistic cathexis, not to excessive amounts or pathological forms of narcissism.

It was from careful clinical observations (richly detailed in all of Kohut's writings) that the assumption of two "separate lines of development for narcissism and object love," the "selfobject transferences," the developmental concept of the selfobject, and structure building through "transmuting internalizations" were derived.

The revision of clinical theory and metapsychology had to lead to a revision of developmental theory. In this connection Kohut could answer Freud's question regarding "the disturbances to which a child's original narcissism is exposed" by reconstructing the development of the "grandiose self" and the "omnipotent, idealized object," both of which are archaic structures that attempt to deal with the normally arising early disturbances to primary narcissism. The archaic idealizations will later be transformed into the narcissistic dimension of the superego, ensuring the power of its values and ideals—a different way of conceiving what Freud called the ego-ideal. In describing the developmental and clinical vicissitudes of these archaic structures, Kohut offered a new view of health and illness in which self-esteem regulation plays a dominant role.

Kohut did not disregard the drives (only drive theory, which is another matter) but saw them in a different light and integrated them within his self psychology. He still considered the duality of libido and aggression a good way to group important inner experiences. The "mirroring" and "idealizing" needs of infancy and childhood, however, appeared to him to be the primary emotional nutrients of psychological development. Freud assumed the inevitability of opposition between sexual and aggressive drives, on the one hand, and the ego's defensive operations (at the behest of the superego), on the other, as primary: the conflict is built into the mental apparatus. Kohut, however, assumed on the basis of his clinical experiences that infants are born preadapted to elicit what they need from their empathic selfobject environment. The selfobject's responses are never perfect; conflicts will always arise. But more important, severe and prolonged selfobject failures will lead to the incomplete or malformed structuralization of the psyche. Here is a crucial (albeit still controversial) difference; the primacy of conflict versus the primacy of deficit and secondary conflict are at the center of contemporary polemics.

From this position it was only a very small step, but a momentous one. to leave narcissism behind and speak about the development of the self from the self-selfobject matrix, without reference to a libido theory. From this vantage point the vicissitudes of the development of the grandiose self, which led at its end point to the pole of self-assertive aggression, and the development of the idealized parent imago, which led to the pole of ideals and values, suggested to Kohut the image of the two poles of the self: the bipolar self. Placed at the center of the psychological universe, the bipolar self could now be seen as a superordinate structure, whose study gave Kohut the impetus to revamp psychoanalysis, just as Freud's new image of the ego in 1923 gave him the impetus to revamp the psychoanalysis of his time.

We should now, in closing, respond to the questions we asked regarding Joffe and Sandler's clinical image of the exhibitionistic child from a self psychological perspective. Faced with exactly the same dilemma, we would be guided by the predominant, sustained transference. This would help us decide whether it was the neurotic conflict over the exhibitionistic wishes that was primary or the need for admiration and praise, whether we were witnessing essentially an oedipal transference (or a regression from it) or a mirror transference. Only the transference context could guide us here. In the case of the mirror transference "drive discharge" would be secondary, in the service of narcissistic needs—for example, the attempt "to do away with underlying feelings of unworthiness, inadequacy, and guilt," as Joffe and Sandler put it, or shame, from a self psychological vantage point. If we are dealing with a mirror transference, interpretations that are focused on drive discharge as if it were primary would make matters worse clinically. In that sense the two views would be antithetical. Drive discharge as a failed effort at restoring self-esteem (when understood from the vantage point of the self) would be very much to the point. This is what Joffe and Sandler mean, I believe, when they speak of this child's maintenance of a particular type of object relationship as well as his technique for gaining admiration and praise.

These are questions that require further empirical study for clearer and more reliable answers. An ongoing exploration of the transferences is crucial, but we also need a clinical epistemology to make possible comparative assessments of the approaches dictated by ego psychology, object-relations theory, and self psychology. At present we do not have such an epistemology (Ornstein, 1987).

REFERENCES

Bing, J. F., et al. (1959). The metapsychology of narcissism. *Psychoanal. Study Child*, 14:9–28.

Fenichel, O. (1945). *The Psychoanalytic Theory of Neurosis*. New York: W. W. Norton.

Freud, S. (1905). *Three Essays on the Theory of Sexuality*. *S.E.* 7:125–243.

———. (1910). *Leonardo da Vinci and a Memory of His Childhood*. *S.E.* 11:59–137.

———. (1911). Psycho-analytic notes on an autobiographical account of a case of paranoia (dementia paranoides). *S.E.* 12:3–82.

———. (1913). *Totem and Taboo. S.E.* 13:1–161.

———. (1914a). On the history of the psycho-analytic movement. *S.E.* 14:3–66.

———. (1914b). On narcissism: An introduction. *S.E.* 14:67–102.

———. (1915). Instincts and their vicissitudes. *S.E.* 14:109–40.

———. (1917). Mourning and melancholia. *S.E.* 14:237–60.

———. (1920). *Beyond the Pleasure Principle. S.E.* 18:3–64.

———. (1921). *Group Psychology and the Analysis of the Ego. S.E.* 8:67–143.

———. (1923). *The Ego and the Id. S.E.* 19:3–66.

———. (1926). *Inhibitions, Symptoms and Anxiety. S.E.* 20:3–74.

Gay, P. (1988). *Freud: A Life for Our Time*. New York: W. W. Norton.

Hartmann, H. (1950). Comments on the psychoanalytic theory of the ego. *Psychoanal. Study Child*, 5:74–96.

———. (1956). The development of the ego concept in Freud's work. *Int. J. Psycho-Anal.*, 37:425–38.

Jacobson, E. (1954). The self and the object world. *Psychoanal. Study Child.*, 9:75–127.

———. (1964). *The Self and the Object World*. New York: International Universities Press.

Joffe, W. G., and Sandler, J. (1968). Some conceptual problems involved in the consideration of disorders of narcissism. *J. Child Psychother.*, 2:56–66.

Jones, E. (1955). *The Life and Work of Sigmund Freud*. Vol. 2. New York: Basic Books.

Kernberg, O. (1975). *Borderline Conditions and Pathological Narcissism*. New York: Jason Aronson.

Kohut, H. (1966). Forms and transformations of narcissism. *J. Amer. Psychoanal. Assn.*, 14:243–72.

———. (1968). The psychoanalytic treatment of personality disorders. *Psychoanal. Study Child*, 23:86–113.

———. (1971). *The Analysis of the Self*. New York: International Universities Press.

———. (1984). *How Does Analysis Cure?* Chicago: University of Chicago Press.

Lichtenstein, H. (1964). The role of narcissism in the emergence and maintenance of primary identity. *Int. J. Psycho-Anal.*, 45:49–56.

May-Tolzmann, U. (1988). Ich- und Narcissmustheorie zwischen 1914 und 1922 im Spiegel der "Internationalen Zeitschrift fuer Psychoanalyse" Manuscript.

Moore, B. E. (1975). Toward a clarification of the concept of narcissism. *Psychoanal. Study Child*, 30:243–76.

Nunberg, H., and Federn, E. (1967). *Minutes of the Vienna Psychoanalytic Society*. Vol. 2, *1908–1910*. New York: International Universities Press.

Ornstein, P. H. (1974). On narcissism: Beyond the introduction. Highlights of Heinz Kohut's contributions to the psychoanalytic treatment of narcissistic personality disorders. *Annual of Psychoanal.*, 2:127–49.

———. (1983). Discussion of papers by Goldberg, Stolorow, and Wallerstein. In J. D. Lichtenberg and S. Kaplan, eds., *Reflections of Self Psychology*. Hillsdale, N.J.: Analytic Press, pp. 339–84.

———. (1987). How do we know what we know in psychoanalysis? Groping steps towards a clinical epistemology. Keynote address to the Academy of Psychoanalysis, New York City, January 15.

Pulver, S. (1970). Narcissism. *J. Amer. Psychoanal. Assn.*, 18:319–41.

Reich, A. (1960). Pathological forms of self-esteem regulation. *Psychoanal. Study Child*, 15:215–34.

Sandler, J., Holder, A., and Meers, D. (1963). The ego ideal and the ideal self. *Psychoanal. Study Child*, 18:139–58.

Wallerstein, R. S. (1983). Self psychology and "classical" psychoanalytic psychology—the nature of their relationship: A review and overview. In J. D. Lichtenberg and S. Kaplan, eds., *Reflections on Self Psychology*. Hillsdale, N.J.: Analytic Press, pp. 313–37.

Narcissism as a Form of Relationship

HEINZ HENSELER

INTRODUCTION AND THESIS

The title of Freud's paper is confusing. Why "Introduction"? We know from Jones that Freud, following a suggestion of Sadger, had introduced the term "narcissism" as early as 1909 at a meeting of the Vienna Psychoanalytical Society on November 10. It first appears in writing in 1910 in a note added to the second edition of the *Three Essays on the Theory of Sexuality*, in which Freud states, in connection with homosexuality, "the future inverts, in the earliest years of their childhood, pass through a phase of very intense but short-lived fixation to a woman (usually their mother), and . . . after leaving this behind, they identify themselves with a woman and take *themselves* as their sexual object. That is to say, proceeding from a basis of narcissism, they look for a young man who resembles them and whom *they* may love as their mother loved *them*" (145 n.).

Similar ideas are to be found in his study of Leonardo da Vinci (1910) and in the case of Schreber (1911). Here, however, as in *Totem and Taboo* (1912–13), he sees narcissism as deriving from a different source: he considered that sexual component instincts already existed at an early stage when there were still no objects. He called this the stage of autoerotism. Freud now assumed that the individual, in his development, "begins by taking himself, his own body, as his love-object, and only subsequently proceeds from this to the choice of some person other than himself as his object" (60). The self would then be the first object. He called this the stage of narcissism. (He subsequently abandoned the idea of a phase of autoerotism.) Finally, in 1914, he introduced narcissism as the original stage of development. He concedes, "we are bound to suppose that a unity comparable to the ego cannot exist in the individual from the start; the ego has to be developed. The auto-erotic instincts, however, are there from the very first; so there must be something added to auto-erotism—a new psychical action—in order to bring about narcissism" (1914, 76–77). But there is no further mention of autoerotism in this paper, and narcissism is seen as primary.

Balint (1960) points out that Freud allowed the different versions of the developmental history of narcissism to subsist side by side even after 1914. One therefore wonders what is ultimately to be taken as primary: the object relation, autoerotism, or narcissism? Or does the fact that these coexist without clarification have a deeper meaning?

My thesis will be that Freud's indecision in this regard is by no means fortuitous but is bound up with the phenomenon of narcissism. Contrary to Freud's equation of narcissism and self-love, I shall try to show that an object-relations structure, albeit of an archaic kind, resides in all narcissistic phenomena. This thesis is not new. What may be new is the demonstration that it follows inevitably from what Freud himself says in "On Narcissism: An Introduction."

NARCISSISM AND SELF-LOVE

In 1914, when Freud wrote the paper with which we are concerned, his interest was directed primarily toward the theory of instincts. The major contributions to metapsychology—"The Unconscious," "Instincts and Their Vicissitudes," and "Repression"—were to appear later, in 1915. The particular aspect of the theory of instincts that interested Freud at this time was the concept of libido, which had undergone a change. In contrast to his view in the *Three Essays* (1905), he no longer regarded libido as excitation that arose in phases and had to be discharged but viewed it as a large reservoir of energy present at all times and constant in quantity, which had to be allocated. In the first section of his paper, Freud therefore tries to explain narcissism in terms of libidinal economy.

Psychopathological phenomena, such as narcissistic perversion, homosexuality, the megalomania of the paraphrenic, and hypochondria, as well as "individual features of the narcissistic attitude . . . in many people who suffer from other disorders" (73), and also phenomena of everyday life, such as the "omnipotence of thought," the "thaumaturgic force of words," magic techniques, human behavior in physical pain or discomfort (such as toothache) or in sleep, and in particular a special type of object choice—all these had led him to suppose "that an allocation of the libido such as deserved to be described as narcissism . . . might claim a place in the regular course of human sexual development" (73).

His "strongest reasons" were therefore based on the discovery of a type of object choice "which we were not prepared for finding." Freud discovered "especially clearly in people whose libidinal development has suffered some disturbance, such as perverts and homosexuals," that they choose their future love object not on the model of their mother but on that of their own person: "They are plainly seeking *themselves* as a love-object." Freud calls the first type of object choice the anaclitic type and the second the narcissistic type; he assumes "that both kinds of object choice are open to each individual, though he may show a preference for one or the other" (88).

He then expounds his ideas on the distribution of the two types of object choice in men and women and attributes the charm of narcissistic women, children, cats, the large beasts of prey, great criminals, and humorists to their narcissistic self-contentment and inaccessibility. "It is as if we envied them for maintaining a blissful state of mind—an unassailable libidinal position which we ourselves have since abandoned" (89).

Freud endeavors to describe narcissism principally in terms of libidinal economy, in metaphors of sending out and drawing back, cathexis, depletion, concentration, damming-up, giving off, persistence, and so on, of amounts of libido. He speaks of secondary narcissism wherein libido is withdrawn from persons and things in the external world and directed toward the ego. The resulting megalomania, however, is "no new creation; on the contrary, it is, as we know, a magnification and plainer manifestation of a condition which had already existed previously"—that is, the condition of primary narcissism. Hence secondary narcissism is "superimposed upon a primary narcissism that is obscured by a number of different influences. . . .

Thus we form the idea of there being an original libidinal cathexis of the ego, from which some is later given off to objects, but which fundamentally persists and is related to the object-cathexes much as the body of an amoeba is related to the pseudopodia which it puts out" (75).

NARCISSISM AND RELATIONSHIP

Freud soon encounters limitations in his attempt to describe narcissistic phenomena in terms of libidinal economy. Although these are not considered explicitly, he turns increasingly, particularly in the second and third sections of his paper, to concepts that denote emotional states and fantasies stemming from the experiential world of relationships. Already in the first section, he is compelled to resort to ideas such as megalomania, the omnipotence of thought, the thaumaturgic force of words, the magical power of gestures, fantasies of the end of the world, and so on. All these notions imply a relation to an object. Megalomania presupposes the comparison: I have to feel bigger than others. Inherent in the omnipotence of thought is the possibility of exerting influence over objects or the surrounding world, and the same applies to the thaumaturgic force of words and the magical power of gestures. Freud interprets the fantasy of the end of the world as the experience of complete object loss.

I consider, however, that the phenomena described by Freud as narcissistic are incompletely interpreted in terms of self-love, and I should like to illustrate this by citing Freud's explanation of primary narcissism, the fundamental concept of his theory of narcissism, on an understanding of which all further considerations depend.

Primary Narcissism as an Archaic Form of Relationship

Freud undertakes to demonstrate the existence of "a primary cathexis of libido [in] the ego" (75). As evidence, he cites observations of the attitude of affectionate parents toward "His Majesty the Baby." "Parental love," he claims, "which is so moving and at bottom so childish, is nothing but the parents' narcissism born again, which, transformed into object-love, unmistakably reveals its former nature" (91). This interpretation is based on the assumption that the parents identify with "His Majesty the Baby," thus reliving their own stage of grandiose and unclouded self-love.

Is this interpretation correct? I believe it is only partly so. By their efforts, the parents do indeed introduce a relationship constellation in which the baby really can feel marvelous. They identify, however, not only with the baby but with the entire interaction of which they are a part.

Freud describes this process in explicit terms: the parents envelop the child not only in loving care and protection but also in wishful dreams of greatness and uniqueness in which they themselves take part. They are under a "compulsion to ascribe every perfection to the child—which sober observation would find no occasion to do—and to conceal and forget all his shortcomings" (91).

The parents' concerns are in fact grandiose: illness, death, renunciation, and the laws of nature and of society are not to touch the child, who will "once more really be the centre and core of creation" (91). The center and core of creation, however, must have something around it if it is to be able to experience itself as the center and core. In reality, the parents' efforts are directed toward the creation of a relationship in which laws do not apply, boundaries dissolve, and subject and object interpenetrate—a relationship in which the bliss of oneness and eternal harmony beckons. This is what they identify with.

Digression: The Form of Relationship of Primary Identification

What Freud calls primary narcissism is inconceivable without an object relation. The object relation concerned is certainly relatively undifferentiated, but it is one for which every human being has a great longing. "As always where the libido is concerned, man has here again shown himself incapable of giving up a satisfaction he had once enjoyed" (94); indeed, "the development of the ego consists in a departure from primary narcissism and gives rise to a vigorous attempt to recover that state" (100).

The international psychoanalytic literature includes an almost unknown paper by Lou Andreas-Salomé (1921),[1] a friend of Nietzsche and Rilke and pupil of Freud from 1912, in which she strongly emphasizes the fact that narcissism is both self-directed and object-directed. She also notes that narcissism is "not merely a primitive point of departure of development but remains as a kind of fundamental continuity in all the subsequent object-cathexes of the libido" (1962, 3). She writes that the "dual disposition of

1. Published in the *Psychoanalytic Quarterly* in 1962.

narcissism . . . [is] turned on the one hand toward self-assertion and on the other toward abandonment in the passive boundless state" (11). She describes the primary narcissistic relationship as "passive absorption in the yet undifferentiated unity" (5). It is the relation of the subject to the object in the sense of the "one-and-all" (15), the primal experience of universal participation, as she puts it.

Plainly without knowing Lou Andreas-Salomé's paper, Balint (compare 1937, 1960) takes up the same idea. He describes the form of relationship in such terms as "harmonic fusion," "intimate penetration," and "mix-up" and illustrates this coalescence of self and object through the images of air and water in the gills of fish (compare also his interpretation of "philobatism").

Balint describes the most primitive form of the primary object in terms of substance and extension without boundaries, on the model of amniotic fluid. It is only gradually that the substances, mixed up in a friendly fashion, turn into objects with solid contours and sharp boundaries. This is why the primary object is also symbolized by water, earth, air, and (more rarely) fire. The ultimate goal of all libidinal striving is to recover the original harmony. This also applies to orgasm. The goal of the mutual orgasm is not only a summit of pleasure but also a summit of mutuality, comparable to the *unio mystica*. Many people can also describe the experience of mutual orgasm in images of unification, coalescence, and the abolition of boundaries.

Countless images of this kind are to be found in the language of religion. One need think only of Romain Rolland's "oceanic feeling"—"a feeling as of something limitless, unbounded" (Freud, 1930, 64, 72). Religious experience makes extensive use of regression to the primary narcissistic state. It is not by chance that Judaism, Christianity, and Islam were born in the desert and that Buddhism stems from meditative experiences. It is not for nothing that one speaks of "submerging oneself" in prayer. The Christian conceptions of heaven involve a never-ending ecstatic experience of happiness, but in an object relation in which the believer joins with the choirs of angels in the glorification of God.

Andreas-Salomé (1921) considers that this primary narcissistic experience also applies to the realm of art. In her view, the poet must have access to the world of experience in which subject and object are not yet clearly separated and in which identifications are predominant. The artist regresses "to these universally inclusive and essential elements . . . on which alone the social enjoyment of art also is based" (24). The artist needs regression to the most infantile state, albeit for the purpose of creativity while in that state. The poet creates from something already present in him from which he merely removes the veil. For this reason, the successfully completed work of art is not the work of a narcissistically isolated subject in an object-free space but the achievement of one who, by his creative act, makes it possible for others to identify without anxiety with his experience (or what I would call his "object-experience").

The other major sphere of cultural achievement, in addition to religion and art, is science, which is in general understood in extremely rationalistic terms. But since Kuhn (1962), if not before, we have become aware that, contrary to the assumptions of most theorists of science, science develops not continuously but in jumps. Kuhn speaks of "changes of paradigms." These are new conceptions of access to one and the same object or phenomenon. Changes of paradigms are induced by observations that are no longer covered by the old paradigms. The creative act, however, lies in a sudden novel understanding of the same phenomenon in a new theoretical frame of reference. Examples of changes of paradigms are Freud's abandonment of the topographical model in favor of the structural model and, after Freud, the change to the object-relations model. Other examples are Einstein's discovery of the theory of relativity, the Copernican revolution, and Darwin's idea of evolution. In my view, such creative acts are based on a profound familiarity with the object of research—a familiarity that may well have the quality of a "primary narcissistic relation."

In 1921, Freud characterized "empathy" as a form of identification but cautiously added, "we are far from having exhausted the problem of identification" (1921, 108). I wonder whether this caution is appropriate. What we do every day in our analyses—alternately empathizing with our patients and reflecting in conceptual and theoretical terms—in my opinion approaches primary identification. After all, it is not for nothing that we also speak of "trial identifications."

In *Group Psychology and the Analysis of the Ego* (1921), Freud returns to the (primary) narcissistic form of relationship connected with the collective feeling of oneness of the individuals in the group. He now distinguishes between object choice and identification and between the wish to have the object and the wish to be like the object. In regard to identification, he also distinguishes between a primary and a secondary form. Secondary identification he attributes to the introjection of disappointing objects. Primary identification (this term appears for a first time in 1923, 31), on the other hand, is "the earliest expression of an emotional tie with another person" (1921, 105). His formulation in 1923 was that the primary identification "is a direct and immediate identification and takes place earlier than any object-cathexis." And subsequent recourse to it involves regression to a stage prior to the object choices.

The concept of primary identification does not remain unequivocal in Freud's successors and is controversial (see Etchegoyen, 1985). But most authors mean by it a symbiotic relationship or fusion of self and nonself before any clear differentiation of subject and object. In my view, the archaic primary narcissistic relationship is one of primary identification in this sense.

A final point of theoretical importance is Freud's distinction between object choice and identification. According to this, the wish for identification is a primary wish and cannot be derived from instincts. This means, however, that we must distinguish between two kinds of pleasure: the orgiastic pleasure of instinctual satisfaction and the pleasure of fusion with the object of identification—a pleasure characterized by security and contentment. J. Sandler has repeatedly drawn attention to this point (for example, 1961–62, 1982; Joffe and Sandler, 1967).

NARCISSISM BEYOND PRIMARY NARCISSISM

If it is true that primary narcissism consists in an intense relationship between an as yet vaguely delineated self and a primary object that is perceived as equally vaguely delineated, with a tendency toward fusion and associated feelings of happiness and harmony, and if it is true that at moments of happiness we can reexperience regressively, in the service of the ego, this form of relationship, which we feel to be ideal, then it must also be possible to rediscover the quality of this form of relationship in the psychic constellations we create for ourselves in order to safeguard our narcissistic equilibrium beyond the stage of primary narcissism.

Let us test this by the two narcissistic constellations mentioned by Freud: our ideal formations and narcissistic object relations.

Ego-Ideal and Ideal Ego

According to Freud, our intense striving to regain primary narcissism—or rather, to secure the quality of primary narcissistic experience for later life—

takes place by way of "the displacement of libido on to an ego ideal imposed from without, . . . satisfaction [being] brought about from fulfilling this ideal" (1914, 100). Beside this ego-ideal he places the conscience, the future superego, "a special psychical agency which performs the task of seeing that narcissistic satisfaction from the ego ideal is ensured and which, with this end in view, constantly watches the actual ego and measures it by that ideal" (95).

There is some lack of precision in Freud's description of the ideal formation. Consider the following passage:

> This ideal ego is now the target of the self-love which was enjoyed in childhood by the actual ego. The subject's narcissism makes its appearance displaced on to this new ideal ego, which, like the infantile ego, finds itself possessed of every perfection that is of value. . . . [Man] is not willing to forgo the narcissistic perfection of his childhood; and when . . . he can no longer retain that perfection, he seeks to recover it in the new form of an ego ideal. What he projects before him as his ideal is the substitute for the lost narcissism of his childhood in which he was his own ideal. (94)

Thus Freud first speaks of the "ideal ego" and then of "the new form of an ego ideal" and "his ideal."

On one occasion Freud says that man "projects [the ideal] before him," but later he states that it is "imposed from without" (100). Do not these imprecisions conceal two different ideal formations, which, owing to the relational structure of narcissism, are closely bound up with each other and are therefore confused by Freud at this point?

We do indeed find exactly this differentiation at different points in the text of Freud's 1914 paper. For instance, he writes: "Observation of normal adults shows that their former megalomania has been damped down and that the psychical characteristics from which we inferred their infantile narcissism have been effaced" (93). Or: "Everything a person possesses or achieves, every remnant of the primitive feeling of omnipotence which his experience has confirmed, helps to increase his self-regard" (98). And Freud explicitly mentions three sources of narcissistic confirmation in the following sentence: "One part of self-regard is primary—the residue of infantile narcissism; another part arises out of the omnipotence which is corroborated by experience (the fulfilment of the ego ideal), whilst a third part proceeds from the satisfaction of object-libido" (100).

It might be assumed on theoretical grounds that the concepts of ideal ego or ideal self (compare the "purified pleasure-ego," 1915b, 136) correspond to the ego-ideal. The representation of "ideal self" is plainly so closely bound up with the ego-ideal that it is often overlooked. Nunberg (1931, 151) speaks of an ideal ego ("the ego which is not yet organized, which feels united with the id"). Jacobson refers to a "wishful concept of the self." To my knowledge, the notion of the ideal self was proposed and comprehensively justified by Sandler, Holder, and Meers (1963). Kernberg is also familiar with it (for example, 1975), and Hanly (1984) pointed once again to the clinical significance of the differentiation between the ego-ideal and the ideal self. The ego-ideal holds before us objectives of perfection to be reached, whereas the ideal self represents an ideal state that we have (or think we have) already reached. The ideal self is not only the derivative of the narcissistically cathected infantile self and hence (as Hanly in particular stresses) an illusory formation; it is also the vehicle of our justified pride concerning ideals and objectives we have achieved. I agree with Hanly that the ideal self exercises a comforting function or a "buffer function" (Henseler, 1974, 79ff.). If a man fails to live up to his ego-ideal, so that his superego torments him and people censure him, his ideal self prevents him from breaking down under the burden of shame or guilt feelings. The ideal self appeases the superego by saying: I admit that I have failed, but this does not leave me completely prey to shame and guilt.

Grünberger (1976, 1984), unlike Freud, views primary narcissism as deriving from prenatal coanaesthesia and from the dual union of mother and baby after birth, which he calls the "monad." This monad remains a part of the psychic structure of the child and of the adult throughout life. I consider that the monad of Grunberger is, at least in part, identical with the ideal self. He refers to the monad in the same terms that Hanly uses for the ideal self: they are both the "guardian angels" of narcissism.

Narcissistic Object Relations

All relations that are based decisively on the object's resembling "what [a person] himself is, what he himself was, what he himself would like to be" or what "was once part of himself" (Freud, 1914, 90) fuel and safeguard the feeling of narcissistic exaltation. But is it true that, in narcissistic object choice, people "are plainly seeking *themselves* as a love-object" (88), that, "strictly speaking, it is only themselves that [narcissistic] women love" (89)?

Is the fascination of these women, as well as the charm of children, cats, beasts of prey, and so on, really due to our envy of their "self-contentment and inaccessibility" (89)?

Freud introduces a different notion in the same paragraph: "Nor does their need [that of women who make a narcissistic object choice] lie in the direction of loving, but of being loved" (89). In other words, they want not to be envied but to be loved! Surely the fascination they exert would be more accurately interpreted as emanating from the unconscious invitation to love them—more precisely, to admire them, to feel one with them, and to identify with them in a state in which wishes can actually or supposedly be fulfilled *in statu nascendi*, so that neediness and envy become superfluous.

The simultaneous orientation of narcissistic object relations toward object and self can again be readily illustrated by the confusing description of the phenomenon of being in love given in the 1914 paper. In terms of libidinal economy, Freud regards being in love as an extreme case of object cathexis. The ego is depleted, as all libido now resides in the object (and he likens this movement to the pseudopodia of the amoeba). In his comparison of men and women (88), the idealization and "sexual overvaluation" that he equates with being in love is for him positive proof that men's love conforms to the anaclitic type and is thus almost purely object-directed. Surprisingly, however, Freud immediately adds that the sexual overvaluation is doubtlessly derived from the child's original narcissism and "thus corresponds to a transference of that narcissism to the sexual object" (88). "Overvaluation" is in fact regarded as a "narcissistic stigma" (91), and the overvaluation of the love object when a person is in love is positively reminiscent of a neurotic compulsion.

To explain these characteristics of being in love, Freud introduces a distinction between ego-libido and object-libido, as if they were two different forms of libido; but this is inconsistent with the earlier amoeba model. He explains: "Being in love consists in a flowing-over of ego-libido on to the object. . . . It exalts the sexual object into a sexual ideal" (100). "In that case a person will love in conformity with the narcissistic type of object choice, will love what he once was and no longer is, or else what possesses the excellences which he never had at all" (101). Thus the extreme case of object love has turned into a narcissistic object relation. But does this mean that being in love is nothing but self-love?

The subject of being in love, and indeed that of narcissistic object relations in general, comes up again in *Group Psychology and the Analysis of the Ego* (1921). This work must be regarded in many respects as a continuation of the 1914 paper, which ends with a reference to the phenomenon of group psychology. The central thesis of this work was set down by Freud in the "formula for the libidinal constitution of groups," as follows: "A primary group . . . is a number of individuals who have put one and the same object in the place of their ego ideal and have consequently identified themselves with one another in their ego" (116). In other words, the individuals in the group are in love with the idealized object and identified with one another in a feeling of grandiose oneness. Suggestibility, the hypnotized state, the wish for submission—all these he ascribes to being in love: identification provides feelings of power and mutuality and even the sensation of losing one's individual boundaries through reciprocal induction into pleasurable experience.

In an attempt to differentiate being in love from identification, Freud again interprets being in love as a form of narcissistic object relation, because "the object serves as a substitute for some unattained ego ideal of our own" (112). But identification, too, is a narcissistic object relation. In this case "the ego has enriched itself with the properties of the object" (113). The difference between identification and being in love is a matter of "whether the object is put in the place of the ego or of the ego ideal" (114).

A few pages later, however, he expresses doubt about the significance of this differentiation: "The influence of suggestion becomes a greater riddle for us when we admit that it is not exercised only by the leader, but by every individual upon every other individual; and we must reproach ourselves with having unfairly emphasized the relation to the leader and with having kept the other factor of mutual suggestion too much in the background" (117–18; see also Anzieu, 1971); since "in many individuals the separation between the ego and the ego ideal is not very far advanced, the two still coincide readily; the ego has often preserved its earlier narcissistic self-complacency" (129).

The answer to the riddle is probably that in both idealization and identification the aim, or at least the tendency, is for a fusion of self and object (see Chasseguet-Smirgel, 1975). Kohut (1971) was later to describe the "grandiose self" and the "selfobjects," which he had previously also called "idealized parental imagos," as the heirs of primary narcissism and to emphasize their importance for an understanding of particular forms of transference: mirror transference and idealizing transference. Although Kohut points out the error of "the frequently made assumption that the existence of object relations excludes narcissism," he says that the narcissistic objects are either "used in the service of the self" or "experienced as part of the self" (1971, xiv). According to Kohut, the objects are after all ultimately in the service of self-love, whereas my thesis, based in particular on the great creative achievements of (primary) narcissistic object relations, tends to place more emphasis on the reality orientation of these relations. This will become clear in what follows.

In a detailed and fair analysis of Kohut's self psychology, Wahl (1985) concludes that "Kohut's perspective is reduced to the univocal self-object experience for the self." This is connected "fundamentally with the omission of the triadic dimension." The "crux of self psychology" is that "the real other appears only as the self-object phenomenon, but I cannot enter into a concrete-real 'transdual' relationship to him as other" (187ff.). "The reflecting (self) object with which I can fuse and which I can idealize without being annihilated in it . . . must at the same time prove to be that 'other' object that is not identical to me but can meet me on a real-sensual plane and initiate a relationship with me; it is only against the other approaching myself (differentiation) that I can experience myself (identity)" (13). Loch (1972, 79ff.) expresses similar ideas.

In what is probably his first contribution on narcissism, Kohut (1966) mentions humor in addition to other transformations of narcissism. Unfortunately, his conception of this transformation remains unclear; nor does he return to the subject in his later works. I presume that he must have sensed that for narcissism to become alive and fertile and not lapse into pathology, the "third dimension" of benevolently critical distance is required, which humor after all provides in exemplary fashion.

How does reality-testing, the perception of the "other" in the object, take place in narcissistic object relations? This for me is a problem in the theory of cognition that has not yet been solved. Let me propose the following, however: if I love or admire someone who is what I myself am, what I myself was, what I myself would like to be, or someone who was once part of myself, this presupposes that I first perceive these characteristics. They initially present themselves to me as "other." Only then can I idealize the object or identify with it. In the case of the narcissistic object relations, however, the "other" must be experienced as something predominantly friendly. It exerts a fascination through which I am invited to enter into a relation with the object that may even be intense and empathic, and that promotes fusion and involves primary identification. It is these fascinating object experiences that give rise to the myths of religions, the works of artists, and the flashes of inspiration of creative scientists. But as soon as the other arouses hatred or envy, the narcissistic relation is ruptured and the limits of the form of perception described are reached.

THE CONCEPT OF NARCISSISM AND THE MYTH OF NARCISSUS

If the equation of narcissism with self-love constitutes a reduction, and if narcissism in fact denotes an archaic form of interaction, are we still entitled to invoke Narcissus, or should we not follow Balint's suggestion and henceforth speak of "primary love" or something similar? We may do so, but need not. After all, to maintain that Narcissus perished because he was in love with himself is to reduce the myth. He did indeed fall in love with his reflected image, which he at first failed to recognize as his own. It was only when he noticed that this image had no existence independent of himself but was an illusion that he despaired and (in Ovid's version) killed himself (see also Wahl, 1985).

In the myth of Narcissus, therefore, it is not a matter of self-love but of the love of a mirror-image object that is tragically taken for a real object. Also, Narcissus' relation to his reflected image in the myth has little to do with wanton egoism; rather, it is presented as an evil fate, as the punishment of a god. The punishment consists in the inability to love real objects. This inability is connected with anxiety: Narcissus certainly yearns for the nymph Echo but not for her body. Echo is to help him find his way out of the forest. Narcissus is pleased to hear and see her, but when she wants to embrace him, he recoils in horror.

According to the myth, the fear of physical nearness is clearly connected with Narcissus' early life. He is an exquisitely beautiful only child, the result of Leiriope's ravishment by the river god Cephisus. Narcissus lacks a father and siblings for his psychic development. All we know about Leiriope is that she is worried about Narcissus' life and therefore approaches the seer Tiresias. And what is he reflected in? He is reflected in the water of the spring whose nymph is his mother, Leiriope!

We now clearly see the anxiety-induced withdrawal from the triadic oedipal relationship, which, by strengthening the sense of reality, would have secured the relation to the primary object as reconcilable with life. We can therefore retain the concept of narcissism; indeed, the myth of Narcissus positively confirms our interpretation.

THE MYTH OF PRIMARY NARCISSISM

What, however, is the reality of primary narcissism in terms of developmental history? Did this harmonious form of relation really exist, or is the theory of primary narcissism only "a myth about the origins, highly idealized by us all" (Etchegoyen, 1985, 5)? Did Freud permit the place of narcissism in its different versions in developmental history to stand side by side because he sensed that narcissistic phenomena were at one and the same time self-oriented and object-oriented?

There is no doubt that primary narcissistic experience exists. But though the term "primary" can be applied to the earliest form of narcissistic experience, it need not denote the earliest form of relation in time, although this is what Freud thought in 1914. But Freud's first mention of primary narcissism already carries a reservation. He concedes that "a unity comparable to the ego" does not of course "exist in the individual from the start"; a "new psychic action" must first "bring about narcissism" (77).

We are told nothing about this action. Logically, however, it is inconceivable that the ego (or rather, the self) should be formed prior to any object relation. On the contrary, it is only unpleasurable experiences with objects that can induce the child to form initial, as yet ill-defined representations of self. "Primary identification," too, cannot possibly be the "earliest expression of an emotional tie with another person" (1921, 105). After all, to identify is something that can be done only by an already existing self with already existing objects. The earliest expression of an emotional tie with another person must be the aggression born of frustration, unless an aggressive relation is not to be regarded as an "emotional tie." Again, Freud writes in "Instincts and Their Vicissitudes": "Hate, as a relation to objects, is older than love" (1915b, 139).

This opens the way to theoretical questions with far-reaching implications. They are concerned with the significance of infantile aggression and the significance of aggression for the theory of narcissism in general. This is, of course, one of the main criticisms leveled at Kohut's self psychology (see, for instance, Kernberg, 1974; Levine, 1979).

Different answers have been given. Balint adheres to the original "harmonious mix-up." I wonder whether Balint is confusing an object relation with what I would suggest to be the original psychophysiological state of low excitation and predominant well-being, of which memory traces can later be triggered.

Melanie Klein has a completely different concept: for her, primary narcissism is identical with oral sadism, which swallows and destroys the object (Etchegoyen, 1985). She is clearly following up Freud's comment that "identification, in fact, is ambivalent from the very first. . . . It behaves like a derivative of the first, *oral* phase of the organization of the libido, in which the object that we long for and prize is assimilated by eating and is in that way annihilated as such" (1921, 105). Freud later gave up this idea (Widlöcher, 1985). Instead of assimilation and destruction, identification came to mean fusion.

But let us again consult Freud. In the description of the reawakening of the parents' narcissism in their attitude toward their child, one of the points he stresses is the unrealistic character of this state. He mentions overvaluation, the relinquishment of sober observation, the failure to recognize realities, the suspension of cultural imperatives, the abrogation of laws, and the replacement of reality by dreams—in other words, a considerable disavowal of reality. It is clear to me that Freud is describing the parents' efforts to make it possible for the baby and themselves to experience (or reexperience) primary narcissism, and this does indeed demand an enormous disavowal of reality. But is it possible that this rich, almost dramatic description of the disavowal of reality contains a hint that the baby, too, must disavow in order to permit itself a primary narcissistic experience? If our considerations regarding the primary frustrating object experience are correct, there can be, from Freud's point of view, only a secondary narcissism, a disavowing, and a regressive plunging into the psychophysiological state prior to any object experience, which only subsequently becomes what Freud and Balint describe so impressively.

But this would mean that primary narcissism and Balint's primary love are not primal experiences but secondary formations. Paradise did not originally exist in this form but was only later constructed, composed out of memory traces of a psychophysiological state, satisfying experiences with objects, and wishful fantasies of happiness and harmony—which can be understood as reaction formations to frustrating reality. Hence, primary narcissism and the narcissistic constellations that later develop from it are a wonderful human achievement, a subsequent invention, offering us universal withdrawal from harsh reality into an "intermediate area" (Winnicott, 1971) in which reality and fantasy can still blend in an agreeable way. Primary narcissism would then be a myth, in the best sense of the word: although never having taken place historically, it yet tells us something true.

CLINICAL CONSEQUENCES

If we are right in our ideas that narcissistic constellations constitute a universal opportunity for withdrawal from the otherness of the other, from the "third dimension" of the object with its setting of boundaries and its sensual reality, into an intoxicating dual union if the otherness is experienced as threatening, then the striking absence of aggression in all narcissistic forms of relation becomes understandable.

The otherness of the other, which is experienced as threatening, the impossibility of incorporating him either by identification or by idealization, gives rise to hatred or envy. Freud (1921) offers as an illustration the cruelty and intolerance of groups—for example, religious communities—toward outsiders. He was not to know that this cruelty and intolerance could reach the magnitude of a holocaust.

Hence, one way of coping with destructive hatred and envy toward a third party in contact with the third dimension in others is to withdraw into a dual union. This signifies a total devaluation of the third party, albeit not experienced consciously. The alternative is a surprised and interested confrontation with the third party, with the result that otherness and boundaries set by the independence of the other are used constructively. Hatred then becomes respect and envy admiration of the other (of course, not without ambivalence), and this at the same time makes possible a consciousness of one's own individuality. Reality-based libidinal and aggressive (rather than destructive) sensual relationships can now come into being.

Favorable developmental conditions in early childhood are necessary in order for this to be possible. Narcissus would have needed a third person, a father, to help him escape from primary narcissistic symbiosis with the overanxious mother. This would have enabled him to turn his libidinal (and aggressive) interest to other objects as well—first the father and later the lovely nymph Echo. But a father was lacking or existed only as a threatening ravisher in fantasy. Siblings were also lacking. Hence, the narcissistic mirror-relationship with the mother could no longer continue to be used flexibly and in the service of the ego but became a rigid fixation. Access to the third dimension remained closed to him. Here, in my view, lies the distinction between healthy and pathological narcissism.

My personal interest in narcissistic phenomena and narcissistic disturbances was aroused when, from 1968 on, I regularly had to treat patients who had attempted suicide. I had expected to encounter people who dealt with aggressive conflicts by turning them against their own persons. Objectively, this was in fact the case, but it sounded quite different as it was told to me by the patients. Aggression did not enter into it at all.

A female patient who had already made five suicide attempts told me, in her first and second interviews, of her life with her boyfriend, an artist. It was a life full of problems but also of fascination. She burnt herself up like a candle for her boyfriend, and he did the same for her. The two were in effect merged into each other seamlessly. She was certain she could cure her lover of his alcoholism. She also felt that she, too, had an aptitude for painting and writing, for conveying to humanity something that it, however, might not be able to understand. Such a life must surely be incomprehensible to me as an average citizen. This life of color and profusion was so intense that death was not a loss but a consummation.

A disobliging remark by her boyfriend had driven her to attempt suicide, but it had not been particularly frightening. "When I think of suicide, I never think of being dead and of everything being over. Instead I think how fantastic the moment of dying must be. This death is, for me, not an end but a beginning. My whole life is there, I am real at the moment of suicide."

On another occasion, the same patient said that when she felt lonely she would sit at her window. "Then I am half inside and half out. I look out over the rooftops, right up into the sky, further and further. It is as if I go out there, evaporate, melt away into space. My feeling of loneliness intensifies. And then a nameless fear overcomes me. I race down the stairs, I rush about, shiver, call out 'Mummy,' and cry."

As part of a research project, I asked fifty unselected, nonpsychotic patients this question, following their suicide attempts: "What did you think before the suicide attempt about what would come afterwards?" Twenty-five patients had no precise ideas at all. They just wanted to get away from where they were, felt that death could only be better. The other half had indeed had certain preconceptions, but these had little to do with their actual knowledge or with their philosophical views about death and dying. Rather, they involved states of repose, relaxation, security, redemption, harmony, and even triumph (Henseler, 1974).

I then understood that suicidal crises (nearly) always arise when a disappointment in a narcissistic object is eliminated by the acting out of a fantasy of fusion with a primary object in a death chosen voluntarily. The hatred of the object that disappoints remains unconscious, and the actual self-destruction is reinterpreted as a narcissistic apotheosis. This process is not identical with the melancholic mechanism described by Freud (1916). What is involved in that case is a partial identification with the disappointing object because at least a part of the self—the superego—continues to rage against the bad introject. In our case, however, it is a matter of a total or primary identification with a purely good object!

Characteristically, about 70 percent of people who have once made a suicide attempt and been rescued do not repeat the attempt. Many of them will talk of their disenchantment. The "death" for which they strove was not so marvelous after all. They are often ashamed of the illusion to which they succumbed. Others remain fixated on this solution to their conflicts. Such patients aroused my particular interest. For the past twenty years, I have constantly had at least one such patient chronically at risk of suicide in analytic treatment. Incidentally, I hesitate to diagnose these people as narcissistically disturbed personalities. They certainly have narcissistic disturbances that become acute in certain crisis situations, but they also exhibit different kinds of conflicts and personality traits (Henseler and Reimer, 1981; Henseler, 1983).

We regularly encounter in these patients the avoidance of hatred and envy, felt to be destructive, in favor of narcissistic object relations, high-flown ideal formations, and a tendency to regress to primary narcissistic forms of experience. Predictably, these patterns also develop in the transference. A matter requiring particularly delicate handling is the alacrity with which these patients form idealizing transferences; they are correspondingly susceptible to disappointment and can switch over into threatening negative transferences. Since I know this, I am constantly on the lookout for it and interpret transference disappointments early on. I even predict them and ask the patients not to run away when they arise but to turn the disappointment into a subject for analysis.

Of course, the correct analytic setting acts as a prophylactic against the temptation to lapse into a harmonious dual union. Again, although I present myself from the beginning as a benevolent and friendly object, I make my third dimension clear. I always say, as an explicit part of the therapeutic contract: if you are absolutely intent on killing yourself, I cannot stop you. I do not offer to save your life. I can only offer you a chance to consider with me why you persist in thinking that you cannot continue to live.

This may sound harsh. In my experience, however, it has a calming effect. The patient senses that I am not afraid, and I escape the possibility of blackmail. In this way it becomes possible to work on the negative transference whenever the patient initiates a narcissistic retreat. The narcissistic disturbance is also mitigated by the more anxiety-free handling of aggression. This, for me, is the strongest proof of the secondary nature of primary narcissism as an aggression-free substitutive relationship.

REFERENCES

Andreas-Salomé, L. (1921). The dual orientation of narcissism. *Psychoanal. Q.*, 31:1.

Anzieu, D. (1971). L'illusion groupalé. *Nouvelle Revue de Psychanalyse*, 4:73–93.

Balint, M. (1937). Early developmental states of the ego: Primary object-love. In M. Balint, *Primary Love and Psycho-analytic Technique*. London: Hogarth Press, 1952.

———. (1960). Primary narcissism and primary love. In *The Basic Fault*. London: Tavistock, 1968.

Chasseguet-Smirgel, J. (1975). *The Ego Ideal*. London: Free Association Books, 1985.

Etchegoyen, R. H. (1985). Identification and its vicissitudes. *Int. J. Psycho-Anal.*, 66:3–18.

Freud, S. (1905). *Three Essays on the Theory of Sexuality. S.E.* 7:25.

———. (1910). *Leonardo da Vinci and a Memory of His Childhood. S.E.* 9:252.

———. (1911). Psycho-analytic notes on an autobiographical account of a case of paranoia (dementia paranoides). *S.E.* 12:3.

———. (1912–13). *Totem and Taboo. S.E.* 13:1.

———. (1914). On narcissism: An introduction. *S.E.* 14:69.

———. (1915a). Repression. *S.E.* 14:143.

———. (1915b). Instincts and their vicissitudes. *S.E.* 14:111.

———. (1915c). The unconscious. *S.E.* 14:161.

———. (1916). Mourning and melancholia. *S.E.* 14:239.

———. (1921). *Group Psychology and the Analysis of the Ego. S.E.* 18:69.

———. (1923). *The Ego and the Id. S.E.* 19:3.

———. (1930). *Civilization and Its Discontents. S.E.* 21:59.

Grünberger, B. (1976). *Vom Narzissmus zum Objekt*. Frankfurt: Suhrkamp.

———. (1984). De la pureté. *Revue franç. de psychanalyse*, 48(3):795–812.

Hanly, C. (1984). Ego ideal and ideal ego. *Int. J. Psycho-Anal.*, 65:253–61.

Henseler, H. (1974). *Narzisstische Krisen: Zur Psychodynamik des Selbstmords*. Reinbek: Rowohlt; Opladen: Westdeutscher Verlag, 2d ed., 1984.

———. (1983). Moby Dick—Überlegungen zur narzisstischen Wut. Jb. Psychoanal., Vol. 15.

Henseler, H., and Reimer, C. (1981). *Selbstnirdgefährdung*. Stuttgart: Frohmann-Holzboog.

Jacobson, E. (1954). *The Self and the Object World*. New York: International Universities Press.

Joffe, W. G., and Sandler, J. (1967). Some conceptual problems involved in the consideration of disorders of narcissism. *J. Child Psychother.*, 2(1):56–66.

Kernberg, O. (1974). Further contributions to the treatment of narcissistic personalities. *Int. J. Psycho-Anal.*, 55:215–40.

———. (1975). *Borderline Conditions and Pathological Narcissism*. New York: Jason Aronson.

Kohut, H. (1966). Forms and transformations of narcissism. In *Self Psychology and the Humanities*. New York: W. W. Norton, 1985.

———. (1971). *The Analysis of the Self*. New York: International Universities Press.

Kuhn, T. (1962). *The Structure of Scientific Revolutions*. Chicago: University of Chicago Press.

Levine, F. J. (1979). On the clinical application of Heinz Kohut's psychology of the self. *J. Phil. Assn. for Psychoanal.*, 4:6–15.

Loch, W. (1972). *Zur Theorie, Technik und Therapie der Psychoanalyse*. Frankfurt: Fischer.

Nunberg, H. (1931). *Allgemeine Neurosenlehre*. 2nd ed. Berne and Stuttgart: Huber, 1959.

Sandler, J. (1961–62). Sicherheitsgefühl und Wahrnehmungsvorgang. *Psyche*, 15:124–31.

———. (1982). Unconscious wishes and human relationships. *Contemp. Psychoanal.*, 17(2):180–96.

Sandler, J., Holder, A., and Meers, D. (1963). The ego ideal and the ideal self. In *Psychoanal. Study Child*, 18:139–58.

Wahl, H. (1985). *Narzissmus?* Stuttgart: Kohlhammer.

Widlöcher, D. (1985). The wish for identification and structural effects in the work of Freud. *Int. J. Psycho-Anal.*, 66:31–46.

Winnicott, D. W. (1971). *Playing and Reality*. London: Tavistock.

Narcissism and the Analytic Situation

BÉLA GRÜNBERGER

This contribution is not intended as a commentary on the whole of Freud's paper. For that one would need to place it in the context of the total body of his work, noting the earlier writings in which the term "narcissism" had been mentioned or where Freud had actually begun to conceptualize it.[1] It should be noted that Freud's interest in narcissism (homosexuality, paranoia, and so on) stemmed from his clinical experience with mental disorders. This is the key to understanding why Freud had to introduce narcissism into psychoanalytic theory and how he did so. The 1914 paper should also be seen alongside another paper dating from the same year—"On the History of the Psycho-Analytic Movement"—in which Freud discusses the dissident views of Jung and Adler. In "On Narcissism," Freud refers directly to these two authors, but his controversy with them can in fact be felt as a presence throughout the text. Like many of his writings, this paper is the fruit of his confrontation with the "dissidents," who

1. *Leonardo* (1910), a note accompanying the second edition of the *Three Essays* (1915), the Schreber case (1911), and *Totem and Taboo* (1912–13) would need to be considered.

indirectly enriched psychoanalysis by inducing Freud to deepen and refine his ideas.[2]

Finally, we should also have to show the breakthrough that the 1914 paper on narcissism represents, while at the same time pointing out that it was in a way "unstable" because Freud was very soon to modify his views and to present narcissism in object terms. So, in "Mourning and Melancholia" (1917), we see the concept that was introduced in 1914 now represented principally in terms of narcissistic identification with an internalized lost object. In melancholia, says Freud, the ego rages against the part of itself that is identified with the lost object and attacks it as though it were the object. It is generally agreed that the part of the ego that attacks the other, "judges it critically, and, as it were, takes it as its object" (1917) foreshadows the superego. Freud also notes in 1917, "Our suspicion that the critical agency, which is here split off from the ego, might also show its independence in other circumstances will be confirmed by every further observation."

When Freud introduced narcissism in 1914, he at the same time introduced the ego-ideal, which is also said—somewhat hastily—to be a precursor of the superego. This is in fact a confusion with the superego introduced in 1923 in *The Ego and the Id*, where Freud uses the terms "superego," "ego ideal," and "ideal ego" indiscriminately. In 1914, the ego-ideal was nothing other than the heir to narcissism:

> As always where the libido is concerned, man has here again shown himself incapable of giving up a satisfaction he had once enjoyed. He is not willing to forgo the narcissistic perfection of his childhood; and when, as he grows up, he is disturbed by the admonitions of others and by the awakening of his own critical judgement, so that he can no longer retain that perfection, he seeks to recover it in the new form of an ego ideal. What he projects before him as his ideal is the substitute for the lost narcissism of his childhood in which he was his own ideal.

Later, Freud says:

> It would not surprise us if we were to find a special psychical agency which performs the task of seeing that narcissistic satisfaction from the ego ideal is endured and which, with this end in view, constantly watches

2. Similarly, *Inhibitions, Symptoms and Anxiety* (1926) cannot be understood without reading Otto Rank's *Trauma of Birth* (1924).

> the actual ego and measures it by that ideal. If such an agency does exist, we cannot possibly come upon it as a discovery—we can only recognize it; for we may reflect that what we call our "conscience" has the required characteristics.

It is therefore clear that the ego-ideal of the 1914 paper does not foreshadow the moral agency. It is the source of plenitude, of perfection, of the absolute and the infinite, toward which the subject, castrated by the loss of his narcissism, is irresistibly drawn. Having been expelled from paradise, he tries to reach heaven (the paradise projected "before him"). Conscience—prefiguring the superego—observes the ego and measures it by the ideal. It is not the ideal. Although this is clinically accurate, what immediately confuses the issue is the mixing of object components with components of pure narcissism. It would be worth separating these elements out for heuristic purposes. The closer Freud approached the introduction of his final topography, the greater became the confusion. The incapacity and impotence affecting the subject constitute a narcissistic wound—an attack on his ideal. It may be convenient to substitute a sense of guilt for the feeling of incapacity. "I am the greatest sinner on earth" may conceal the unbearable idea of being nothing at all. Conscience, which lays down boundaries and prohibitions, may save narcissism and the feeling of self-regard. The melancholic dies not of an "excess" of superego but of an "excess" of ideal—and the megalomaniac ideal may disguise itself as a pitiless superego, as a last resort against a feeling of annihilating inadequacy. I shall return to this point later.

I am inclined to try to make a separate study of narcissism and its vicissitudes, on the one hand, and instinctual conflicts, on the other. In my commentary on Freud, I shall attempt principally to show the importance of the concept of narcissism in the understanding of the analytic situation itself. My study of narcissism published in 1956 was based precisely on the analytic situation and the process it initiates. In that work I sought to distinguish the object-related and instinctual transference components from the narcissistic components. I tried to show that the analytic situation gives rise to a narcissistic regression that induces specific sensations and feelings: elation, the "end-of-session syndrome" (giddiness and disorientation, as described by Ferenczi in 1914, which I connect with the narcissistic regression promoted by the session, from which the patient is expelled), and a particular cathexis of the analysis and the analyst whereby they often supplant the patient's religious and ideological interests, which have suddenly fallen by the wayside, so that the ego-ideal becomes projected onto the analyst. These phenomena, associated with the narcissistic regression, are essential elements in the treatment and form part of what some authors call the therapeutic alliance. When, at the beginning of an analysis, a female patient has a dream that expresses the essentials of her object conflicts and the problems these have led to in the establishment of her sexual identity, and she hears a voice telling her: "That will be all right; you will be having lessons from a teacher of higher mathematics," are we really to believe that this identification of the analyst constitutes a defense against destructive instincts and results from a split between an idealized good object and a persecutory bad object? Is it not rather the reconstitution in fantasy of a particular narcissistic state brought about by the analytic situation?

In my writings on narcissism I have emphasized its prenatal origin. Freud, however, makes no mention in his 1914 paper of the fetal state as the origin and model of absolute narcissism. Indeed it was not until 1921, in *Group Psychology and the Analysis of the Ego*, that he was to write: "Thus, by being born we have made the step from an absolutely self-sufficient narcissism to the perception of a changing external world and the beginnings of the discovery of objects." Now during intrauterine life (subjective) self-sufficiency is satisfied. As a result, the self is omnipotent, in a state where time and space do not exist, since these result from the gap between the appearance of a need and its satisfaction. The memory of this state exists in us in the form of unconscious traces that reappear in the idea of God (God is the omnipotent fetus before becoming the Father [or mother]) in the various mystical systems, in the "oceanic feeling," in the elation afforded by the contemplation of works of art or immersion in the world of music, in the belief in a Paradise Lost, a Golden Age, and so on.[3] Now the projection onto the analyst of the lost omnipotence tends to re-create the fetal state in which the fetus was, thanks to its host—the mother—absolutely content, without needs and without "problems" (the teacher of higher mathematics who can solve all problems).

I am inclined to distinguish between these projections of the lost omnipotence onto the analyst and the transference proper. The narcissistic regres-

3. I consider here only the re-creations through myth, which are more or less universal and "normal," of the state of prenatal completeness and felicity. The intrauterine state may be troubled, but there are nevertheless moments when it approaches absolute perfection and as such subsists asymptomatically.

sion in the analytic situation and the projections of the ego-ideal to which it gives rise are virtually universal. This is not a transference proper, although, as Freud showed (in *Inhibitions, Symptoms and Anxiety*, 1926, after Ferenczi, "Stages in the Development of the Sense of Reality," 1913), the mother in postnatal life constitutes a substitute for the lost womb: "What happens is that the child's biological situation as a foetus is replaced for it by a psychical object-relation to its mother" (1926). This reconstitution of what I have called the "monad" (1984) is what occurs in the analytic situation. It is what forms the background on which the components of the historical transference proper and the object conflicts will be inscribed.

As we know, after birth, the people who surround the child tend, in fortunate cases, to reconstitute the lost womb; in addition, the psychic apparatus endeavors to achieve satisfaction through hallucination. Eventually, however, it becomes impossible for the baby to continue in this state. Depending on the attitude of those around him, the change may take place relatively gradually or suddenly; in the latter case the human young is plunged into a state of abandonment linked to his actual fundamental powerlessness, his distress resulting from having been born in an unfinished state (his helplessness, as Freud puts it). The human child is a fallen god who has to confront a narcissistic trauma inherent in the human condition just at the moment when the vicarious means of continuing in the prenatal state fail. The analytic situation is first experienced as offering the patient an opportunity to recover his fetal omnipotence and thereby to repair a fundamental traumatic situation. In order to begin to translate this scheme into reality, the patient must be able to project his aspirations for omnipotence onto the analyst, with whom he fuses. Hence the analytic situation, if it is narcissistic, contains virtually another dimension, that of the object relation. The patient regresses to the intrauterine situation but is at the same time ready to establish with the analyst the monad that replaces the fetal state after birth. As Freud says in his 1914 paper, man is incapable of giving up a satisfaction once enjoyed. He had already written, in "Creative Writers and Day-Dreaming" (1908), "Actually, we can never give anything up; we only exchange one thing for another."

The patient must be able to emerge from an absolute, autarkic, and in fact paranoid narcissism in order to reconstitute his lost omnipotence in the analysis and with the analyst. It is noteworthy that the coordinates of the treatment encourage this tendency. This regression is induced by the fundamental rule, the fact that the patient can say anything at all, and the position of the analyst outside the analysand's field of vision. The patient's position on the couch and the blocked access to motility give the session the semblance of a dream.[4] The regularity and fixity of the sessions are guaranteed by the analyst, the guardian of the setting and hence of the narcissistic regression in which he allows the patient to immerse himself but from which he also lets him emerge. For me, the analytic situation is characterized much more by the narcissistic regression than by the transference. What I mean is that the transference—and here I am faithfully following Freud—is a universal phenomenon: people have a transference to their cardiologist, to their milkman, to the caretaker of their block of flats. It is true that the analytic situation constitutes a laboratory where the manifestations of the transference are observed in a privileged and, as it were, aseptic manner (by virtue of the neutrality of the analyst, who "does not reply" but interprets). But the analytic coordinates, more than anything else, set in motion the narcissistic aspects of the psyche. It must be added, however, that if there is this narcissistic regression in the background and the hope placed in the analysis and the analyst of regaining the lost omnipotence and repairing the narcissistic wound, then the analysis must gradually enable the patient to tackle his object conflicts and integrate the instinctual aspect by interpreting the historical transference proper.

Some symptoms disappear very quickly in analysis, before the interpretation has been made of the conflicts underlying them. Such recovery is connected with the analytic situation but not with the analysis proper. It was probably the operative factor in the short analyses that prevailed in the early days of psychoanalysis. The flight into recovery is encouraged by the narcissistic elation of the opening stages, which the patient (unconsciously) refuses to replace by the object solution through analysis of the historical transference. The specific narcissistic regression proper to the analytic situation initiates the analytic process, which supplies the motive power for the treatment. The transference, for its part, is grafted onto this process, which is independent of it and, so to speak, autonomous. It seems to me that we must avoid including in the term "transference" everything that happens between the analyst and the analysand, everything the analytic situation induces. If prenatal life is the model for narcissistic regression in the analytic situation, it is not identical to the historical transference that reproduces the patient's accidental and personal experiences.

In fact, I have found it necessary to introduce the idea of a dialectic between narcissism and instincts, based on the fact that the newborn has to

4. Bertram Lewin said this first, and others later developed the idea.

confront a change of regime. Whereas in the uterus his needs were automatically satisfied and some of his physiological functions were nonexistent (for example, respiration), dormant (the musculature), or in a more or less latent state (the sensorium), he must now suddenly face up to his instincts and take possession of his corporeity. The analysis, by virtue of its narcissistic dimension, should ideally allow instinctual life and the body which is its source to become integrated, without the instincts and their support continuing to be experienced as antagonistic to narcissism, as ego-dystonic.

In his 1914 paper, Freud says:

> The relations of self-regard to erotism—that is, to libidinal object-cathexes—may be expressed concisely in the following way. Two cases must be distinguished, according to whether the erotic cathexes are ego-syntonic or, on the contrary have suffered repression. In the former case (where the use made of the libido is ego-syntonic), love is assessed like any other activity of the ego. . . . When libido is repressed, the erotic cathexis is felt as a severe depletion of the ego, the satisfaction of love is impossible, and the re-enrichment of the ego can be effected only by a withdrawal of libido from its objects. (99–100)

Again:

> One part of self-regard is primary—the residue of infantile narcissism; another part arises out of the omnipotence which is corroborated by experience (the fulfilment of the ego ideal), whilst a third part proceeds from the satisfaction of object-libido. (100)

I should like to emphasize that the first opposition between narcissism and the instincts follows from what I have just said—prior to object conflicts, the Oedipus complex, the superego, and so on. Of course, in cases of neurosis, this fundamental antagonism is not only less pronounced but also concealed by a multiplicity of much more developed conflicts that have masked and even transformed it to the point of making it invisible and unrecognizable. The same does not apply to more serious pathologies, particularly melancholia. Note that in the 1914 paper Freud mentions the following pathological disorders in connection with narcissism: the perversions, homosexuality, the paraphrenias, hypochondria, and paranoia; but he does not mention melancholia, about which, as I have already pointed out, he was to write a paper discussing narcissism in terms of objects (narcissistic identification). It is precisely in connection with melancholia that we can best see the results of the absence of coordination between narcissism and instinctual maturation. The statement of narcissism in object terms in "Mourning and Melancholia" is, of course, mitigated by the idea that the lost object is a narcissistic object, that what is involved may be an abstraction, and that the loss is a loss of ego. Freud even wonders whether "a loss in the ego irrespectively of the object . . . may not suffice to produce the picture of melancholia."

In fact, in my view (see "The Suicide of the Melancholic," 1966b), melancholia involves a withdrawal of narcissism from the overall ego of the subject, from his body, and from his instinctual life. The overall ego undergoes idealization with the sign reversed. It is fecalized and identified with filth that has to be swept away. It is often found that suicides, shortly before they kill themselves, appear to feel better and regain a certain tonus and energy—to an extent that the act, when it occurs, surprises those around them (I am not talking about patients in the hospital). This is because their decision has been taken and is an enormous relief to them: their bodily ego ("rags and tatters"—*guenille*, Molière) is about to disappear, and their narcissism, liberated from its "bag of guts" (*enclos de tripes*, Céline), will triumph. At last complete, absolute, external, and unlimited, the subject has returned to the state he experienced before birth; instead of being excrement, he has once again become God (Grünberger, 1987). So I would stress again the degree to which the irrational and the mystical in man—sources of the best and the worst—are illuminated by the idea of prenatal self-sufficiency and felicity.

It seems to me that the root of the belief in the body-mind duality lies in the newborn's appropriation of his body when he enters into the instinctual regime. The mother and those around the newborn must thus help him to cathect narcissistically his new mode of being and his instincts. Owing to a failure in the gradual carryover of narcissism into instinctual life, the latter is liable to be violently rejected at a certain point in time, as in the case of melancholia, where the subject sacrifices his unworthy (unsatisfying, mutilated, "dirty") body in order to regain the plenitude of his "pure," glorious, and immortal soul.

Freud and many analysts after him conferred object status on religious phenomena, just as Freud stated narcissism in object terms in "Mourning and Melancholia." God is thus, for Freud, essentially a projection of the father, able to protect us from fate (*The Future of an Illusion*, 1927); the "oceanic feeling" is a manifestation of religious need, which is nothing other than the longing for the father (*Civilization and Its Discontents*, 1930). Freud was afraid of mysticism and was justifiably anxious lest psychoanalysis be engulfed by it. We know, however, that we cannot really escape from problems by flight or disavowal. Although part of the concept of God may be regarded as stemming from the father complex (particularly in the Jewish religion of Freud's forefathers), it has another important source in the state of lost fetal omnipotence.

The following quotation from Pascal's *Pensées* features in the epigraph to my book on narcissism:

> What is it then that this desire and this inability proclaim to us, but that there was once in man a true happiness of which there now remains to him only the mark and empty trace, which he in vain tries to fill from all his surroundings, seeking from things absent the help he does not obtain in things present? But these are all inadequate, because the infinite abyss can only be filled by an infinite and immutable object, that is to say, only by God Himself.

This hypothesis of the importance of the traces left behind in us by prenatal life not only offers at least a partial explanation for man's thirst for the absolute—one of the most specific of human characteristics, which perhaps most radically distinguishes man from the lower animals—but also has important consequences for our understanding of psychopathology.

After all, even if Freud subsequently abandoned his 1914 distinction between transference neuroses and narcissistic neuroses, this distinction remains historically and clinically interesting. It helps us understand how narcissism can constitute a major obstacle to treatment, whereas in other cases it actually furnishes the motive power for it. If my view is accepted that it is absolutely vital for the child to achieve a synthesis between his narcissism and his instincts (this is the ideal, which is never fully accomplished; only a relative balance can possibly be achieved between the narcissistic and instinctual streams), it must be strongly emphasized that this synthesis is feasible only with the help of those around him, chiefly the mother. Being loved and understood (but true love includes understanding) is equivalent to (partial) restoration of the first narcissistic state, which I regard as synonymous with the fetal state, or rather, to regaining partially the feeling of value connected with this state.[5] Any narcissistic restoration achieved

5. Obviously, it may be thought that the feeling of value is projected retrospectively, in contrast to the affect connected with the postnatal narcissistic wound.

with the aid of the people around the child provides a subsequent foundation for hope when a new figure appears on the scene. The analyst, then, before being a promise of instinctual satisfactions, appears in the patient's psychic field as a promise of narcissistic restoration. It is because the patient has experienced or even glimpsed, however incompletely, the possibility of narcissistic restoration through his first objects that he will be capable of accepting the analyst as a hope.

When those around the baby have repeatedly failed in the task of helping him to recover, if only partially, his lost feeling of completeness, the subject will hesitate and sometimes refuse to cathect the new figure represented by the analyst. His aggressiveness will often be tantamount to a simple rejection of this intruder, who withdraws libido from his ego after he had found a relative solution to the problem of dressing his own wounds. It is this second form of narcissism that is often studied today, as it is encountered more and more frequently (in particular, in the narcissistic and borderline characters discussed by Otto Kernberg). I certainly do not wish to deny the importance of this pathology or of the publications devoted to it. But it seems to me essential to emphasize that narcissism is involved both in the transference neuroses (to use Freud's terminology again) and in the narcissistic personality disorders (which we now know not to be the prerogative of the "narcissistic neuroses" alone, in the 1914 sense—that is, the psychoses). I have said that, in the first case, it helped the treatment become established, it underlay the analytic process, and it paved the way for the emergence of the historical transference and for the working over of object and instinctual conflicts; in the second case, it blocked them, sometimes fatally, at any rate necessitating modifications of technique.

In 1966 I wrote a study entitled "*L'Oedipe et le narcissisme*" (The Oedipus Complex and Narcissism, 1966a), in which I elaborated on the antithesis I had previously described between the narcissistic and instinctual dimensions, an antithesis that tends to give rise to a dialectical situation. Here I stressed the infantile helplessness that Freud emphasized. I said it was obvious that, although man was born helpless, he was not so during his fetal life:

> Thus at birth, man is, on the one hand, holder of a narcissistic heritage whose support, linked to fetal life, has been torn away and, on the other hand, bearer of a sexual apparatus that is not yet functional, though there are unmistakeable indications of a sexual tension very early seeking to activate this apparatus. The infant, then, is an outcast

> of both worlds. . . . he clings desperately to his mother, or rather to what she represents for him at that time: the possibility both of prolonging his prenatal narcissistic state and of integrating it into a new universe with an instinctual base.

The child will be induced to replace the narcissistic trauma (stemming from his intrinsic impotence) by an external prohibition, which is infinitely less wounding to his narcissism. At least a part of the ban on incest in man is due to the time lag between the appearance of the oedipal wish and the ability to satisfy it. Morality stems *partly* from human impotence and immaturity. This is one reason morality is so easily swept aside when the possibility of a narcissistic fulfillment is glimpsed on the horizon. The narcissistic wound gives rise to morality; obliteration of the wound, or the promise of its obliteration, is capable of extinguishing morality.

This brings us back to the 1914 paper. Freud ends his study by pointing out that "the ego ideal opens up an important avenue for the understanding of group psychology. . . . Originally this sense of guilt was a fear of punishment by the parents, or, more correctly, the fear of losing their love; later the parents are replaced by an indefinite number of fellow-men." Another part (but not yet the whole) of morality arises from the need of the child, and then of the man, to re-create with his mother, and later with his fellow human beings, an "environment" to replace the primal womb. In order for this "environment" to perform its function as a supplier of narcissistic food, the child, and later the man, must win it over—that is, cause it to love him. This is why the child or man may wish to be loved by this "environment" at all costs, including that of morality, which stems from another human dimension—namely, the instinctual and object aspect of the psyche.[6]

I should like to make one final point. In the 1914 paper, Freud speaks of the charm of narcissistic beings: children, cats, and large beasts of prey, great criminals, humorists, and finally, narcissistic women who are full of self-satisfaction. (This type of woman admittedly exists, but there are also "seducers," Casanovas, who are no less narcissistic). All the same, considering that Freud constantly regards women as marked by lack and by envy, it is surprising to see him here associate their charm with their self-satisfaction. Perhaps it is because he characterizes the object choice of men as representing "complete object-love," conforming to the anaclitic type, whose model

6. This is, however, beyond the scope of this essay. I wish in particular to show that the dialectic of narcissism/instincts also plays an important part in morality.

is the mother who nurses the child. Does he not then project onto women (as substitutes for the nursing mother) the lost fetal self-sufficiency recovered by fusion with the mother who replaces the uterine environment? Thus the most highly developed form of love, as we already know, contains the balm (the philter or elixir) capable of healing the wound with which we are "plunged into the world."

REFERENCES

Ferenczi, S. (1913). Stages in the development of the sense of reality. In *First Contributions to Psycho-Analysis*. London: Hogarth Press, 1952.

———. (1914). Sensations of giddiness at the end of the psycho-analytic session. In *First Contributions to Psycho-Analysis*. London: Hogarth Press, 1952.

Freud, S. (1905). *Three Essays on the Theory of Sexuality. S.E.* 7.

———. (1908). Creative writers and day-dreaming. *S.E.* 9.

———. (1910). *Leonardo da Vinci and a Memory of His Childhood. S.E.* 1.

———. (1911). Psycho-analytic notes on an autobiographical account of a case of paranoia (dementia paranoides). *S.E.* 12.

———. (1912–13). *Totem and Taboo. S.E.* 13.

———. (1914). On narcissism: An introduction. *S.E.* 14.

———. (1917). Mourning and melancholia. *S.E.* 14.

———. (1921). *Group Psychology and the Analysis of the Ego. S.E.* 18.

———. (1923). *The Ego and the Id. S.E.* 19.

———. (1926). *Inhibitions, Symptoms and Anxiety. S.E.* 20.

———. (1927). *The Future of an Illusion. S.E.* 21.

———. (1930). *Civilization and Its Discontents. S.E.* 21.

Grünberger, B. (1956). The analytic situation and the process of healing. In *Narcissism*. New York: International Universities Press, 1979.

———. (1966a). The Oedipus Complex and Narcissism. In *Narcissim*, New York: International Universities Press, 1979.

———. (1966b). The suicide of the melancholic. In *Narcissism*, New York: International Universities Press, 1979.

———. (1984). La monade. Manuscript.

———. (1987). Don Quijote—Narziss—sein Kampt und sein Scheitern. In *Forum der Psychoanalyse*, 3(1):1–15 (Berlin: Springer Verlag).

Rank, O. (1929). *The Trauma of Birth*. London: K. Paul, Trench, Trubner. (First published in 1924 in German.)

List of Contributors

WILLY BARANGER is training and supervising analyst of the Instituto de Psicoanálisis, Buenos Aires. He is honorary president of the Uruguayan Psychoanalytic Association, former president of COPAL (now FEPAL), and an honorary member of the Peru Psychoanalytic Society.

DAVID BELL is consultant at the Cassel Hospital, Richmond, London, and a member of the British Psychoanalytical Society.

R. HORACIO ETCHEGOYEN is training and supervising analyst of the Buenos Aires Psychoanalytic Association. He previously served as chairman of psychiatry and medical psychology (U.N.C.), president of the Buenos Aires Psychoanalytic Association, and vice-president of the IPA.

PETER FONAGY is senior lecturer in psychology, University College London; coordinator of research at the Anna Freud Centre, Hampstead; the Freud Memorial Professor Designate, University of London, and a member of the British Psychoanalytical Society.

LEÓN GRINBERG is training and supervising analyst of the Madrid Psychoanalytical Association. He holds the Chair of Psychoanalysis in the Ateneo de Madrid.

BÉLA GRÜNBERGER is a member of the Paris Psychoanalytical Society.

HEINZ HENSELER is professor of psychoanalysis and director of the Department of Psychoanalysis, Psychotherapy, and Psychosomatics, University of Tübingen; training and supervising analyst, German Psychoanalytical Association; and past president of the German Psychoanalytical Association.

OTTO F. KERNBERG is associate chairman and medical director, New York Hospital-Cornell Medical Center, Westchester Division; professor of psychiatry, Cornell University Medical College; and training and supervising analyst, Columbia University Center for Psychoanalytic Training and Research.

PAUL H. ORNSTEIN is professor of psychiatry and co-director of the International Centre for the Study of Psychoanalytic Self Psychology, Department of Psychiatry, University of Cincinnati; and training and supervising analyst, Cincinnati Psychoanalytic Institute.

ETHEL SPECTOR PERSON is director and training and supervising analyst at the Columbia University Center for Psychoanalytic Training and Research and professor of clinical psychiatry, College of Physicians and Surgeons of Columbia University. She is chairperson of the Publications Committee of the IPA.

JOSEPH SANDLER is the Freud Memorial Professor of Psychoanalysis, University of London, and director of the Psychoanalysis Unit, University College London. He is training and supervising analyst at the British Psychoanalytical Society and president of the IPA.

HANNA SEGAL is a fellow of the Royal College of Psychiatry, training and supervising analyst of the British Psychoanalytical Society, and vice president of the IPA. She has served as president of the British Psychoanalytical Society.

NIKOLAAS TREURNIET is faculty member and training and supervising analyst of the Dutch Psychoanalytical Society.

CLIFFORD YORKE is psychiatrist in charge, Anna Freud Centre, Hampstead, and training and supervising analyst of the British Psychoanalytical Society.

Index

For Product Safety Concerns and Information please contact our EU representative GPSR@taylorandfrancis.com
Taylor & Francis Verlag GmbH, Kaufingerstraße 24, 80331 München, Germany

www.ingramcontent.com/pod-product-compliance
Ingram Content Group UK Ltd.
Pitfield, Milton Keynes, MK11 3LW, UK
UKHW022204190926
475702UK00003B/187